Leadership, Diversity, and Social Justice

Cognella Series on Advances in Culture, Race, and Ethnicity

Leadership, Diversity, and Social Justice

Culture as a System for Resistance and Emancipation

Antonio Jiménez-Luque, Ph.D.

University of San Diego

Series edited by Miguel Gallardo, Psy.D.; Allen Ivey, Ed.D., ABPP; Joseph E. Trimble, Ph.D.; Norweeta G. Milburn, Ph.D.; and Sumie Okazaki, Ph.D.

cognella®
SAN DIEGO

Bassim Hamadeh, CEO and Publisher
Amy Smith, Senior Project Editor
Abbey Hastings, Production Editor
Jess Estrella, Senior Graphic Designer
Alexa Lucido, Licensing Manager
Natalie Piccotti, Director of Marketing
Kassie Graves, Senior Vice President, Editorial
Jamie Giganti, Director of Academic Publishing

Cover image courtesy Marta Jiménez-Luque.

Printed in the United States of America.

cognella® | ACADEMIC PUBLISHING
3970 Sorrento Valley Blvd., Ste. 500, San Diego, CA 92121

Brief Contents

Foreword   **xi**
  Joseph E. Trimble, PhD

Introduction   **xv**

Chapter 1. Culture as a System of Domination in a Postcolonial World   1

Chapter 2. Leadership as a Social Myth for Domination or Emancipation   15

Chapter 3. Culture, Resistance, and Social Movements   33

Chapter 4. Organizational Culture and Change   53

A Work of Deconstruction and Reconstruction   53

Chapter 5. A Case Study of the Macro Context of the Organization   77

History, External Relationships, and Current Challenges   77

Chapter 6. A Case Study of the Micro Context of the Organization   99

Internal Relationships, Understandings, and Meanings   99

Chapter 7. Critical Intercultural Leadership Process   133

Conclusions and Recommendations   **165**
Afterword   **175**
Index   **181**

Detailed Contents

Foreword **xi**
  Joseph E. Trimble, PhD

Introduction **xv**

Chapter 1. Culture as a System of Domination in a Postcolonial World 1
  Culture: A Framework to Make Sense and Meaning of the World 1
    Characteristics of Culture and Cultural Differences 2
  Hegemony and Culture 3
    Culture, Hegemony, and Social Control 4
  Doxa and the "Indisputable" 8
  Conclusion 12
  Discussion Questions 12
  References 12

Chapter 2. Leadership as a Social Myth for Domination or Emancipation 15
  Relational Sociology 18
  Evolution of Leadership Theory 19
    Dualisms, Complexity, and Critical Leadership Studies 20
    Leadership and The Cultural and Symbolic Approach 22
    The Ontological Challenge of Leadership and Processes 23
    Process Studies 23
    Misplaced Leadership Focus 24
    Leadership Refocused: A Process of World-Making 25
    Frameworks to Make Sense/Meaning of the World 27
    Actions to Create and Transform the Social Order 28
  Conclusion 29
  Discussion Questions 29
  References 29

Chapter 3. Culture, Resistance, and Social Movements 33
  Culture and Critical Consciousness 33
  Critical Consciousness 35
    Awakening of Critical Consciousness 35
  Identity Development and Ethnogenesis 38
    Ethnogenesis Studies 39
    Resistance Against Domination and Oppression 41

Culture as a Field for Struggle   42

Social Movements and Culture   43

 Evolution of Social Movements and Cultural Studies   43

 Social Movements and Culture Production   45

 Collective Action and Frames to Produce Culture   47

 Ethnic Identity, Social Movements, and Critical Interculturality   47

Conclusion   49

Discussion Questions   49

References   49

Chapter 4. Organizational Culture and Change:
A Work of Deconstruction and Reconstruction   53

Culture and Organizations   54

Organizational Culture   54

Levels of Culture Within an Organization   55

 Artifacts   56

 Espoused Beliefs and Values   56

 Basic Underlying Assumptions   57

Organizational Culture from an Academic Approach   57

 Combining Integration, Differentiation, and Fragmentation   58

 Organizational Culture and Social Movements Organizations   60

Macrocultures, Cultures, and Subcultures   60

How Culture Emerges in New Groups   61

Culture Formation in Organizations   62

Shared Experiences of the Group   63

Transmission of Knowledge and Communication   63

How Actors Create, Embed, and Transmit Organizational Culture   64

 Primary Embedding Mechanisms   66

 Secondary Embedding Mechanisms   66

How Culture Changes   67

Toward an Intercultural Society   70

Conclusion   72

Discussion Questions   73

References   73

Chapter 5. A Case Study of the Macro Context of the Organization:
History, External Relationships, and Current Challenges   77

History and Background   78

Foundation and Evolution: The "Dream" Comes True   79

Characteristics: A Diverse Organization as a Holistic Process   82

The Employees: A Combination of Openness, Empathy, and Awareness   85

External Formal and Informal Relationships   87

A Sanctuary to Balance Asymmetries of Power and Decolonize   90

Raising Awareness and Educating Hegemonic Institutions   91
Current Challenges   94
Conclusion   97
Discussion Questions   98
References   98

Chapter 6. A Case Study of the Micro Context of the Organization: Internal Relationships, Understandings, and Meanings   99
Formal and Informal Internal Relationships   100
Diversity of the Staff   100
Encouragement for Creativity and Fluidity of Organizational Structures   110
Commitment with Social Justice and Cultural Resistance   114
Particularities of the Leadership Process   119
Tacit and Explicit Understandings and Meanings   122
Curiosity, Openness, and a Lack of Fear   123
Intercultural Society and a Common Identity/Purpose   124
Safe Space and Sanctuary for Social Justice and Cultural Resistance   127
Social Justice   129
We Shall Overcome: Cultural Resistance   131
Conclusion   132
Discussion Questions   132

Chapter 7. Critical Intercultural Leadership Process   133
Making Visible the Invisible: The Sanctuary   135
We Struggle, Therefore I Am: The Platform   141
Empowerment Through Frameworks of Collective Action   142
Deconstructing and Reconstructing Social Structures   144
Balancing Asymmetries of Power   147
United by Our Differences: The Intercultural Society   149
Valuing Different Cultures   149
Navigating Between Cultures to Develop a Multiple Consciousness   150
Enhancing a Sense of Belonging Through a Common Purpose   151
Emancipatory Doxa/Pluri-Doxa and Transformation: The Lines in the Sand   153
Resilience: Flexibility and Capacity to Adjust   154
Embracing Change and Transformation   156
Leadership and Organization as Processes   157
Drawing Lines in the Sand   158
Conclusion   160
Discussion Questions   160
References   161

Conclusions and Recommendations   165
Afterword   175
Arthur W. Blume, PhD

Index   181

Foreword

Joseph E. Trimble, PhD

In August of 2012 Jean Lau Chin, the prominent multicultural clinical psychologist, invited me to collaborate with her on a book emphasizing the influences of cultural diversity and leadership, a topic that had not received much serious consideration in the leadership field. Since I did then and still do consider myself to be a multicultural psychologist, I enthusiastically agreed to collaborate with her. We subsequently published two books on diverse cultural influences on leadership and coauthored conference presentations, journal articles, and book chapters on the emerging topic (see Chin & Trimble, 2014; Chin et al., 2017).

In 2019 Jean and I initiated a column series for the International Leadership Association's (ILA) Intersections series titled *Global & Culturally Diverse Leadership in the 21st Century*. Our column series emphasized how leaders view leadership, including the social and cultural perspectives that influence their own leadership styles. The series also invited leaders and scholars to focus columns on the ways their perspectives have gained prominence in the training and practice of organizational psychology as the world's population grows and changes. Specifically, we encouraged contributors to focus columns on how we prepare ourselves, our communities, businesses, educational institutions, as well as our citizens to live, work, and practice in the world of the future.

Our very first column was written by Antonio Jiménez-Luque, titled *Decolonial Leadership: From a Local and Hegemonic Paradigm Toward a Global and Intercultural Perspective of the Field*. In his thoughtfully crafted column, Antonio argued that what today are universal and global theories of leadership are quite ethnocentric and local and that many current theories still reflect the Eurocentric colonial mentality of dominance and power. He argued that new leadership theories and practices should be developed with non-Western, non-Eurocentric perspectives, for they can balance asymmetries of power in society and contribute to "decolonize our minds" and overcome the obstacles that hinder effective global and intercultural leadership. He concludes, "The challenge is immense, but since the field of leadership has the potential for impacting in a beneficial way issues of equity, diversity, and social justice, the creation of a new paradigm of leadership thought from decolonial, global and intercultural perspectives cannot wait anymore" (Jimenez-Luque, 2019, p. 9).

As I assisted Antonio with his column, I felt a strong partnership emerging between us. We shared common interests in multicultural topics, particularly those pertaining to leadership theory and practice, and we continued to collaborate on projects of interest to both of us. Unfortunately, Jean Lau Chin passed away in May 2020. I invited Antonio and Gayle Skawen:-nio Morse to join me in sponsoring and editing the ILA column series, and our collaborative partnership continues today.

The thesis and theme of Antonio's book represents a thoughtful, well-researched extension of his ILA column. In his book Antonio carefully and thoroughly explores aspects of the influence cultural diversity has on leadership styles. He examines the challenges to oppression through a well-crafted case study of leadership in a Native American Indian urban community. The study focuses on the process of collective emancipation and decolonization within a context of coloniality.

Antonio's exploration of the critical intercultural leadership process that emerges to effectively organize cultural resistance and emancipation offers new insights regarding more inclusive and diverse leadership that go beyond the Euro-American canon. His study's results will contribute to better understanding how leadership influences and shapes organizational cultures. Importantly, with his study Antonio sheds light on processes of social change leadership, providing a developmental model of culture change for organizations that can be reproduced in other contexts.

His case study and its influences on emancipation and leadership is framed in a uniquely crafted model called critical intercultural leadership. The model describes a process of struggle of an ethnic social movement organization from a postcolonial world toward an intercultural society. The model consists of four stages beginning with Eurocentric leadership and progresses to a deconstruction and reconstruction phase. The four thematic sections serve as the focus for the book's comprehensive chapters, offering avenues for new paradigms of cultural diversity leadership.

Emerging 20th-century views of leadership challenge the significance of power in leader-centric models. Power inherent in the social identities of members of out-groups and in-groups in society plus their contribution to group and organizational dynamics is central to a new paradigm of diversity leadership. The lived experiences of subordinate groups within a culture or country share an experience of being marginalized or oppressed. As world leadership shifts, new paradigms of diversity leadership are essential for a 21st-century view.

While democracies have prevailed as ideal leadership structures, 21st-century models must consider alternative structures of leadership, such as reluctant leadership styles, which have been effective and favorably accepted in different countries throughout the world. Though masculinized contexts of leadership have prevailed, 21st-century models must also consider feminist and humane orientations to leadership.

Antonio Jiménez-Luque's book is well framed and rich with scholarly arguments and case study findings that will assist all those who study and work in the leadership field to further explore and advance culturally diverse leadership education as well as practices that foster civility, respect, appreciation, and greater understanding among peoples of the world.

Joseph E. Trimble, PhD
Bellingham, WA, United States
January 22, 2022

References

Chin, J. L., & Trimble, J. E. (2014). *Diversity and leadership*. Sage.

Chin, J. L., Trimble, J. E., & Garcia, J. E. (Eds.). (2017). *The culturally diverse leader: New dimensions, opportunities and challenges for business and society*. Emerald Group Publishing Limited.

Jimenez-Luque, A. (2019). Decolonial leadership: From a local and hegemonic paradigm toward a global and intercultural perspective of the field. In J. L. Chin & J. E. Trimble (Eds.), *Global & culturally diverse leadership in the 21st century* (pp. 1–12). International Leadership Association.

Introduction

The postcolonial world of today is the result of the processes of modernity and its darker side, colonialism. *Modernity* is a period in history that resulted in socioeconomic and cultural changes in Western Europe and the appearance of Eurocentrism, the belief that Europeans and their culture were the pinnacle of humanity and its history and the exclusive bearers, creators, and protagonists of modernity (Quijano, 2010). The other side of modernity is colonialism, the formal political domination of one country by another in which the relationship between the two nations is always one of economic exploitation, although the dominant nation may pretend otherwise (Kloby, 2006).

Modernity can ultimately be summarized as a set of ideas surrounding a capitalist economy, the modern nation-state, and Enlightenment rationalism (Martin, 1999). It is a process based on reason, as it considers that human reason would illuminate both the darker aspects of nature and human relations. Modernity offers a discourse of salvation, as it liberates human beings from religious and political dogmas (O'Neill, 1999). As Condorcet (1955) stated, "The sun will shine only on free men who know no other master but their reason; when tyrants and slaves, priests and their stupid or hypocritical instruments will exist only in works of history and on the stage" (p. 179).

To date, no consensus exists on when modernity began. Some scholars argue that its origin can be traced to the year 1436, with Gutenberg's adoption of moveable type; some to the year of 1520, with Luther's rebellion against Church authority; and others maintain that it was with the American Revolution of 1776 or the French Revolution of 1789 (Toulmin, 1992). The disagreement about the precise date of modernity's origin can be placed between the 15th and 17th centuries in what was a process in Europe from south to north and from the east to the west. In essence, this was a movement that started with the Italian Renaissance, through the Lutheran Reformation and the scientific revolution of the 17th century, culminating in the bourgeois political revolution in England, North America, and France (Dussel, 2005).

Hence, this narrative of modernity only "represents an 'intra' European, Eurocentric, self-centered, and ideological view, from the perspective of the centrality of Northern Europe that has prevailed since the 18th century, dominating even up to our own days" (Dussel, 2005, p. 12). Although modernity is seen as a European phenomenon, it is constituted in a dialectical relation with a non-European alterity as its ultimate content. In essence, modernity appears when the "center" of world history shifts to Europe and the other continents become its "periphery" (Mignolo & Escobar, 2010).

Moreover, what is established through this worldview is a linear concept of the history of human civilization that departs from a primitive stage and culminates in its more "sophisticated" phase, Europe. Thus, while Europe represents "modern civilization," other regions are labeled as "primitive," and these differences are considered natural and not consequences of a history of power relations (Quijano, 2010).

This phenomenon, when western Europeans thought of themselves as the most developed and sophisticated culture in the history of humanity and protagonists of modernity, is called Eurocentrism (Quijano, 2010). To better understand Eurocentrism and how this concept became the dominant frame of reference, it is necessary to situate this critique outside the European continent in the realization that Europe was never the center of world history until the Industrial Revolution at the end of the 18th century as a consequence of colonialism. According to Dussel (2005), the history of modernity was distorted thanks to the mirage of Eurocentrism that situated Europe at the heart of the entirety of prior world history. In essence, during modernity, a Eurocentric leadership process that created a framework to make sense and meaning of the world founded on exclusion and exploitation was imposed.

The Darker Side of Modernity: Colonialism

Throughout humanity's history, there were great civilizations, like ancient China and Egypt, Greece and Rome, and the Inca and Aztec Empires. Because the Western civilization that resulted from the Renaissance and the Enlightenment was the most recent in that time, Europeans considered themselves very modern and sophisticated and tried to "save" the world by making other people be like them (Mignolo, 2011). Through this mindset, Europe was obliged to bring "light" to the world in the name of progress and civilization and develop and spread its new economic system, capitalism (Mignolo, 2011). Thus, within a capitalist system, the need for resources—what Karl Marx (1867/1977) called "primitive accumulation"—provided another foundation for colonialism.

Modern colonialism began shortly after the great boom in global exploration symbolized by the travels of Christopher Columbus. However, it is generally agreed to have peaked in the late 1800s and the beginning of the 20th century, even if some European countries kept their colonies for decades after (Kloby, 2006). One such example is the conquest of America. Quijano (2010) describes how the conquest of the Indigenous societies that inhabited this continent began the constitution of a new world order that 500 years later covered the whole planet (Quijano, 2010). Europeans established this new global order through direct, political, social, and cultural domination over the conquered. Thus, America was constituted as the first space/time of a new model of power at a global level (Europe was separated from America—and its primitive people—in space and from Middle Ages in time), which formed the first identity of modernity (Quijano, 2000). There were two historical processes to produce that space/time: One was the codification of differences between conquerors and the conquered through the idea of race, with which the people of America, and later the world, were classified within this new model of power. The other process was the constitution of a new structure of labor control and its resources and products. This new structure "was an articulation of all historically known previous structures of control of labor, slavery, serfdom, small independent commodity production and reciprocity, together around and upon the basis of capital and the world market" (Quijano, 2000, pp. 533–534). In associating new historical identities with social roles and geo-historical places, "both race and the division of labor remained structurally linked and mutually reinforcing, in spite of the fact that neither of them were necessarily dependent on the other in order to exist or change" (Quijano, 2000, p. 536).

This domination, at least its political aspects, has been defeated in many parts of the world. At the same time, its successor, Western imperialism, "is an association of social interests between dominant groups ('social classes' and/or 'ethnic groups') of countries with unequally articulated power, rather than an imposition from the outside" (Quijano, 2010, p. 22). This structure of power still produces the current social discriminations of race, ethnicity, or nationality that are presented as objective and scientific categories (Quijano, 2010). The relationship that began during the 16th century between Western culture and other cultures continues to be one of colonial domination whose results are a relationship that consists, in the first place, of a colonization of the imagination of the dominated (Quijano, 2010). In other words, a Eurocentric leadership process resulting in a colonial matrix of power (i.e., coloniality) was imposed, and it is still the framework within which different social relations operate.

Coloniality

As a consequence of these socioeconomic and cultural processes, modernity can be considered a narrative that originates from Europe and "builds Western civilization by celebrating its achieving while hiding at the same time its darker side, coloniality" (Mignolo, 2011, pp. 3–4). There is no modernity without coloniality, because these are two sides of the same coin, with modernity representing the light and coloniality the shadow. Thus, this darker side of modernity produced two main effects at a global level: a system known as the colonial matrix of power, understood as a framework of world-making, and social structures that designed new asymmetric power relationships.

Colonial Matrix of Power

According to Quijano (2000), the colonial matrix of power (CMP) is the first effectively global model in human history in several respects:

> To begin with, it is the first where in each sphere of social existence, all historically known forms of control of respective social relations are articulated, configuring in each area only one structure with systematic relations between its components and, by the same means, its whole. Second, it is the first model where each structure of each sphere of social existence is under the hegemony of an institution produced within the process of formation and development of that same model of power. Thus, in the control of labor and its resources and products, it is the capitalist enterprise; in the control of sex and its resources and products, the bourgeois family; in the control of authority and its resources and products, the nation-state; in the control of

intersubjectivity, Eurocentrism. Third, each of those institutions exists in a relation of interdependence with each other. Therefore, the model of power is configured as a system. Fourth, this model of global power is the first that covers the entire planet's population. (pp. 544–545)

On the other hand, Puerto Rican sociologist Ramón Grosfoguel (2010) proposes a broader definition of this matrix of power, defining it as an intersectionality of hierarchies of "sexual, political, epistemic, economic, spiritual, linguistic and racial forms of domination and exploitation where the racial/ethnic hierarchy of the European/non-European divide transversally reconfigures all of the other global power structures" (p. 71). This intersectionality of hierarchies could not be possible without assigning negative cultural value to differences and diversity. This Eurocentric process of leadership explained and, at the same time, legitimized the domination of one group by another in terms of class, race, gender, or culture. Thus, alleged differences are often said to be natural, universal, or eternal, based on biology or God's teachings. In this respect, both religion and science played a key role in rationalizing domination (Rothenberg, 2006).

Concerning race, Memmi (1996) affirms that the first form of racism consisted of stressing the difference between accuser and victim. However, revealing a characteristic differentiating two individuals or two groups does not, in and of itself, constitute a racist attitude. Rather, it depends in part on how difference is perceived. In its modern meaning, the idea of race does not have an easily trackable history before America's colonization. However, from then on, social relations founded on the category of race produced new social identities (e.g., Indian, Black, mestizo, etc.) and redefined others (Quijano, 2000). Thus, identities such as European, American, Asian, African, and, much later, Oceanian were produced, and along with them, relations of domination that constituted hierarchies, places, and corresponding social roles of the model of colonial domination were imposed (Quijano, 2000).

In summary, from the 16th century on, Western Europe became the center of the modern world system, and this ethnocentrism, associated with a universal racial classification, explains why Europeans felt "not only superior to all the other peoples of the world, but, in particular, naturally superior" (Quijano, 2000, p. 541). First with the hegemony of the coasts of the Mediterranean and the Iberian Peninsula and later with the northwest Atlantic coast, the CMP, imposed through a Eurocentric leadership process, has proven to be the most effective instrument for implementing universal domination through the creation and maintenance of unfair socioeconomic and cultural structures (Quijano, 2000).

Social Structures of Asymmetric Relations of Power

A *structure* is a set of patterned arrangements that are repeated. Hence, a *social structure* can be defined as an arrangement situated in any geographical space that influences or limits individuals' choices and opportunities (Barker, 2005). However, other definitions of "social structure" maintain that rules themselves are reaffirmed if they are followed. In essence, structural properties of social systems are mediums that influence the outcome of practices that constitute social systems (Giddens, 1979).

In terms of modernity and coloniality, the latter was the first global system where all forms of control in social relations were articulated, and as a result of this process, a unique suprastructure emerged between the different components of the entire system (Quijano, 2000). Each structure of every social sphere was under the control of an institution that produced a process in the creation of the CMP. As we have seen, the institution of capitalism controlled labor and its resources. The bourgeois concept of the family did the same with sex and its resources and products, as did the nation-state with authority and resources and products. Finally, Eurocentrism did the same with its totalizing intersubjectivity (Quijano, 2000). In short, a global system of socioeconomic stratification based on the place and the time took form, a system that evolved later toward what we currently understand by concepts such as classism, racism, sexism, and the epistemicide or elimination of other forms of knowledge.

Colonial administrations have almost completely been eradicated from the capitalist world system. Nevertheless, colonial situations and mental frameworks still exist. According to Grosfoguel (2010), these situations represent "cultural, political, sexual, spiritual, epistemic and economic oppression/exploitation of subordinate racialized/ethnic groups by dominant racialized/ethnic groups with or without the existence of colonial administrations" (p. 74). In short, colonialism is almost over, but coloniality still affects the minds and social imaginaries of both the oppressors and the oppressed. For example, if we look to the core zones of the capitalist world economy today, one cannot help but notice the overlap with predominantly White Euro-American societies, such as Western Europe, North America, and Australia. On the other hand, if we compare the peripheral zones, they overlap with previously colonized non-European peoples. Japan is the only exception, but curiously, it was never colonized or dominated by Europeans, and similar to the West, they had a colonial empire (Grosfoguel, 2010). It is worth pointing out that this system of coloniality also includes Global South migrants in the racial/ethnic hierarchy of global cities, suggesting that there is a periphery outside and inside the core zones and a core inside and outside the peripheral regions (Grosfoguel, 2010).

The "decolonization of the world" during the 19th century in Latin America and the 20th century for the largest part of the rest of the planet is a myth that has contributed to the invisibility of coloniality today. Decolonization and decoloniality are different concepts, as were colonization and coloniality (Grosfoguel, 2010). Thus, we cannot think of decolonization in terms of conquering power over the juridical-political boundaries of a state alone, as all the old national liberation and socialist strategies pretended. This is because global coloniality is not reducible to the presence or absence of a colonial administration or the political/economic structures of power (Grosfoguel, 2010).

In terms of power, the social structures identified above were central in defining individuals' and groups' possible choices, particularly the position they occupied in the CMP. According to Arendt (1970), "Power is never the property of an individual; it belongs to a group and remains in existence as long as the group keeps together" (p. 44). In other words, what defined power was determined by one's group and then one's position in the matrix of power. Bourdieu (1977, 1990) also elaborated a similar concept by combining power and identity, arguing that today there is a struggle for social recognition as a type of power he called "symbolic power." This is a struggle "to win everything which, in the social world, is of the order of belief, credit and discredit, perception and appreciation, knowledge and recognition—name, renown, prestige, honor, glory, authority, everything which constitutes symbolic power as recognized power" (Bourdieu, 1984, p. 251).

Social groups try to acquire symbolic power as well as an increase in the value of existing assets "to impose the taxonomy most favorable to its characteristics, or at least to give to the dominant taxonomy the content most flattering to what it has and what it is" (Bourdieu, 1984, pp. 475–476). Thus, each group seeks to impose its worldview and frameworks to make sense and meaning of reality as being most valuable to secure symbolic power. However, if a group fails to promote its values, it will be forced to accept its inferiority. As Bourdieu (1984) states, "Adapting to a dominated position implies a form of acceptance of domination. The sense of incompetence, failure or cultural unworthiness imply a form of recognition of dominant values" (p. 389). In short, and as a result of the struggles for symbolic power, the CMP supposed a design of a global social system that "distributed" power in an asymmetric way in terms of class, race, gender, and culture. Again, this was according to the position one occupied in the already existing power hierarchy. In our current society, this design is still operative; therefore, without an awareness of one's biased processes of symbolic power, social and cognitive justice will be impossible.

The Postcolonial World Today

Although today we have terms such as "postmodernity" and almost all former colonial regimes have disappeared, the 21st-century world system is still based on Eurocentric leadership processes of modernity and colonialism. Among the main consequences derived from these processes and narratives that prevent dialogue among cultures are social hierarchies such as (a) classism, (b) racism, (c) sexism, and (d) cultural epistemicide, along with (e) a general system of domination and oppression.

Classism

One barrier to social and cognitive justice among cultures that we are witnessing is classism. It is a system derived from the CMP and the negative value of difference and the capitalist structure that controls labor and its resources. Classism is depicted as "prejudice and discrimination based on socioeconomic level or class" (Blumenfeld & Raymond, 2000, p. 25). As a result of classism, while the wealthiest have privileges and are assigned a high status, poor and working-class people and their cultures are stigmatized and disadvantaged (Fiske-Rusciano & Cyrus, 2005). In essence, classism is a tangible result of social and economic inequity and "the umbrella under which all other forms of oppression are connected" (Zrenchik & McDowell, 2012, p. 102).

Classism is also widely internalized by both rich people and poor people. This is what is understood as hegemonic, a governing power that wins consent to its rule from those it subjugates when "those whose labor is being exploited believe those who benefit from this exploitation to be of greater value" (Zrenchik & McDowell, 2012, p. 104). As Marx (1867/1999) argued, to maintain the status quo and the hierarchies, "the maintenance and reproduction of the working class is, and ever must be, a necessary condition" (p. 332).

Racism

When the capitalist structure developed in Europe, the control of labor and its resources was based on social classes to legitimize the exploitation of big sectors of society. However, after Europeans arrived in America in 1492, they justified their exploitation of Indigenous communities and enslaved Africans, emphasizing race. According to McGoldrick and Giordano (1996), race is not a cultural or genetic matter but an issue of strictly political oppression. It is constructed through fictions, which is not to say that race is a fiction (Eisenstein, 2006). It is an idea always in part fixated on the body, with a meaning always contextualized, yet the meaning of race precedes its context.

Colors, noses, and hair are defined before they are seen, yet one sees them only through the context of their world (Eisenstein, 2006). Today, the theme of racism is "less biological heredity and more the insurmountability of cultural differences. Historical cultures outline the 'other'; the language of incompatibility displaces the superior/inferior divide. Boundary lines are therefore being constantly redrawn and must remain flexible" (Eisenstein, 2006, p. 188). Racism is old and new, static and changing, tied to skin color, and pluralized to encompass ethnic/cultural meanings beyond the idea of the inferior–superior divide (Eisenstein, 2006).

Sexism

The third barrier that hinders social and cognitive justice is sexism, which resulted from a bourgeois concept of family that utilized patriarchy, a former system of domination, to control sex, its resources, and its products. From a Marxist perspective, the bourgeois concept of the nuclear family performs ideological functions for capitalism, teaching passive acceptance of hierarchy, being central for consumption, and reproducing class inequality when wealthy families pass down private properties to their children (Engels, 2010).

Patriarchy, a historic creation formed by men and women in a process that took nearly 2,500 years to complete, "appeared as the archaic state. The basic unit of its organization was the patriarchal family, which both expressed and constantly generated its rules and values" (Lerner, 2006, p. 253). This family structure has varied throughout history, but one common element is the male dominance in the public realm, institutions, and government (Lerner, 2006). Further, the family not only mirrors the social order in the state upon which it educates its children to follow but also reproduces and reinforces it (Lerner, 2006).

The basic relations in a patriarchal system are controlled by, and submissive to, those who rank higher in terms of age and gender: Duties and obligations are strictly defined along these two axes. "They are marked by inequality but legitimized through the concept of 'complementarity,' which means that while roles and responsibilities are dissimilar and unequal, they are idealized as reciprocal and therefore of equal value" (Lerner, 2006, p. 258). For Rothenberg (2006), "The institutionalization of hierarchies of age and gender signifies that older men have more power than younger men, and men in general have more power than women" (p. 258).

Epistemicide

The last system identified as a consequence of the design of the CMP (along with its negative value of differences) is the epistemicide of other types of knowledge. Through Eurocentrism and its Eurocentric leadership process, intersubjectivity is dominated, and the world is only conceptualized from a Western worldview, which makes the achievement of social and cognitive justice nearly impossible. Santos et al. (2007) call epistemicide the extermination of knowledge and ways of knowing and argue that it is impossible to have social justice without global cognitive justice.

The epistemic privilege of the Western world is the result of four epistemicides that took place throughout the 16th century: Jewish and Muslim populations in Spain; Indigenous people in the conquest of the Americas; Africans enslaved in the Americas; and women in Europe being accused of witchcraft and burned alive (Grosfoguel, 2013). Thus, the canon of thought in the social sciences and humanities is based on the knowledge produced by a few men from among five countries: Italy, France, England, Germany, and, later, the United States (Grosfoguel, 2013). Their knowledge is considered superior to all other countries' knowledge, and they monopolized the authority of such knowledge around the world (Grosfoguel, 2013).

As Maldonado-Torres (2008) affirms, the other side of René Descartes's famous quote "I think, therefore I am" is the racist/sexist structure of "I do not think, therefore I am not." It is the control of intersubjectivity by the CMP, and "it is a 'coloniality of being' where all of the subjects considered inferior do not think and are not worthy of existence because their humanity is in question" (Grosfoguel, 2013, pp. 86–87).

Domination and Oppression

Modernity and its darker side, coloniality, resulted in asymmetric power relations that are translated today into relationships of domination and oppression. *Oppression* is a process by which "one segment of society achieves power and privilege through the control and exploitation of other groups, which are burdened and pushed down into the lower levels of the social order" (Pincus, 2006, p. 145). Besides, oppression and domination define injustice (Young, 2011). The former is the institutional constraint on self-development, whereas the later represents the institutional constraint on self-determination. In essence, without developing and exercising one's capacities and experiences and without determining one's actions and conditions, there is no justice or symmetric power relations; therefore, there is no possibility for social justice. According to Young (2011), a group is oppressed when it experiences one of the following five dimensions of oppression: exploitation, marginalization, powerlessness, cultural imperialism, and violence. In short, through these five dimensions, an individual belonging to a specific group cannot develop and/or exercise their capacities and experiences (oppression) or determine their actions and conditions (domination).

Oppression also refers to systemic constraints on groups and "is structural, rather than the result of a few people's choices or policies" (Young, 2011, p. 40). Marilyn Frye (1983) defines oppression as "an enclosing structure of forces and barriers which tends to the immobilization and reduction of a group or category of people" (p. 11). In essence, "we cannot eliminate this structural oppression by getting rid of the rulers or making some new laws, because oppressions are systematically reproduced in major economic, political, and cultural institutions" (Young, 2011, p. 40).

The terms of race, class, gender, and culture are defined as "a constellation of 'positionalities' (e.g., social locations) that classify, categorize, and construct the social value that is assigned to individuals according to various components (e.g. beliefs, concepts, and structures that define social practice)" (Harley et al., 2002, p. 220). Positionalities "possess rank, have value, and are constructed hierarchically, particularly those that are visible and discernible" (Robinson, 1999, p. 73). Reducing racism and classism to the beliefs, ideas, or overt behaviors of individuals is inadequate (Bonilla-Silva, 1996) because racism and classism refer to systems of oppression that occur at multiple levels (Bell, 1997). For example, at an individual level, individuals demonstrate either overt or covert personal prejudices and discriminatory behavior toward Black, Indigenous people of color (BIPOC) or lower social classes (Holley & VanVleet, 2006). On the other hand, institutional discrimination is evidenced through "the day-to-day practices of organizations and institutions that have a harmful impact on members of subordinate groups" (Kendall, 1997, p. 306). According to Bonilla-Silva (1996), "Racial practices that reproduce racial inequality in contemporary America are increasingly covert, are embedded in normal operations of institutions, avoid direct racial terminology, and are invisible to most Whites" (p. 476).

As a result of this system of domination and oppression, there are disadvantages for members of subordinated groups and unearned privileges for members of dominant groups (McIntosh, 1998). However, while at an individual level an oppressed person needs an oppressor, in terms of structures, it is not necessary, because "while structural oppression involves relations among groups, these relations do not always fit the paradigm of conscious and intentional oppression of one group by another" (Young, 2011, p. 41). It is here where, along with the systems and structures of classism, racism, sexism, and the epistemicide that need to be transformed, social and cognitive justice become impossible to realize in today's postcolonial contexts, absent a critical intercultural leadership process aimed at decolonizing our minds and articulating more inclusive and broader frameworks of world-making. The goal is to seek cultural groups' emancipation and their different epistemologies that remain "invisibilized" by the dominant culture and its hegemonic epistemology, positivism which, as other theories of science is not based on scientific arguments (but rather on other social, economic, and political arguments) and because of its position of power neglects the internal plurality of science.

Culture as a System for Resistance and Emancipation

The phenomenon of leadership is influenced by culture (Peterson et al., 1994). However, while culture influences leadership, the dynamics of leadership also shape and determine cultural practices (Guthey & Jackson, 2011) and are central in articulating frameworks with which to make sense of reality (Drath & Palus, 1994). At a global level, the current postcolonial world has become the prison of a monologue: the monologue of a dominant culture and worldview. This dominant culture has been imposed through a process of Eurocentric leadership that started in the 16th century with modernity and its darker side, colonialism (Quijano, 2000). With this process that situated Western culture at the top of a social hierarchy and the rest of cultures in subordinated positions, the hegemonic culture became a system of domination, social exclusion, and control. However, different ethnic organizations and social movement have emerged in recent decades that challenge this system of oppression, its imaginaries, and social structures, from their own ethnic-identity perspective (Jimenez-Luque, 2021). Viewing culture as a field for struggle, these organizations and social movement organizations (SMOs) have decided to initiate processes of "critical intercultural leadership" to confront hegemonic narratives, cultural assumptions, and social structures, with the aim of building a new intercultural society (Walsh, 2010).

Conceptual Framework

This conceptual framework depicts a process of critical intercultural leadership as a spiral developmental model that brings change from a postcolonial world to an intercultural society (see Text Boxes 1 and 2 in Figure 0.1). For this transition to be effective, I suggest a leadership process that includes four stages with a relationship of growth that goes from the smaller to the bigger:

- eurocentric leadership: culture and doxa as a system of domination and control
- critical intercultural leadership: from critical consciousness to culture as a field for struggle
- ethnic organizations and SMOs: organizational culture for ethnogenesis
- ethnogenesis, a stage that is divided in two:
  o deconstruction
  o reconstruction (see concentric circles in Figure 0.1)

All four stages occur and are experienced within a global sphere of what can be thought of as doxa, which can grow or shrink depending which type of society is created: either an inclusive society (broader doxa) or an exclusive one (narrower doxa; see Circle 5 in Figure 0.1). To build an intercultural society, a critical intercultural leadership model that focuses on developing a more inclusive doxa of all different ways of thinking, doing, and being is needed. However, this process must be reviewed constantly to avoid reproducing oppression and domination with other subjects or social groups (see Text Box 3 in Figure 0.1).

This study is an ethnographic case study (chapters 5 and 6) that includes observations, artifacts collection, and interviews and was conducted in a city in the Northwest of the United States within a Native American organization that struggles for cognitive and social justice and is part of a bigger social movement of decolonization in the country. From perspectives of critical theory and intercultural studies, adapting a relational-centered approach that overcomes dichotomies between individual/social, agency/structure, and national/international, I examine how the members of the organization understand culture as a field for struggle, developing frameworks and structures to shape an organizational culture that raises critical consciousness among its members while unfolding a process of emancipatory ethnogenesis. The four findings of my research are:

- Making visible the invisible: the sanctuary
- We struggle, therefore I am: the platform
- United by our differences: the intercultural society
- Emancipatory doxa/Pluri-doxa and transformation: the lines in the sand

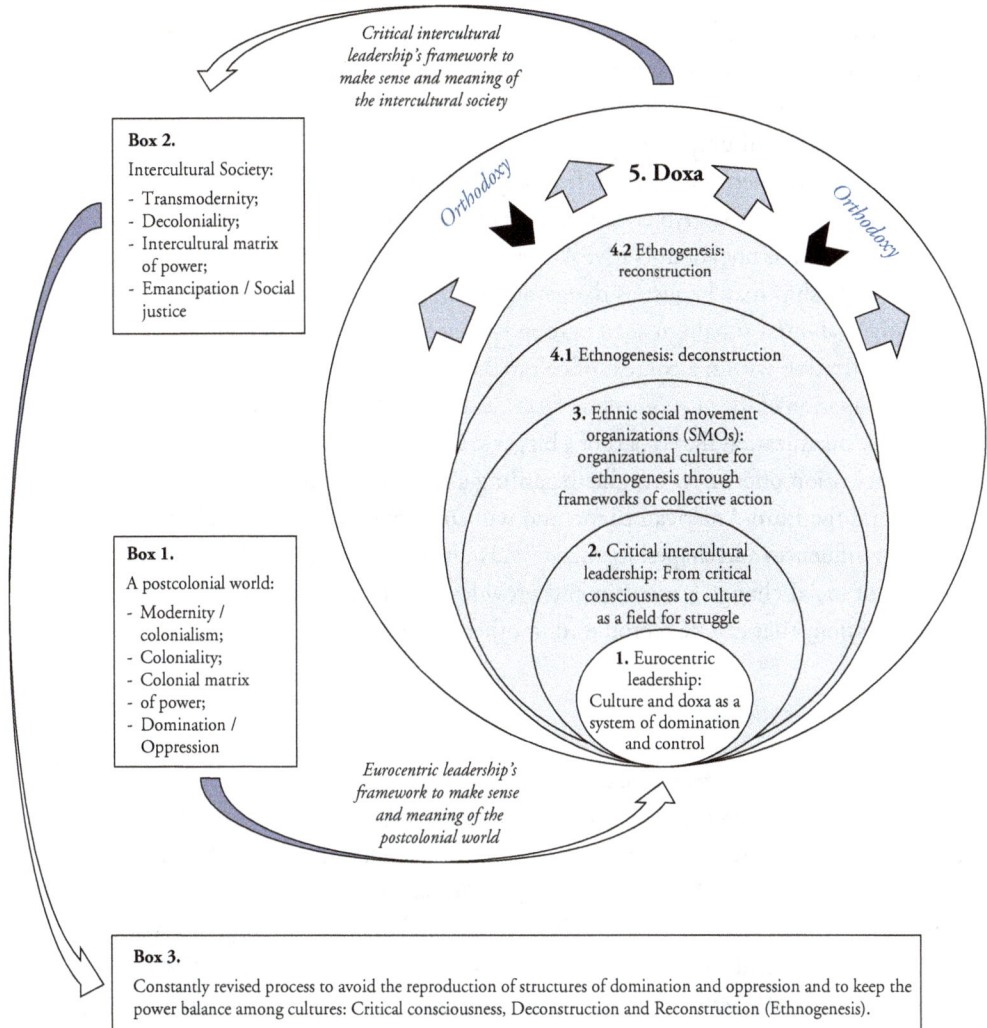

FIGURE 0.1   Critical Intercultural Leadership: A Process of Struggle of an Ethnic Social Movement Organization from a Postcolonial World Toward an Intercultural Society.

I conclude that subordinated social groups seeking recognition and political representation to balance asymmetries of power within postcolonial societies need to prioritize a struggle for the categories that make this possible.

This study contributes to postcolonial discourse in leadership and organization studies by applying a decolonial lens and offering empirical research about an emancipatory process of leadership within a context of coloniality. Also, this research illuminates the relationship between cultural identity as a resource and leadership, which can help to advance our understanding of how social change leadership happens. Finally, this study also implements a more collective approach to leadership analysis, incorporating a social and cultural perspective grounded in sociology, anthropology, and an ethnographic methodology of research.

The study was designed not to understand the processes of this organization as representative of Native American leadership but as an example of a subaltern social group—more specifically, a marginalized social group that resists and struggles in a collective way against the dominant worldview and uses cultural identity to balance asymmetries of power and challenges the dominant order. Today, there are over 500 federally recognized tribes in the United States (Warner & Grint, 2006), and urban American Indians in the same city belong to many different tribes. Thus, this research is not about Native American leadership, since the notion of a homogenous "Native" leadership may be just as dangerous as the idea of a universal theory of leadership. This study is about a subaltern social group engaged in a process of collective emancipation and decolonization within a context of coloniality.

This exploration of the phenomenon of a critical intercultural leadership process that emerges in an ethnic organization that is part of a bigger social movement to organize cultural resistance and emancipation offers new insights regarding a more inclusive and diverse leadership that goes beyond the Euro-American canon and will contribute to a better understanding of how leadership influences and shapes organizational culture. Additionally, this study sheds light on processes of social change leadership and provides a developmental model of culture change for organizations that can be reproduced in other contexts.

References

Arendt, H. (1970). *On violence*. Penguin.

Barker, C. (2005). *Cultural Studies: Theory and Practice*. Sage.

Bell, L. A. (1997). Theoretical foundations for social justice education. In M. Adams, L. A. Bell, D. J. Goodman, & K. Y. Joshi (Eds.), *Teaching for diversity and social justice* (pp. 1–14). Routledge.

Blumenfeld, W. J., & Raymond, R. (2000). Prejudice and discrimination. In M. Adams, W. Blumenfeld, R. Castaneda, H. Hackmanh, M. L. Peters, & X. Zuniga (Eds.), *Readings for diversity and social justice: An anthology on racism, antisemitism, sexism, heterosexism, ableism and classism* (pp. 21–30). Routledge.

Bonilla-Silva, E. (1996). Rethinking racism: Toward a structural interpretation. *American Sociological Review, 62*, 465–480.

Bourdieu, P. (1977). *Outline of a theory of practice*. Cambridge University Press.

Bourdieu, P. (1984). *Distinction: A social critique of the judgment of taste*. Harvard University Press.

Bourdieu, P. (1990). *The logic of practice*. Stanford University Press.

de Sousa Santos, B., Nunes, J. A., & Meneses, M. P. (2007). Opening up the canon of knowledge and recognition of difference. In B. de Sousa Santos (Ed.), *Another knowledge is possible* (pp. xix–lxii). Verso.

Drath, W. H., & Palus, C. J. (1994). *Making common sense: Leadership as meaningmaking in a community of practice*. Center for Creative Leadership.

Dussel, E. (2005, June 1–4). *Anti-Cartesian meditations: On the origin of the philosophical Antidiscourse of modernity* [Paper presentation]. Second Annual Conference of the Caribbean Philosophical Association, San Juan, PR, United States.

Eisenstein, Z. (2006). Hatred written on the body. In S. P. Rothenberg (Ed.), *Beyond borders. Thinking critically about global issues* (pp. 180–195). Worth Publishers.

Engels, F. (2010). *The origin of the family, private property, and the state.* Penguin.

Fiske-Rusciano, R., & Cyrus, V. (2005). *Experiencing race, class and gender in the United States* (4th ed.). McGraw Hill.

Frye, M. (1983). *The politics of reality.* The Crossing Press.

Gallissot, R., Kilani, M., & Rivera, A. (2000). *L'imbroglio ethnique en quatorze mots clés.* Sofedis.

Giddens, A. (1979). *Central problems in social theory: Action, structure and contradiction in social analysis.* Macmillan.

Grosfoguel, R. (2010). The epistemic decolonial turn: Beyond political-economy paradigms. In W. Mignolo & A. Escobar (Eds.), *Globalization and the decolonial option* (pp. 65–77). Routledge.

Grosfoguel, R. (2013). The structure of knowledge in westernized universities. Epistemic racism/sexism and the four genocides/epistemicides of the long 16th century. *Human Architecture: Journal of the Sociology of Self-Knowledge, 11*(1), 73–90.

Guthey, E., & Jackson, B. (2011). Cross-cultural leadership revisited. In A. Bryman, D. Collinson, K. Grint, B. Jackson, & M. Uhl-Bien (Eds.), *The Sage handbook on leadership* (pp. 165–178). Sage.

Harley, D. A., Jolvette, K., McCormick, K., & Tice, K. (2002). Race, class, and gender: A constellation of personalities with implications for counseling. *Journal of Multicultural Counseling and Development, 30*(4), 216–238.

Holley, L. C., & Van Vleet, R. K. (2006). Racism and classism in the youth justice system: Perspectives of youth and staff. *Journal of Poverty, 10,* 45–67.

Jimenez-Luque, A. (2021). Reframing the past to legitimate the future: Building collective agency for social change through a process of decolonizing memory. *Leadership, 17*(5), 586–605. https://doi.org/10.1177/1742715021999892

Kloby, J. (2006). The legacy of colonialism. In S. P. Rothenberg (Ed.), *Beyond borders. Thinking critically about global issues* (pp. 99–106). Worth Publishers.

Lerner, G. (2006). The patriarchal family. In S. P. Rothenberg (Ed.), *Beyond borders. Thinking critically about global issues* (pp. 253–255). Worth Publishers.

Maldonado-Torres, N. (2008). *Against war.* Duke University Press.

Martin, J. (1999). The social and the political. In F. Ashe, A. Finlayson, M. Lloyd, I. MacKenzie, J. Martin, & S. O'Neill (Eds.), *Contemporary social & political theory* (pp. 155–177). Open University Press.

Marx, K. (1977). *Capital: A critique of political economy.* Vintage Books. (Original work published 1867)

Marx, K. (1999). *Das kapital: An abridged edition* (D. McLellan, Ed.). Regnery. (Original work published 1867)

McGoldrick, M., & Giordano, J. (1996). Overview: Ethnicity and family therapy. In M. McGoldrick, J. Giordano, & J. K. Pearce (Eds.), *Ethnicity and family therapy* (pp. 1–27). Guilford.

McIntosh, P. (1998). White privilege and male privilege: A personal account of coming to see correspondences through work in women's studies. In M. L. Andersen & P. H. Collins (Eds.), *Race, class and gender: An anthology* (3rd ed., pp. 94–105). Wadsworth.

Memmi, A. (1996). Assigning value to difference. In S. P. Rothenberg (Ed.), *Beyond borders. Thinking critically about global issues* (pp. 173–179). Worth Publishers.

Mignolo, W. (2011). *The darker side of western modernity. Global futures, decolonial options.* Duke University Press.

Mignolo, W., & Escobar, A. (Eds.). (2010). *Globalization and the decolonial option.* Routledge.

O'Neill, S. (1999). Rationality. In F. Ashe, A. Finlayson, M. Lloyd, I. MacKenzie, J. Martin, & S. O'Neill (Eds.), *Contemporary social and political theory* (pp. 1–24). Open University Press.

Peterson, M. F., Brannen, M. Y., & Smith, P. B. (1994). Japanese and U.S. leadership: Issues in current research. *Advances in International and Comparative Management, 9*, 57–82.

Pincus, F. L. (2006). *Understanding diversity: An introduction to class, race, gender and sexual orientation.* Lynne Rienner.

Quijano, A. (2000). Coloniality of power, eurocentrism, and Latin America. *Nepantla: Views From South, 1*(3), 533–580.

Quijano, A. (2010). Coloniality and modernity/rationality. In W. Mignolo & A. Escobar (Eds.), *Globalization and the decolonial option* (pp. 22–32). Routledge.

Robinson, T. L. (1999). The intersection of dominant discourses across race, gender, and other identities. *Journal of Counseling & Development, 77*, 73–79.

Rothenberg, S. P. (2006). *Beyond borders. Thinking critically about global issues.* Worth Publishers.

Toulmin, S. (1992). *Cosmopolis.* The University of Chicago Press.

Walsh, C. (2010). Interculturalidad crítica y educación intercultural. In J. Viaña, L. Tapia, & C. Walsh (Eds.), *Construyendo interculturalidad crítica* (pp. 75–96). Instituto Internacional de Integración.

Warner, L. S., & Grint, K. (2006). American Indian ways of leading and knowing. *Leadership, 2*(2), 225–244.

Young, I. M. (2011). *Justice and the politics of difference.* Princeton University Press.

Zrenchik, K., & McDowell, T. (2012). Class and classism in family therapy praxis: A feminist, neo-Marxist approach. *Journal of Feminist Family Therapy, 24*(2), 101–120.

Chapter 1

Culture as a System of Domination in a Postcolonial World

Objectives

The main idea of this chapter is the connection between culture and hegemony and how culture can be used as a system of control and domination, imposing the view of a powerful social group upon others. Additionally, every culture creates a doxa, assumptions of what is taken for granted, and this space for thinking limits what can be thought and questioned. For creating social change, subaltern social groups need to challenge the hegemonic doxa that dominant groups have imposed and that they might have internalized.

Culture: A Framework to Make Sense and Meaning of the World

Culture is a collective phenomenon shared in a certain way among people who live within the same social environment or are in contact with it. According to Hofstede et al. (2010), "Culture consists of the unwritten rules of the social game. It is the collective programming of the mind that distinguishes the members of one group or category of people from others" (p. 5). Thus, culture is learned from a specific social environment because human beings observe the environment and transmit their experiences with other humans. "The personality of an individual, on the other hand, is his or her unique personal set of mental programs that needn't be shared with any other human being" (Hofstede et al., 2010, p. 7). In essence, when human beings learn their culture, what they do is absorb the influence of a collective programming and specific personal experiences (Hofstede et al., 2010).

As Trice and Beyer (1993) argue, cultures are

> collective phenomena that embody people's responses to the uncertainties and
> chaos that are inevitable in human experience. These responses fall into two major

categories. The first is the substance of a culture—shared, emotionally charged belief systems that we call ideologies. The second is cultural forms—observable entities, including actions, through which members of a culture express, affirm, and communicate the substance of their culture to one another. (p. 2)

Martin (2002) defines culture "as consisting of in-depth, subjective interpretations of a wide range of cultural manifestations (a generalist rather than a specialist view), both ideational and material" (p. 120). Besides, culture is a phenomenon below the surface within the unconscious, powerful in its impact but at the same time invisible and creates within us ways of thinking and frames of reference (Schein, 2010). "Just as our personality and character guide and constrain our behavior, so does culture guide and constrain the behavior of members of a group through the shared norms that are held in that group" (Schein, 2010, p. 14).

Characteristics of Culture and Cultural Differences

According to Schein (2010), there are four main characteristics of culture:

- structural stability: not only what is shared but also defines the group, and it is valued because it provides meaning and predictability
- depth: the essence of a culture; the unconscious part of a group that also provides stability
- breadth: the capacity that culture has to cover and influence all of a group's functioning
- patterning or integration: the ability of culture to tie together and to give harmony to the different cultural manifestations in order to internalize the natural and social order. In other words, integration is the answer to reduce disorder and anxiety through a view of how things are and ought to be that brings consistency and predictability. (Trice & Beyer, 1993)

Moreover, there are different ways of manifesting cultural differences, and they can be grouped in four categories: (a) symbols; (b) heroes; (c) rituals; and (d) values (Hofstede et al., 2010). Symbols are "words, gestures, pictures, or objects that carry a particular meaning that is recognized as such only by those who share the culture" (Hofstede et al., 2010, p. 8). These symbols can be developed or copied from other groups and can be destroyed or become "old" and disappear. Heroes are persons, alive or dead, real or imaginary, with highly valued characteristics in a certain culture, and they represent a model to follow by the other members of society (Hofstede et al., 2010). Rituals are collective activities that, although they seem superfluous and not effective, are considered essential within a culture. Through gathering and discourses, they reinforce group cohesion or allow the leaders to assert themselves (Hofstede et al., 2010). In terms of values, these are considered "broad tendencies to prefer certain states of affairs over others. Values are feelings with an added arrow indicating a plus and a minus side" (Hofstede et al., 2010, p. 9). However, values of inclusion for a community can create values of exclusion for members of another, resulting from moral circles.

Thus, from childhood, "people draw a mental line around those whom they consider to be their group. Only members of the moral circle thus delineated have full rights and full obligations" (Hofstede et al., 2010, p. 12). In other words, the moral circle can be applied to political parties, religions, or nations; it "is the key determinant of our social lives, and it both creates and carries our culture" (Hofstede et al., 2010, p. 13). However, the moral circles can be broader or narrower, more inclusive, or more exclusive depending upon the culture. According to Hofstede et al. (2010), "We live in societies that are so large that blood ties cannot be the only, or even the most important, way to determine moral rights and duties" (p. 15). Besides, every person has multiple identities, "and almost everyone belongs to a number of different groups and categories at the same time" (Hofstede et al., 2010, p. 18), carrying different layers of mental programming within themselves. Therefore, solidarity of class among nonhegemonic cultures that focuses on shared identities of domination and oppression could be a feasible project to broaden the moral circle through a critical intercultural leadership process.

Notwithstanding, to broaden that moral circle, the key issue is the depth of the layers of mental programming or layers of culture. In other words, changing a culture is going to be easier or more complicated depending on the depth of the layer where this cultural practice is situated. According to Schein (2010), culture is like the image of an onion with different layers where the outer ones are labeled as practices and the ones at the core are the values. Thus, cultural change can be fast for the practices of a culture but slow for the values, which were learned during childhood and give stability to a culture (Schein, 2010).

Within the core of culture, we find values such as gender or nationality; thus, it will be easier to understand how to change the culture in general and assumptions and values in particular within organizations because even if changing organizational cultures is not easy, the fact that its members joined the organization as adults makes it feasible (Hofstede et al., 2010). Culture is a dynamic phenomenon that is not static and flows because the culture is constantly created, recreated, and even destroyed by our interactions with others. "When we are influential in shaping the behavior and values of others, we think of that as 'leadership' and are creating the conditions for new culture formation" (Schein, 2010, p. 3). Thus, when constructing and reconstructing culture, we can seek either domination and social control or emancipation and social justice. Eventually, the leadership process involved in shaping culture and creating social structures and frameworks for world-making will be central to defining how culture can define the organization of a society.

Hegemony and Culture

Within modernity, culture has become an element of social exclusion and control to legitimize domination and oppression and a hegemonic discourse presented as universal and eventually internalized by society (Bourdieu, 1977). According to Fairclough (1992), "A discourse is a social practice not just of representing the world, but of signifying the world, constituting and constructing the world in meaning" (p. 64). Besides, a discourse or narrative has material effects because it (a) contributes to construct social identities and to define social positions for social subjects and types of self; (b) helps construct social relationships between people; and (c) creates systems of knowledge and belief and has the potential to transform society (Fairclough, 1992). Thus, due to asymmetries of power relations and resources between social groups and cultures, the dominant sectors of society have more possibilities of establishing a specific framework and doxa, which is what is taken for granted in any particular society, the experience by which "the natural and social world appears as self-evident" (Bourdieu, 1977, p. 162). In essence, doxa establishes the borders of what is allowed to be thought and said, limiting a narrative or worldview.

Culture, Hegemony, and Social Control

One of the main impediments Marx and Engels (1970) identified to create consciousness of class, political organization, and social change was the integrative role of hegemony. According to their thesis, the dominant capitalist class controls the means of production (i.e., material) and the means of mental production (i.e., ideas). Thus, Marx and Engels (1970) argue that every ruling class in the history of humanity

> is compelled, merely to carry through its aim, to present its interests as the common interest of all the members of society. ... It has to give its ideas the form of universality, and represent them as the only rational, universally valid ones. (pp. 65–66)

Marx understands culture as ideology and compares it to a "camera obscura" that distorts social reality through the production of ideas, concepts, and consciousness and affects all that can be said, imagined, or conceived in the fields of politics, law, morality, religion, metaphysics, and so on (Marx & Engels, 1970). In other words, thoughts and ideas are socially constructed, and culture, as an ideology, can be conceived for domination or emancipation through either a Eurocentric or critical intercultural process of leadership.

For Marx and Engels (1970), ideology is the superstructure that legitimizes the social structures, and they describe the concept of "hegemony of the spirit" as the consensual aspect of ruling-class domination or hegemony that would be followed later by Gramsci (1995) when he coined the term "cultural hegemony," understood as the process of domination implemented through ideological means that result in spontaneous consent. Stated simply, social sectors are successful in holding power over social institutions. Through them, these dominant groups influence the rest of society's thoughts and behaviors, establishing normative ideas, values, and beliefs that eventually will become the hegemonic worldview of society (Strinati, 1995). Cultural hegemony functions by achieving the consent of the masses to abide by social norms and the rules of law by framing the worldview of the ruling class—and the social and economic structures that go with it—as just, legitimate, and designed for the benefit of all (Strinati, 1995). Besides, hegemony has different facets, and the hegemonic groups succeed in providing "a unison of economic and political aims" and "intellectual and moral unity" (Strinati, 1995, p. 181). This is how the idea of common sense is created, implemented, and embedded in the social imaginaries of society. Thus, the supremacy of the bourgeoisie is based on two equally important facts: economic domination and intellectual and moral leadership (Forgacs, 2000)—that is, power relations through capital and a Eurocentric leadership of exploitation and exclusion to legitimize social inequities.

Regarding the concept of hegemony, Gramsci (1995) made a distinction between rule and hegemony. Rule is expressed through political forms that, in times of crisis, use either direct or effective coercion (Williams, 1995). However, "the more normal situation is a complex interlocking of political, social, and cultural forces, and hegemony, according to different interpretations, is either this or the active social and cultural forces which are its necessary elements" (Williams,

1995, p. 595). Hegemony as a concept goes beyond the concepts of culture and ideology. The former is the whole social process where individuals define and shape their whole lives, while the latter is the projected system of meanings and values of a particular class interest (Williams, 1995). According to Williams (1995), "'Hegemony' goes beyond 'culture,' as previously defined, in its insistence on relating the 'whole social process' to specific distributions of power and influence" (p. 595). In our current societies, social inequalities prevent individuals from defining and shaping their own lives because they are limited by social structures that are barriers to self-development and determination. This is what Gramsci (1995) defined as domination and subordination. Additionally, the concept of hegemony also goes beyond ideology because it is not enough with that conscious system of ideas and beliefs but the whole lived social process organized by a dominant perspective (Williams, 1995). Ideology is an articulated system of meanings, values, and beliefs, understood as a worldview or class perspective (Williams, 1995). Therefore, hegemony is a conglomerate of practices and expectations, "a lived system of meanings and values—constitutive and constituting—which when experienced as practices, appear as reciprocally confirming" (Williams, 1995, p. 596). Hegemony gives a sense of an absolute reality for the people in a society, a "culture" understood as the lived dominance and subordination of specific social classes (Williams, 1995). As Williams (1995) argues, a lived hegemony is a process that cannot be reduced, except analytically, to a system or structure, because it includes experiences, relationships, and activities with tensions and limits that are constantly changing. In other words, hegemony is complex and needs to be renewed, maintained, or changed, much as a leadership process of power relations that, at the same time, is resisted and challenged, producing the emergence of counter-hegemony and alternative hegemony.

The second system of cultural control analyzed by two critical theorists from the Frankfurt School, Horkheimer and Adorno (1996), is the idea of "culture industry." For Horkheimer and Adorno (1996), the age of myth is continued with the Enlightenment and modernity, which keeps fulfilling the myths from medieval ages and ancient times. As Horkheimer and Adorno (1996) state, "Myth is already enlightenment, and enlightenment reverts to mythology" (p. xvi). Thus, one of the main promises of modernity, such as to put an end to myth and superstition, was not true and has led us to a path of destruction in the name of reason (Horkheimer & Adorno, 1996).

Moreover, the Enlightenment's rational program aimed to differentiate humankind from nature and, eventually, in taking over nature, also took humans' own nature, repressing feelings, urges, and desires and separating the mind from the body. This separation of the mind from the body resulted in a constant oppression that has taken over all aspects of human life and is limited to human rationality designed to exploit nature, including human beings. Thus, after the Enlightenment, humankind becomes a master of nature, and a connection between Enlightenment and the scientific method is established, situating science as the only legitimate model of explanation for reality, overcoming tradition, and liberating us from myth and superstition (Horkheimer & Adorno, 1996). Along with reason and science comes bureaucracy and technology, making invisible other epistemologies and other knowledge beyond the rational knowledge.

For Horkheimer and Adorno (1996), the systems of fascism and capitalism position human beings as numbers and develop a culture industry and popular culture in subduing the masses.

As the authors argue, popular culture means producing standardized cultural goods in an effort to manipulate mass society and transform people into passive actors. These accessible pleasures of popular culture render people docile and content, no matter their economic circumstances. Besides, culture industry creates false psychological needs that only the capitalist system can satisfy (Horkheimer & Adorno, 1996). In conclusion, this system of control and domination creates a framework to make sense of reality that makes us believe a discourse, a narrative, because "the whole world is made to pass through the filter of the culture industry" (Horkheimer & Adorno, 1996, p. 126).

Marcuse (1991), another representative of the Frankfurt School following the idea of culture industry, coined the concept of "mass culture," which refers to a system wherein the people are dispossessed of their capacity for critical thinking due to the imposition of a one-dimensional worldview. Marcuse argues that consumerism is a form of social control and that our democracies are authoritarian systems where privileged social sectors dictate our perceptions of freedom. Thus, consumers act irrationally, buying more than they need, ignoring environmental degradation and sustainability issues, and not being conscious of their domination and oppression. "All liberation depends on the consciousness of servitude, and the emergence of this consciousness is always hampered by the predominance of needs and satisfactions which, to a great extent, have become the individual's own" (Marcuse, 1991, p. 7). As a result of this system of control, individuals lose their humanity and become a means to an end of a consumer machine that never stops and is never satisfied.

For Marcuse (1991), two dimensions represent the coexistence of the present system with its negation, which in terms of culture would be expressed in the role of culture as a critique of the social order. This critique is needed to unfold any possibility of social change because the two dimensions create a space between what can be thought and what exists wherein critical thinking can emerge. Within this gap, society can "enable its slaves to learn and see and think before they know what is going on and what they themselves can do to change it" (Marcuse, 1991, p. 40). However, this system of social control eliminates the gap between these two dimensions and imposes a unique single dimension that makes it impossible to think beyond this system's frame.

This process of closing the gap and imposing an authoritarian system that does not accept other alternative frameworks is implemented in different manners. One of them is the introduction of consumerism culture and public opinion into the public sphere through television, radio, state officials, and so forth. Now, social control is exercised through the satisfaction of needs created by the system and produces conformity and an idea of happiness that is aligned with the system's values. Thus, Western democracies are not really democratic, because people are manipulated not to think critically and are only offered choices that remain within the system's dominant framework (Marcuse, 1991). Even dissent is controlled and reduced to opinions that do not challenge the system, giving the impression that democracy appears to be "the most efficient system of domination" (Marcuse, 1991, p. 52). As Marcuse (1991) states, "Contemporary society seems to be capable of containing social change—qualitative change which would establish essentially different institutions, a new direction of the productive process, new modes of human existence" (p. xliv). It is a universal project that controls discourses, action, and culture, "an omnipresent system which swallows up or repulses all alternatives" (Marcuse, 1991, p. xlix). Additionally, systems of domination have evolved: "They have become increasingly technological, productive, and even beneficial; consequently, in the most advanced areas of industrial society, the people have been coordinated and reconciled with the system of domination to an unprecedented degree" (Marcuse, 1991, p. vii).

Additionally, Foucault (1995) states that science is a powerful force used by elites to govern modern societies. Since the Enlightenment, science acquired a hegemonic status as a discourse that substituted the narrative of religion. According to Foucault, discourses and narratives establish the limits for the thought of a society, and when acquiring a status of truth, they can dominate the world and exclude alternative discourses. However, they require power mechanisms to reinforce and reproduce them, called "disciplinary technologies of power." Through those technologies (e.g., classification, standardization, surveillance, individualization, totalization, etc.), dominant groups control the daily practices of members of a society in an unconscious form because within a specific belief system, certain views, ideas, or actions become undeniable truths and then it is not possible to think beyond them (Foucault, 1995).

While Foucault shows how power works with institutional discourses and disciplinary practices, Bourdieu uncovers how power embeds its logics into individuals' daily practices. Thus, the fourth system of cultural control is symbolic violence, when violence is exercised with the complicity of a person (Bourdieu & Wacquant, 1996). *Symbolic violence* is the imposition of what can be thought and perceived upon the dominated, who then think this social order of domination is just and incorporates unconscious structures that aim to perpetuate social structures of domination (Bourdieu & Wacquant, 1996). However, Bourdieu (1991) goes beyond a dualism of freedom and determinism and states that "all symbolic domination presupposes, on the part of those who submit to it, a form of complicity which is neither passive submission to external constraint nor a free adherence to values" (pp. 50–51). For Bourdieu (1991), it is an even more organic process than the idea of hegemony for Gramsci (1995) because Bourdieu considers that individuals, through the experience of the social world and its institutions and structures, start taking for granted forms of thinking and behaving. As Bourdieu (1988) argues:

> More concretely, the legitimation of the social world is not, as some believe, the product of a deliberate and purposive action of propaganda or symbolic imposition; it results, rather, from the fact that agents apply to the objective structures of the social world structures of perception and appreciation which are issued out of these very structures and which tend to picture the world as evident. (p. 21)

Bourdieu's work was focused on recognition instead of interest, and for him, symbolic violence is an act of nonrecognition that is outside the control of consciousness and connected with his idea of habitus (Bourdieu, 1977). By habitus it is understood when men and women internalize particular forms of perception and appreciation within a specific context and acquire different dispositions for politics, art, science, regarding their different social classes or ethnic groups that situate them in a specific position in the social order.

Symbolic violence, then, is the incorporation of unconscious structures that tend to perpetuate the structures of action of the dominant while the dominated accept their position as "right" (Webb et al., 2002). Thus, the more the internalized thoughts and actions are used and shown to "work," the more cemented they become within the unconscious (Bourdieu, 1990). Therefore, symbolic violence removes the victim's agency and voice and, in some senses, is much more powerful than physical violence since it is embedded in the very modes of action and structures of individual's cognition and imposes the specter of legitimacy of the social order.

Doxa and the "Indisputable"

In *Outline of a Theory of Practice*, Bourdieu (1977) uses the term "doxa" in relation to his concept of the habitus, which supposes an explanation to how the social space that a group of people shares works at a micro level and determines their practices. In this context, *practice* is defined as the embodied activities and competencies that individuals learn and carry out in social spaces that in turn enable individuals to negotiate interactions with other individuals in that particular social space (Bourdieu, 1977). Additionally, from these social spaces, individuals and groups develop *dispositions*, understood as inclinations toward certain responses and tendencies to make one choice over another, privileging one specific action over another (Bourdieu, 1977). In other words, the habitus enacts the worldview of an individual or a group through their practices.

According to Bourdieu (1977), some structures shape the character of particular shared environments, such as "material conditions of existence" (p. 72), which constitute the specific social spaces inhabited by different groups. However, what differentiates habitus and makes it function as a basis for enhancing certain dispositions and practices in all those individuals who are within a particular habitus is the fact that there is a range of practices and dispositions for each specific habitus, which corresponds to what can be thought within that habitus (Bourdieu, 1977). In essence, there is a limit and a constraint to the possibilities in any habitus due to its specific perceptual framework: This is what Bourdieu calls "doxa."

Social orders are constructed in arbitrary ways. Nevertheless, this arbitrariness tends to be naturalized. "Of all the mechanisms tending to produce this effect, the most important and the best concealed is undoubtedly the dialectic of the objective chances and the agents' aspirations, out of which arises the sense of limits, commonly called the sense of reality" (Bourdieu, 1977, p. 164). As a result of these mechanisms, the different systems of classification that reproduce the objective classes (e.g., sex, age, class, etc.) contribute to the reproduction of the power relations of which they are the result, legitimizing the arbitrariness of the social order (Bourdieu, 1977). According to Bourdieu (1977), "In the extreme cases, this is to say, when there is a quasi-perfect correspondence between the objective order and the subjective principles of organization (as in ancient societies) the natural and the social world appears as self-evident" (p. 164). This is how, through schemes of thought and perception, the subjective order can be presented as objective and experienced as natural and taken for granted (Bourdieu, 1977). Thus, the instruments of knowledge of the social world are political instruments presented as self-evident and cannot be disputed. Besides, "the political function of classifications is never more likely to pass unnoticed than in the case of relatively undifferentiated social formations, in which the prevailing classificatory system encounters no rival or antagonistic principle" (Bourdieu, 1977, p. 164).

In other words, the symbolic power to impose the principles to construct social reality is central for political power.

To extend the field of doxa, stable objective structures and their reproduction in the agent's dispositions are needed. Thus, when these structures are internalized as a result of the logic of reproduction and the political order is not perceived as arbitrary "but as a self-evident and natural order which goes without saying and therefore goes unquestioned, the agents' aspirations have the same limits as the objective conditions of which they are the product" (Bourdieu, 1977, pp. 165–166). Thus, the subjective necessity of the common sense world is validated by an objective consensus on the sense of the world.

What is essential goes without saying because it comes without saying: The tradition is silent, not least about itself as a tradition. Customary law is content to enumerate specific applications of principles that remain implicit and unformulated. Unquestioned, the play of the mythico-ritual homologies constitutes a perfectly closed world, each aspect of which is, as it were, a reflection of all the others, a world that has no place for opinion as liberal ideology understands it. Additionally, nothing is further from the correlative notion of the majority than the unanimity of doxa, the aggregate of the "choices" whose subject is everyone and no one because the questions they answer cannot be explicitly asked (Bourdieu, 1977).

However, even if the social order's arbitrariness is internalized, naturalized, and legitimated, this legitimacy arises from competition and conflict between groups claiming to possess it. Besides, when there is either "cultural contact" or political and economic crisis, doxa is questioned. All of a sudden, there appears a critique that brings what is indisputable into dispute, what is not formulated into formulation, "which, in breaking the immediate fit between the subjective structures and the objective structures, destroys self-evidence practically" (Bourdieu, 1977, p. 167). However, even the most radical critique will be limited by the objective conditions of the social order.

Thus, "crisis is a necessary condition for a questioning of doxa but is not in itself a sufficient condition for the production of a critical discourse" (Bourdieu, 1997, p. 167). On one side, there is a field of opinion of what can be questioned and, on the other, the field of doxa, of what is beyond question as a result of tacit accords to follow social convention. For Bourdieu (1977), both fields are a fundamental objective for a class struggle, "which is the struggle for the imposition of the dominant systems of classification" (p. 168), like the system that was imposed through modernity and that is still in place within our postcolonial societies.

To be successful, the dominated need to have "the material and symbolic means of rejecting the definition of the real that is imposed on them through logical structures reproducing the social structures (i.e., the state of the power relations) and to lift the (institutionalized or internalized) censorships which it implies" (Bourdieu, 1977, p. 168). Thus, dominant groups of society, when they feel threatened, impose censorship through an orthodox discourse that establishes the "official way of speaking and thinking [about] the world," and an overt opposition "between 'right' opinion and 'left' or 'wrong' opinion" (Bourdieu, 1977, p. 170), which is a strategy for limiting the universe of possible discourses and narratives.

Thus, to question doxa is an act of heresy, "for it is to question the very basis on which not just particular practices or dispositions ultimately rest, but on which the very system that is the basis of all practices in a habitus ultimately rests" (Chopra, 2003, p. 426). Doxa is a space of presuppositions, the taken-for-granted, the unconscious, the untheorized, and liberal, radical, conservative, or orthodox thought developed within doxa does not challenge it (Chopra, 2003). However, as noted above, what is doxa for people of one habitus need not necessarily be doxa for the inhabitants of another habitus due to the different structures that constitute a particular type of environment that produces habitus (Bourdieu, 1977). Notwithstanding, what if there were a singular agency shaping these habitus by creating social structures across the breadth of a society? If so, each habitus would be embedded by the same discourse of what counts as doxa. A specific discourse, narrative, or tool for shaping habitus and creating structures.

For Bourdieu (2000), this singular agency that can create social structures and shape habitus that will impose doxa as the indisputable truth is the state. As Bourdieu (1998b) argues:

> The construction of the state is accompanied by the construction of a common historical transcendental immanent to all its subjects. Through the framing it imposes upon practice, the state establishes and inculcates common forms and categories of perception and appreciation, social frameworks of perceptions, understandings, or memory in short state forms of classification. It thereby creates the conditions for a kind of immediate orchestration of habituses which is the foundation of consensus over this set of shared evidences constitutive of (national) common sense. (p. 54)

The state holds a "metacapital" (sum of different capitals) that enables it "to exercise power over the different fields and over the different particular species of capital, and especially over the rates of conversion between them" (Bourdieu, 2000, pp. 40–41). Regarding the concept of "field," it is understood as how a social space in society functions and is composed, and it is opposed to Bourdieu's theorization of the habitus. Thus, the social space can be comprised of different fields, corresponding to different spheres of activity and practice, such as the cultural, economic, social, and political.

When it comes to the cultural field, each group brings its own set of cultural practices into the field. However, "the criteria for what counts as culture is decreed by the dominant class in that field, which is the class that possesses the most cultural capital, and whose interest that particular structure of the field serves" (Chopra, 2003, p. 427). Thus, the struggle of any group to improve their position within the system and increase their power will only reinforce the structure that serves the interests of the dominant class (Chopra, 2003). In other words, the struggle is not just about increasing the capital of nonhegemonic groups but redefining the terms of the conversation to challenge doxa.

At the level of field, what constitutes doxa is the *nomos*, a fundamental law that limits what can be thought within the field (Bourdieu, 2000). Besides, nomos is the regulative principle that orders the functioning of a field, and it is a view that is historically shaped and reflects the interests of the groups in dominant positions in a field. The cultural field is not only about struggling to increase the amount of capital different groups possess but also determining which criteria will define what is considered genuine cultural capital and the right to define that nomos (Bourdieu, 2000). In essence, all participants in a field are increasing their capital through exchange, negotiation, or struggle. Participation in this game contributes in an unconscious way to reaffirm "the structure of the field, that is, the reaffirmation of those practices that serve a dominant class as the most authentic incarnation of that sphere of social activity" (Chopra, 2003, p. 428). Therefore, the goal is not improving one's situation within the field; it is challenging doxa and the nomos of the field. It is not about getting a bigger piece of the cake; it is about changing the cake.

For Bourdieu (1977), "What goes without saying and what cannot be said for lack of an available discourse represents the dividing-line between the most radical form of misrecognition and the awakening of political consciousness" (p. 170). Thus, the space of doxa must be challenged and broadened through new discourses, narratives, and frameworks that will say what until then cannot be said within a narrower and exclusive doxa. It is Marx's equation that language is both real and practical consciousness, Weber's Ausseralltäglichkeit as an extraordinary discourse in times of crisis that is connected with charisma, or Sartre's expression, "words wreak havoc." It is when a name for what was nameless has been found (Bourdieu, 1977). In essence, any language that can command attention is an "authorized language," invested with the authority of a group: The things it designates are not simply expressed but also authorized and legitimated. By extension, what is applied in terms of language can also be applied for discourses, narratives, and worldviews; and those that do not fit within the space of orthodoxy-heterodoxy are not considered legitimate and are labeled as heretic. Thus, a group has power when it has "the capacity to objectify unformulated experiences, to make them public—a step on the road to officialization and legitimation—and, when the occasion arises, to manifest and reinforce their concordance" (Bourdieu, 1977, p. 170).

There is, therefore, a "dialectical relationship between authorized, authorizing language and the group which authorizes it and acts on its authority" (Bourdieu, 1977, p. 171). One example of imposing doxa was with modernity and its darker side, colonialism: when hegemonic groups imposed a hegemonic discourse through a process of Eurocentric leadership that was presented as a self-evident truth about the human and social order and that was and still is undisputable. Doxa is "what gives the dominant discourse its strength" (Bourdieu, 1998a, p. 29), and today it is re-created through partisan groups of those in the fields of academia, media, and business and others who spread ideas that reinforce and contribute to the acceptance of the propositions of a system that is seen as an inexorable truth about the social world (Bourdieu, 1998a). Within globalization and the society of information, "to name things is to bring them into existence" (Melucci, 1995, p. 296). Thus, there is power in naming because "it is language that meets the challenge of meaning or its reduction to signs. It is through language that, today, even nature can be named or erased" (Melucci, 1995, p. 296).

Going from language and naming to dialogue means to transition to "the encounter between men,[1] mediated by the world, in order to name the world" (Freire, 2012, p. 88). As Freire (2012) states, this dialogue is not possible "between those who want to name the world and those who do not wish this naming—between those who deny others the right to speak their word and those whose right to speak has been denied them" (p. 88). As a result of this impossibility, the dominated must claim the right to name the world because, in doing so, they will start to

---

1   Personally, I would prefer to use the word "human," but Freire uses "men" when he refers to humanity.

transform it. This is a critical intercultural leadership process that is not thought to bring to the dominated "a message of 'salvation,' but in order to come to know through dialogue with them both their objective situation—the various levels of perception of themselves and of the world in which and with which they exist" (Freire, 2012, p. 95).

Conclusion

Culture works as a framework for sense- and meaning-making. On the one hand, culture gives us the stability that we need to live in a complex reality, but on the other hand, it limits and constraints our views of the world. When culture is seen as a field for struggle where different social groups try to impose their vision of the world, culture becomes a system for social control, but it can be a system for resistance too. As we will see in the following chapter, leadership is central in these processes because although leadership is influenced by culture, it also creates and shapes culture. Leadership can be defined as a collective process of sense- and meaning-making to define the world and create a social order.

Discussion Questions

1. How are leadership and culture interconnected? Culture and power?
2. How can leadership create or shape culture?
3. How can doxa, or the cultural assumptions of leaders and followers, be challenged?
4. How can we create more inclusive societies through the challenge of assumptions and unconscious biases?

References

Bourdieu, P. (1977). *Outline of a theory of practice*. Cambridge University Press.

Bourdieu, P. (1990). *The logic of practice*. Stanford University Press.

Bourdieu, P. (1998a). The 'myth' of globalization and the welfare state. In P. Bourdieu (Ed.), *Acts of resistance: Against the tyranny of the market* (pp. 29–45). The New Press.

Bourdieu, P. (1998b). *Practical reason: On the theory of action*. Stanford University Press.

Bourdieu, P. (2000). *Pascalian meditations*. Polity Press.

Bourdieu, P., & Wacquant, L. (1996). *An invitation to reflexive sociology*. Polity.

Chopra, R. (2003). Neoliberalism as doxa: Bourdieu's theory of the state and the contemporary Indian discourse on globalization and liberalization. *Journal of Cultural Studies*, *17*(3–4), 419–444.

Fairclough, N. (1992). *Discourse and social change*. Blackwell.

Forgacs, D. (Ed.). (2000). *The Gramsci reader: Selected writings 1916–1935*. New York University Press.

Foucault, M. (1995). *Discipline and punish: The birth of the prison*. Vintage Books.

Freire, P. (2012). *Pedagogy of the oppressed*. Bloomsbury.

Gramsci, A. (1995). *Selections from the Prison Notebooks*. International Publishers.

Hofstede, G., Hofstede, G. J., & Minkov, M. (2010). *Cultures and organizations: Software of the mind.* McGraw Hill.

Horkheimer, M., & Adorno, T. (1996). *Dialectic of enlightenment.* Continuum.

Marcuse, H. (1991). *One-dimensional man.* Beacon Press.

Marx, K., & Engels, F. (1970). *The German ideology.* Lawrence and Wishart.

Melucci, A. (1995). The global planet and the internal planet. In M. Darnovsky, B. Epstein, & R. Flacks (Eds.), *Cultural politics and social movements* (pp. 287–298). Temple University Press.

Schein, E. (2010). *Organizational culture and leadership* (4th ed.). Jossey-Bass.

Strinati, D. (1995). *An introduction to theories of popular culture.* Routledge.

Trice, H. M., & Beyer, J. M. (1993). *The cultures of work organizations.* Prentice Hall.

Webb, J., Schirato, T., & Danaher, G. (2002). *Understanding Bourdieu.* Sage.

Williams, R. (1995). Selections from Marxism and literature. In N. B. Dirks, G. Eley, & S. B. Ortner (Eds.), *Culture, power, history: A reader in contemporary social theory* (pp. 604–608). Princeton University Press.

Chapter 2

Leadership as a Social Myth for Domination or Emancipation[1]

Objectives

The main idea of this chapter is that leadership is a relational process that emerges within a particular context to achieve a goal. More specifically, leadership is a collective process of sense- and meaning-making to define the world and create a social order—a process of "world-making" through framing and action. Thus, leadership needs to be studied holistically, drawing from a process study approach and relational sociology. Additionally, leadership is relational, and any relationship involves power and resistance.

Leadership can be understood as a social myth that functions to legitimize a specific social order. Moreover, "the major significance of most recent studies on leadership is not to be found in their scientific validity but in their function in offering ideological support for the existing social order" (Gemmill & Oakley, 1992, p. 115). In mainstream conceptualizations of leadership, there is an unquestionable assumption that leaders and hierarchies are necessary for organizations to function, and this approach has real consequences when it comes to the practice of leadership (Gemmill & Oakley, 1992). For critical leadership studies, it is central to better understand the existing social order that mainstream leadership approaches support.

---

1 Although most of the literature about leadership studies talks in terms of leaders and followers, in this study, I want to problematize the word "follower" since it implies being behind or below somebody. Thus, I prefer to use the word "supporter" since a supporter can be behind but also next to or in front of a leader. Therefore, although "leader" and "supporter" might still imply a hierarchical order, the combination of these two concepts does not establish such a clear vertical relation as the relationship between leader and follower does.

Most of today's social orders around the world are the result of colonialism. These social orders are characterized by Eurocentric colonial structures of power, also known as "coloniality," that still produce specific social discriminations codified by racial, ethnic, anthropological, or national forms (Quijano, 2010). The Eurocentric perspective naturalizes domination and oppression and universalizes a hegemonic worldview and its social order as superior to the rest. This dominant social order establishes a hierarchy between races, cultures, and identities, resulting in an asymmetrical distribution of power, recognition, and value (Mignolo, 2011).

In the United States, race, culture, and identity are functional to establish social orders and distribute power in asymmetrical ways. White people are situated at the top of the social hierarchy and their identity implies recognition and prestige, while marginalized social groups experience exclusion and stigma. However, today, many subaltern social groups in the country are unfolding emancipatory leadership processes that emphasize the work and struggle of culture and identity to challenge the dominant social order (Jimenez-Luque, 2021). The first focus is on the decolonization of the marginalized groups since they might have internalized the oppression, then on actions and strategies to decolonize the dominant society.

Since mainstream leadership is functional to legitimize a Eurocentric social order with colonial power structures based on race, culture, and identity, it becomes central for critical leadership perspectives to study in-depth critical and intercultural leadership processes seeking social justice. These emancipatory processes emerge within a context of coloniality and struggle against the social order using culture and identity as resources for resistance and social change (Jimenez-Luque, 2021). Besides, because the dominant social order is supported by internalizing assumptions of individualistic and vertical views of leadership where a leader at the top accumulates all the power, it is key to make visible more distributive and participatory ways of exercising leadership. Instead of annihilating people, shared leadership approaches can empower them in a more collective and emancipatory way (Jimenez-Luque, 2021).

Leadership can be interpreted as transformation (Burns, 1978), mobilization of people (Heifetz & Sinder, 1988), and "the process by which 'social order' is constructed and changed" (Hosking & Morley, 1988, p. 90). Brown and Hosking (1986), in their critical work about distributed leadership and skill performance within social movement organizations, describe the skills involved in achieving, maintaining, and changing social organizations and orders and how leadership is central to create social orders. Also, Zoller and Fairhurst (2007) examine leadership's role in mobilizing collective resistance in organizations to transform structures of domination. Additionally, Ospina and Su (2009), in their research about race, ethnicity, and the work of leadership in social change organizations, show how the participants of their study understand race/ethnicity as a resource to advance their goals, revealing details about the roles of these social identities in the work of leadership.

In terms of creating and/or transforming a social order, Bourdieu (1989) argues that "to change the world, one has to change the ways of world-making, that is, the vision of the world and the practical operations by which groups are produced and reproduced" (p. 23). However, for any social group, the idea of change and transformation produces anxiety; thus, to gain support for world-making, it is necessary to unfold a leadership process that develops a collective framework, a vision that gives stability, and a collective action that creates structures and institutions that provide sustainability to this social order.

For the implementation of these frameworks that transform, mobilize, and create new social orders to be successful, they need to make sense and be meaningful for the people involved in the process of leadership. According to Luhmann (1995), the essence of any social system is its specific mode of meaning creation, and it is not possible to articulate any social configuration without meaning production. "Meaning-making enables organizational members to work together towards a common interpretation of reality. Without such shared understanding, organizational activity lacks coherence and common direction" (Ladkin, 2010, p. 102). For Drath and Palus (1994), leadership is a social process where people of a community of practice interact and make sense of the world by creating frameworks within which their actions have meaning according to their different cultural approaches. Gaining consensus and commitment is central in a process of world-making focused on making framing and action part of the leadership process. When there is no consensus and commitment, there is no leadership. However, consensus and commitment may be "offered" because the leader has manipulated the supporters who believe the existing framework and the social order that results from that vision and discourse is the best suited for them even if this framework limits and constrains their capabilities and potential as human beings. Thus, consensus and commitment are the measure to determine whether or not leadership is manipulative, whether the supporters can develop their capabilities and potential within a social order and are not limited or constrained, for example, because of lack of money, the color of their skin, their gender, and so on. As noted in Chapter 1, concepts such as "spontaneous consent" (Gramsci, 1995), "one-dimensional man" (Marcuse, 1991), and "symbolic violence" (Bourdieu, 1991) can explain the commitment and consensus of supporters while being manipulated by their leaders. It is important to note that even when there is manipulation to gain consensus and commitment, the phenomenon of leadership is present. In other words, leadership can be a process toward oppression *or* emancipation.

According to Ladkin (2010), "Meaning-making and its alignment is facilitated by ongoing dialogue and discussion in which those involved disclose their intentionalities, perspectives and emotional responses around the situation in question" (pp. 124–125). Additionally, since there are individuals and groups engaged in the conversation from different cultural perspectives in a critical intercultural leadership process, translation of meaning to articulate frameworks to create and change a social order is central. "A hermeneutic rendering suggests that once the overarching purpose is identified and articulated; gathering the individuals, providing the space and facilitating translating across discourses are key tasks for those taking up the leader role" (Ladkin, 2010, p. 125). This process will be central to move from meaning-making to action.

However, there are asymmetries of power in any relational process that, when excessively high, result in a social order of domination and oppression among human beings even with the spontaneous consent of the people. During modernity, a colonial matrix of power (CMP) was imposed and is still the mental framework of making sense and meaning of the world, legitimizing inequities such as racism, sexism, and classism (Quijano, 2000). Thus, sense-making is political because meaning is political (Fairclough, 1992), and in any relationship where power is involved, resistance emerges (Foucault, 1995). In other words, the Eurocentric leadership process imposed since the 16th century through modernity and colonialism generated the appearance of subaltern leadership processes of cultural resistance that started to deconstruct the internalization of that system of domination and oppression while creating a more holistic and inclusive framework for world-making.

In the following sections, an introduction to relational sociology will be followed by a chronological description of leadership theory's evolution and then some critiques from a critical leadership studies perspective. I will conclude by presenting the perspective used for this study: leadership as a relational process for world-making.

Relational Sociology

According to Emirbayer (1997), "The key question confronting sociologists in the present day is not 'material versus ideal,' 'structure versus agency,' 'individual versus society,' or any of the other dualisms so often noted; rather, it is the choice between substantialism and relationalism" (p. 282). Most of the current approaches in sociology and other disciplines have as their point of departure the notion that units of inquiry are comprised of substances (e.g., things, beings, or essences) (Emirbayer, 1997). For Elias (1978), this "substantialist" way of thinking results from grammatical patterns that configure Western languages. These languages only depict constant movement or change using verbs and imply that there is an isolated object that is resting first and then starts a movement. For example, the idea of a river flowing or the wind blowing carries an assumption that both concepts are a thing at rest at a given point in time (Elias, 1978). In essence, what we do with our languages is to reduce processes of flow and change to static conditions. However, opposed to the different existing varieties of substantialism, there is the perspective of transaction proposed by Dewey and Bentley (1949) that takes place when systems that describe and name are implemented "to deal with aspects and phases of action, without final attribution to 'elements' or other presumptively detachable or independent 'entities,' 'essences,' or 'realities,' and without isolation of presumptively detachable 'relations' from such detachable 'elements'" (p. 108). This is a relational perspective where the meaning of the different units involved in the transaction is the result of the roles they play within the space for the transaction. This "dynamic, unfolding process becomes the primary unit of analysis rather than the constituent elements themselves" (Emirbayer, 1997, p. 287).

Individual persons, moreover, cannot be separated from the transactional spaces within which they act. For example, when Marx (1867/1977) depicts the concept of capital, he affirms that "capital is not a thing, but a social relation between persons which is mediated through things" (p. 932). Therefore, the idea of agency is not a property that acts on passive substances (individuals or groups) but an inseparable element from the fluxes and dynamics that are constantly occurring within the fields/spaces of interactions among people (Emirbayer, 1997). According to Bourdieu and Wacquant (1996), "We may think of a field as a space within which an effect of field is exercised. … The limits of the field are situated at the point where the effects of the field cease" (p. 100).

Regarding leadership studies, the same substantialist approaches are reproduced at both an individual and external level. Thus, the focus on leaders and followers as separated essences with an agency that is also separated from the field of interactions is not acknowledging that, in the same way consciousness is consciousness of something (Husserl, 1960), agency is "agency toward something" (Emirbayer, 1997, p. 294). In other words, the leadership discipline needs to acknowledge that the phenomenon of leadership is broad and holistic because while at an internal level the agency is toward persons, places, or meanings, at an external level, it would be toward culture or structures—and all of them within fields of constant interactions, changes, and struggles.

Evolution of Leadership Theory

According to Horner (1997), "In some cases, leadership has been described as a process, but most theories and research on leadership look at a person to gain understanding" (p. 270). Hence, leadership has typically been defined by the traits, qualities, and behaviors of a leader and, more recently, by relations of power and influence and the importance of context: cognitive and situational theories, and cultural and symbolic approaches.

The first leadership studies trend was centered on identifying which internal qualities great leaders had, with the intention to recognize them in future leaders (Bernard, 1926). Thus, the focus of the research was on personality and physical and mental characteristics. The prevailing idea was that great leadership is "reserved" to only a few privileged individuals who possess a set of innate traits that cannot be developed (Galton, 1869). These leadership traits were understood as patterns of personal characteristics that make leaders consistently effective across different groups and organizations (Zaccaro et al., 2004).

A second major approach was to study what great leaders do to train their behavior (Halpin & Winer, 1957). Although Stogdill (1948) and Mann (1959) found similar traits across several studies they undertook, there was evidence suggesting that leaders in one situation may not necessarily be leaders in another. Thus, the emphasis of leadership studies shifted away from leaders' traits to behaviors, and new research on behavior came up, such as Blake and Mouton's (1964) recognized model of five different leadership styles, centered on the concern that leaders have for people and for achieving their purposes. As a result of the behavioral approach, the idea of "the born leader" was substituted with the idea that "the leader can be made," which contributed to developing leadership methods to teach employees in different organizations how to be a great leader (Saal & Knight, 1988).

A third approach that emerged was the research interested not only in traits, qualities, and behaviors of the leaders but also in theories of power and influence that considered "leadership in terms of the source and amount of power available to leaders and the manner in which leaders exercise that power over followers through either unilateral or reciprocal interactions" (Bensimon et al., 1989, p. 7). In 1959, French and Raven developed a model that includes five bases of power: reward, coercion, legitimate, expert, and referent. Raven added informational power as a new base of power in 1965, and this is central in terms of power and influence (Raven, 1992). From here, additional leadership theories have emerged, such as transactional leadership, which uses the position of power of the leader to get followers to accomplish tasks (Burns, 1978; Bass, 1985), or transformational theories, which are focused on motivating followers by satisfying their needs and engaging them in the processes of work (Burns, 1978; Bass, 1985).

Under the category of "power and influence" emerged the connection between leadership and motivation, wherein leaders have to create "the right environment, one in which people want to be involved and feel committed to their work" (Horner, 1997, p. 273). In essence, this perspective emphasizes the people being led, not the leader, even if the leader continues at the center of the research. However, even if motivation theories are thought to control the employees from a hierarchical perspective where the leader is at the top, this approach opens indirectly the inclusion of another actor within the leadership studies, the follower, along with the environment the leader creates and the culture where all the relations are embedded.

A fourth leadership approach focuses on how the situation, context, task, and environment could affect the leader's decision. Situational and contingency theories state that what leaders do depends upon characteristics of the particular situation and the context within which they act (Hemphill, 1949). Thus, leadership scholars started to consider the possibility that leadership could be different according to every situation (Saal & Knight, 1988), which paved the way for more realistic and complex views of the leadership phenomenon that started to go beyond the image of the leader and the follower.

With a broader perspective of studying leadership, culture came later to the equation with cultural and symbolic approaches. These approaches suggest that if leaders want to be effective, they need to understand their organizations' culture and, in particular, how culture evolves and changes to adapt to external factors (Schein, 2010). According to Schein (2010), "Culture is both a 'here and now' dynamic phenomenon and a coercive background structure that influences us in multiple ways. Culture is constantly reenacted and created by our interactions with others and shaped by our own behavior" (p. 3).

Other perspectives, such as the one proposed by Manz and Sims (1989), started to focus on self-leadership, conceptualizing leadership as a process in which everyone involved in the leadership phenomenon participates. This relates to Gardner's (1990) definition of leadership as "the accomplishment of group purpose, which is furthered not only by effective leaders but also by innovators, entrepreneurs, and thinkers; by the availability of resources; by questions of value and social cohesion" (p. 38). Under this perspective, leadership was thought of as a more holistic phenomenon involving a group, a purpose, leaders, innovators, and thinkers, taking away the idea of leadership resting solely in one person, a leader. Leadership may be rotated among the members of an organization formally or informally, each person may hold leadership responsibility for specific tasks at work, or informal leaders can emerge within the organization (Wilson et al., 1994). Gradually, leadership theories started to lay "the groundwork for examining leadership as a process, taking the emphasis away from an individual" (Horner, 1997, p. 278). This naturally makes the study of leadership more complex: "The focus of leadership research cannot be a specific person, even if that person is designated as the team leader, if a comprehensive understanding of the leadership process is expected" (Horner, 1997, p. 280).

Dualisms, Complexity, and Critical Leadership Studies

According to Harter (2006), when it comes to leadership studies, "dualisms pop up everywhere" (p. 90). Thus, we have dualisms such as leadership/management; leaders/followers; self/ contexts; born/made leaders; task/people orientation; transactional/transformational; organic/

mechanistic; or autocratic/participative, to name a few examples. This dualist view is prevalent in mainstream leadership research when it comes to traits, styles, contingency theories, paths, goals, charisma, and so on, "where leaders' personas and practices have tended to be privileged and psychological perspectives and positivist methodologies predominate" (Collinson, 2014, p. 39). However, a dualist leadership perspective can have very negative effects on the leadership field because dualism tends to oversimplify "the complex, inter-connected, and shifting relationships that characterize leadership dynamics. It emphasizes differences by making excessive separations between distinctions and treating these as immutable polarities" (Collison, 2014, p. 39). Besides, from a critical perspective, dualism also contributes to increasing asymmetries of power when privileging, marginalizing and excluding, and as a consequence, "important issues, particularly around power, ambiguity, tension, paradox, and contradiction tend to disappear from view" (Collinson, 2014, p. 39).

Particularly in the United States, positivist approaches represent the dominant perspective (Martin & Collinson, 2002), and critical visions "may decide to work 'within' or 'alongside' the mainstream functionalist and positivist perspectives rather than try to engage in thoroughgoing critique" (Collinson, 2014, p. 46). Notwithstanding, there are more and more leadership scholars around the world interested in the tensions, paradoxes, and contradictions that the phenomenon of leadership produces, and new research on leadership effectiveness suggests that it "is more closely associated with versatile, agile and ambidextrous practices that require a capacity to deal with uncertainty, unpredictability, paradox, simultaneity, and ambiguity in more subtle ways" (Collinson, 2014, p. 43). Storey and Salaman (2009) recommend leaders embrace these tensions and contradictions and advocate for organizational systems that "thrive on paradox" because that is the "the essence of leadership" (p. 22).

Dualism is not exclusive of leadership studies, however. Social theory is embedded with binaries between subject and object, individual and society, or action and structure (Collins, 2014), same as organizational theory and dualisms such as centralized and decentralized, differentiation and integration, formal and informal, or change and stability (Dale, 2001). Dualism is very connected with modernity and its frame for reason and practice, based on opposition in general and dichotomy in particular. According to Bauman (1991), "Intellectual visions that turn out tree-like images of progressive bifurcation reflect and inform the administrative practice of splitting and separation" (p. 14). For the modern human being, ambiguity means chaos and anarchy, and the new framework of modernity seeks stability and order through binary classifications. However, this project of modernity is unachievable because ambiguity will always emerge, producing more ambiguity that could not be classified (Bauman, 1991).

Therefore, to overcome dualism and embrace complexity, critical leadership studies (CLS) offer an approach to better understand leadership's phenomenon more holistically and comprehensively. Critical leadership studies are a growing area of research that views power as key to leadership dynamics (Alvesson & Spicer, 2012). Critical perspectives "focus on the situated power relations and identity dynamics through which leadership discursive practices are socially constructed, frequently rationalized, sometimes resisted, and occasionally transformed" (Collison, 2014, p. 37). Additionally, CLS also recognizes that, besides positional leaders in positions of formal authority, leaders can emerge informally in subordinated positions and oppositional organizations (Knowles, 2007) or revolutionary social movements (Rejai, 1979).

In the following sections, I will focus on the two main perspectives that I used for this study in terms of leadership: cultural and symbolic leadership and leadership as a process from a CLS perspective. I used a cultural and symbolic approach focused on how systems of shared beliefs and values that give meaning to organizational life are maintained, reinterpreted, or changed. However, this perspective is still very centered on the role of leaders, and even if I consider this idea very important due to the privileged position of authority and power that leaders have to implement their vision or framework, my research was not solely concerned with the role of leaders but more specifically with the constant flux of interactions and changes between different members of the organization and understanding leadership as a process that includes leaders, supporters, environment, culture, context, and purpose to be achieved. Thus, I followed the three main principles of CLS: (a) followers' agency, expertise, and potential for resistance; (b) the fact that leadership dynamics can create unexpected and contradictory consequences beyond the leader's understanding or anticipation; and (c) the interconnection and complexity of leadership that cannot be reduced to a dualism between two static subjects (Collison, 2014).

Leadership and The Cultural and Symbolic Approach

According to De Giosa (2009), cultural and symbolic approaches "focus on what culture actually does, by privileging once more an analysis of the processes rather than thinking of culture as an entity and focusing on a description of its structures" (p. 172). In terms of leadership, this perspective is centered on leaders within an organization because it is understood that they have the strongest influence on the organizational culture due to their position of authority and power. Leadership and organizational culture are seen as "management of culture" in organizations "because leadership organizes its contents and manages its modes of construction" (De Giosa, 2009, p. 172). From this perspective, organizational culture and leadership are the two sides of a coin, and the focus is on the leaders because they play "the role of leading actor in this process, the point of reference of the social and organizational set-up" (De Giosa, 2009, p. 172). For example, Weick (1995) argues that a true leader must act as an evangelist, a person who identifies and points out the meanings of things to the other members of an organization or community. Thus, to impact or facilitate this vision or framework to the other members of the organization, power is a central element.

Power within organizations "means the ability of a subject to influence others' behaviours within social relationships" (De Giosa, 2009, p. 176). Power expresses a relation but within an organization or society can also represent an objective position resulting from an organizational structure (De Giosa, 2009). This position is more related to the concept of *authority*, which is defined as "the power to make decisions which guide the actions of another. It is a relation between two individuals: one 'superior,' the other 'subordinate'" (Simon, 1945, p. 179). Thus, in each organization, it is the authority that shapes its formal structure (De Giosa, 2009), and a person without a recognized formal status or position will have more difficulty convincing the other members of the organization about their vision and framework (Simon, 1945). As a result of these asymmetries of power, individuals in leadership positions within an organization are an important unit of inquiry to understand the organizational culture. However, leadership is a broader phenomenon that goes beyond leadership positions because "the formal scheme of an organization will always be different from the way in which the organization itself operates, that is, through a number of interpersonal relations, which are absent from a formal scheme" (De Giosa, 2009, p. 180). While it is vital to focus on individuals in leadership positions because they have more power and impact on implementing their frameworks and visions, it is also important to consider the informal aspects of organizations that are related to interpersonal relations and strongly influence the culture of an organization. Therefore, the interest is focused not only on the positional leader but also on the relationships within the organization and with external actors that eventually configure the organization's culture. In summary, this study has taken into account several formal or positional leaders within an organization (and also supporters), but the center of the research is the process that contributes to making sense and meaning of reality with the aim of, as Pfeffer (1981) argues, constructing and conserving systems of meanings, paradigms, languages, and common cultures.

The Ontological Challenge of Leadership and Processes

The assumption that leaders have essential traits and abilities that can be measured and trained explains the individualistic approach from a psychological perspective often at the origin of leadership theories and research (Wood, 2005). This assumption around leadership in general and leaders in particular "presupposes only certain individuals can be leaders, only certain leaders are appropriate for certain contingencies, or only certain individuals have sufficient flexibility in their leadership styles to match the needs of a number of different situations" (Wood, 2005, p. 1102). Moreover, there is the idea that leaders are the only ones to create meaning, make sense of reality (Hosking, 1988), and inspire and transform people and organizations (Maccoby, 2000). However, this is a very limited and simplistic approach to the study of a broad phenomenon such as leadership, and with this study, I argue leadership is best understood as a process rather than a property or substance.

From a perspective of process, each element can be understood as permeable and combines with another element without dissolving into independent parts so "the actual character of leadership extends into a portion of another as a relation or continuity of flow rather than a solid state" (Wood, 2005, p. 1103). Leaders are the result of past events, relations, and actions but at the same time are in the process of becoming different people because they constantly experience new events, encounters with other people, and acting through daily practices.

Process Studies

Process metaphysics is a distinctive branch of philosophical tradition opposed to a dominant Western metaphysic that affirms the nature of reality is "here, now, immediate, and discrete" (Whitehead, 1933/1967b, p. 180). Thus, process metaphysics presents the nature of reality as a process and argues that "processes rather than things best represent the phenomenon that we encounter in the natural world about us" (Rescher, 1996, p. 2). It is focused on becoming instead of being (Chia, 1996) because "process is the concrete reality of things" (Griffin, 1986, p. 6).

When it comes to leadership, concepts such as leaders, followers, and organizations are "simple appearances we employ to give substantiality to our experience, but under whose supposed 'naturalness' the fundamentally processual nature of the real is neglected" (Wood, 2005, p. 1104). This is the dominant approach used currently that separates the individual actor from the "different" rest, disregarding the significance of the internal diversity, or "milieu," of individuals (Deleuze, 1994, p. 211). Whitehead (1925/1967a) defines this perspective as "the fallacy of misplaced concreteness," which consists of mistaking abstract conceptualizations for concrete things without considering past, present, and future events.

The key issue in process studies is how an actor "condenses within itself ... a multitude of social dimensions and meanings" (Cooper, 1983, p. 204) because leadership is not situated in "the autonomous, self-determining individual with a secure unitary identity [at] the centre of the social universe" (Alvesson & Deetz, 2000, p. 98). Therefore, leadership is understood as a "systematic complex of mutual relatedness" (Whitehead, 1925/1967a, p. 161) where conceptual interpretations are always "an incompletion in the process of production" (Whitehead, 1929/1978, p. 327). For Cooper (1983), leadership is "the point of difference" (p. 204), and Wood (2005) suggest it "is already a 'complete' relation, where the relation is the thing itself and each part necessarily refers to another, but without 'completion' in a straightforward way" (p. 1105). In other words, the phenomenon of leadership "is the unlocalizable 'in' of the 'between' of each, a freely interpenetrating process, whose 'identity' is consistently self-differing" (Wood, 2005, p. 1105).

Misplaced Leadership Focus

According to Smircich and Morgan (1982), people look to leaders to create a framework for defining their reality. Notwithstanding, what is seen as real is normally the result of power relations (Wood, 2005). Whitehead (1925/1967a) argues that there is a misperception of reality that makes us believe there exists an order of "completed" things and that individuals can comprehend it without realizing they are social first. Thus, concepts connected with leadership such as "charisma, effectiveness, vision, and transformation only appear as personal qualities because we have mistaken our abstraction of them for concrete reality" (Wood, 2005, 1106). In other words, when we identify a leader or we identify ourselves with a leader, it is through a process of abstraction that emerges from an indeterminate ultimate reality (Griffin, 1986) but is not the essence of the person themselves (Wood, 2005). This inaccurate perspective results in understanding leadership as the person at the top of a hierarchy (Barker, 2001) or as a relation between things where one aspires to be like the other (Wood, 2005). In essence, "the origin of individuality, therefore, is thought to be either an idealized social actor exercising influence on external circumstances, or a discrete relation capable of reconciling singular terms" (Wood, 2005, p. 1107). Mainstream leadership situates the leader at the center and "forgets this individual is already a synthesis of differences, not linked through some principle of identity, but through irreducibly heterogeneous processes, which surround and suffuce it" (Wood, 2005, p. 1107).

New leadership perspectives have started to focus on leadership as a process of individuation rather than as a static individual, positioning leadership as a process of transformation and change (Barker, 2001). Simondon (1992) argues that "to grasp firmly the nature of individuation, we must consider the being not as a substance, or matter, or form, but as a tautly extended and supersaturated system" (p. 301). Thus, the process of individuation is understood "as something to be explained, rather than as something in which the explanation is to be found" (Simondon, 1992, p. 299).

According to Tsoukas and Chia (2002), these contributions to the idea of leadership as a process have been central to advancing this topic. However, they are only going to be fully developed "if their calls for a greater attention to process lead to a consistent reversal of the ontological priority" (Tsoukas & Chia, 2002, p. 570). Hosking (2001) describes the constant connections that construct social realities and refuses to reproduce taken-for-granted elements about processes and relations, and Barker (2001) criticizes the assumptions that a person can explain a concept as complex and fluid as leadership. Leadership is "the complex and continuous relationships of people and institutions," and these relationships need to be the center of leadership studies (Barker, 2001, p. 483). Leadership can be defined as a "dissipative system … continually renewing itself within a dynamic context" (Barker, 2001, p. 487). So what we are experiencing is in constant transformation within a system composed of microsystems.

Leadership Refocused: A Process of World-Making

As noted at the beginning of this section on leadership theory, I understand leadership as a collective process of world-making with both leaders and supporters as active actors. This process seeks stability and is exercised by leaders and supporters who, despite having the agency to shape and influence, are influenced by the environment, the culture, the context, and the purpose to be achieved, which is based on the combination of framing and action and requires consensus and commitment to emerge.

Leadership takes place between people's relationships with other peoples and with institutions (Barker, 2001) and, to make sense and meaning of a complex and uncertain world, emerges in the transaction between leaders and supporters to create frameworks seeking for social stability on the one side and leaders and supporters with the structures and institutions they create looking for sustainability on the other.

Describing the configuration of a social order, Elias (2000) states:

> This basic tissue resulting from many single plans and actions of men can give
> rise to changes and patterns that no individual has planned or created. From this
> interdependence of people arises an order sui generis, an order more compelling and
> stronger than the will and reason of the individual people composing it. It is the order
> of interweaving human impulses and strivings, the social order, which determines
> the course of historical change; it underlies the civilizing process. (p. 366)

Therefore, what leaders and supporters would do is point out a direction articulating frameworks that provide stability to create a social order because, as Elias (2000) argues, the relations between individuals with their actions, plans, and purposes, cannot be foreseen simply because multiple combinations cannot be calculated.

When it comes to the concept of leaders, Hosking (1988) defines them as "those who consistently make effective contributions to social order" (p. 153). However, as Rost (1993) argues, the contributions or changes of social order are just "intended" because the changes may take place in the future or not take place at all, although the leadership phenomenon had emerged and unfolded. According to Stacey (2012), the existing tools and techniques for leaders and managers based on "instrumental rationality" are useless because they "cannot enable leaders and managers to choose the future of their organizations; nor can they enable leaders and managers to control the process of realizing whatever choices they make" (p. 122). Notwithstanding, some individuals, regardless of their position or power, contribute to building and changing the social order and gaining consensus and commitment of other individuals. Those individuals who receive support become leaders, and those who gave their support become supporters, configuring what is described as the phenomenon of leadership in this study. In other words, leaders and supporters are two sides of the same coin: There are no leaders without supporters, and there are no supporters without leaders.

In terms of supporters, they are the individuals who offer their consensus and commitment to the proposals of social order of other individuals who, in gaining support, become leaders. However, the relationship between leaders and supporters is very fluid because not only can the leaders at any time lose their support and therefore their condition of leaders but also the supporters can seize the initiative and contribute to social order, gaining consensus and support of leaders who, in becoming supporters, transform the former supporters in leaders. Therefore, "leader" and "supporter" are not exclusive identities or identities that "kill" each other and cannot coexist, as Maalouf (2009) argues, and they can exist simultaneously at a given time regardless of the position within an organization or community.

Notwithstanding, in this study, I view leadership as a process that goes beyond leaders and supporters influencing each other, and there are other elements, such as the environment, culture, context (where I include social structures and institutions), and the purpose to be achieved, that also influence the process of leadership. All those elements are interconnected, and it is not only in the "in between" of the relationship between leaders and supporters where the phenomenon of leadership emerges (i.e., "leadership moment," according to Ladkin [2010]) but also in the "in between" of the relations of leaders and followers with the rest of the elements (see Figure 2.1).

Since leaders and supporters have agency, leadership is exercised by actors through their relationships. However, it is necessary to deconstruct heroic or romantic views of leaders as powerful individuals who control the whole process (Meindl & Ehrlich, 1988; Stacey, 2012). Within the process of leadership, leaders are not only influenced by the resistance of supporters who, at a given time, can withdraw their support and become leaders of another proposal when gaining consensus and support of other individuals who then will become supporters but also for the multiple combinations of relationships and environmental and contextual events that leaders cannot control. Leaders influence the process of leadership and contribute to achieving a purpose, but they cannot control the whole process of leadership, because the phenomenon of leadership is an extremely deep and complex process with many elements involved that cannot be controlled, just influenced. However, to understand that heroic and glorious designs of leadership do not work "does not mean abandoning any idealistic concern with improving the human conditions of life. It simply means taking a humbler stance and working realistically in our own local interactions" (Stacey, 2012, p. 127). According to Hernes (2008), actors within a process "intervene on the assumption that something will become; they assume that there is something there to be reckoned with, and they assume that through organization something

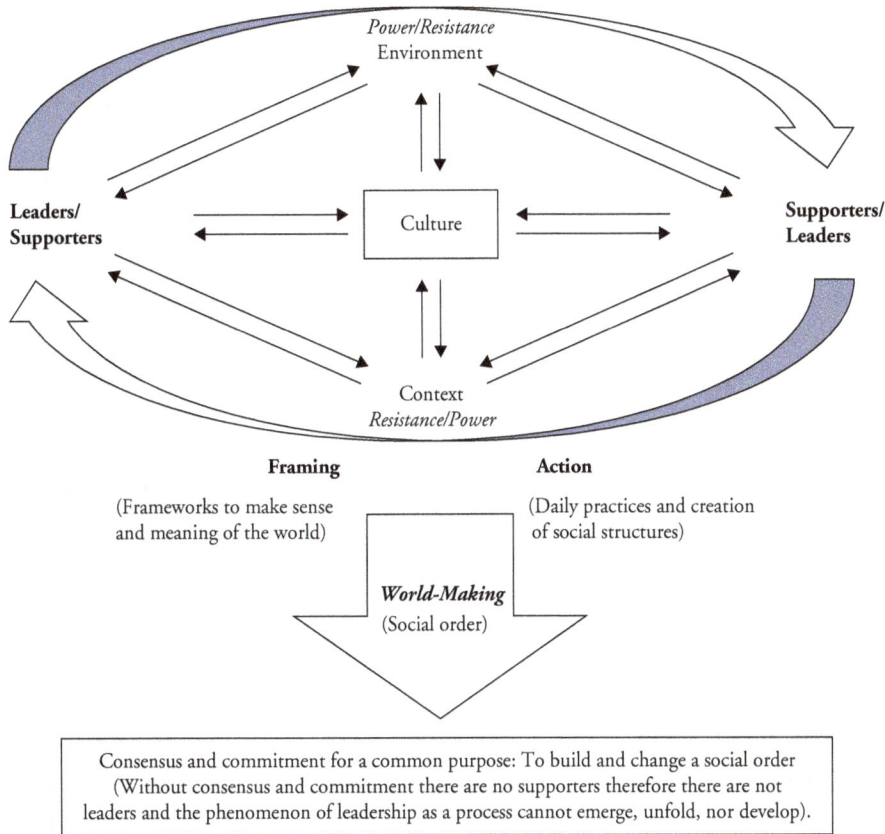

Power/Resistance
Environment

Leaders/
Supporters

Culture

Supporters/
Leaders

Context
Resistance/Power

Framing

(Frameworks to make sense
and meaning of the world)

Action

(Daily practices and creation
of social structures)

World-Making
(Social order)

Consensus and commitment for a common purpose: To build and change a social order
(Without consensus and commitment there are no supporters therefore there are not
leaders and the phenomenon of leadership as a process cannot emerge, unfold, nor develop).

FIGURE 2.1   Leadership as a Process: Framing and Action for World-Making.

will be achieved in a tangible stable, state" (p. 128). Therefore, meaning- and sense-making are essential in the process of leadership. When analyzing leadership as a process to build and change the social order, it is important to focus on leaders and supporters because both have agency and certain influence at giving some order, redirection, or 'stabilization to the process. However, it is central to consider how leadership unfolds, considering the different elements that, although they can be influenced and shaped by leaders and supporters, influence them. This social order is constructed through two subprocesses that combined represent the process of leadership in this study:

- designing collective frameworks to make sense and meaning of the world and a particular social order
- developing collective practices to produce and reproduce a particular social order

Frameworks to Make Sense/Meaning of the World

For Drath and Palus (1994), "Making sense is the process of arranging our understanding of experience so that we can know what has happened and what is happening, and so that we can predict what will happen; it is constructing knowledge of ourself and the world" (p. 2). Through a constructivist perspective, human beings create a coherence out of their experiences (Kegan, 1982; Piaget, 1954) and try to understand "using meaning-making structures to construct knowledge about experience so that one is able to interpret, anticipate, and plan" (Drath & Palus, 1994, p. 3).

To make sense of an experience, one creates a frame that explains how the world is and helps the person act and behave in the world (Bruner, 1986). It is a process of construction of reality developed at an internal level (Kegan, 1982) and at a societal level when constructing experience together (Berger & Luckman, 1966) to communicate and organize in groups for world-making. Instead of being told what to do, what people need are frameworks within which all their actions will make sense (Drath & Palus, 1994). As noted above, in a complex and uncertain world, although leaders cannot control events or the whole process of leadership, they do control "the context under which events are seen if they recognize a framing opportunity" (Fairhurst, 2011, p. 2). Cultural frames and framing have material consequences because it is through them that "we create the realities to which we must then respond" (Fairhurst, 2011, p. 27) and from where we create social structures and institutions to produce and reproduce a specific social order.

People commit to other people, ideas, values, goals, and, on a more general level, to ways of being, acting, and understanding the world (Kegan, 1982). This social and collective level of meaning-making is the culture where we are embedded when we are born (Goodman, 1978), limiting and constraining what can be said or thought. From this perspective, the most general tool in a society to make meaning is culture, and processes of leadership "are connected to the larger cultural frame within which they occur culture-building is the primary process of meaning-making in collective experience and thus the primary leadership process" (Drath & Palus, 1994, p. 10).

Actions to Create and Transform the Social Order

As noted before, leadership is transformation (Burns, 1978), mobilization of people (Heifetz & Sinder, 1988), the construction and change of a social order (Hosking & Morley, 1988). In essence, leadership is about sense-making (Weick, 1995; Pye, 2005) to enable people to act, transform, and, more specifically, in this study, struggle to deconstruct social structures of domination and oppression to reconstruct new structures for liberation and emancipation.

Melucci (1995) argues that collective action is a social construction with purpose and meaning. This purpose and meaning emerge from framing to legitimate the actions (Snow & Benford, 1992). However, framing is also defined throughout collective action, transforming the dominant culture, bridging, amplifying, or transforming other frames (Snow et al., 1986). Therefore, framing influences action, but action influences framing when preexisting beliefs or oppositional values that emerge during the struggle are incorporated within the group's frames (Taylor & Whittier, 1995). There is an interconnection between framing and action (Snow & Benford, 1992), and both influence each other in creating a shared reality (Fairhurst, 2011), a new social order. Framing and action configure the process of world-making to transform society and are the glue that brings together and makes sense and meaning of the different elements involved in the leadership process: leaders, supporters, environment, culture, context, and purpose to be achieved.

Conclusion

Leadership needs to be viewed from a critical perspective because, as a relational process, it involves power and resistance. Additionally, leadership within organizations and societies is central to identity formation and legitimizing social orders. Thus, leadership can create hierarchical social orders where there are a few chosen ones at the top and the rest need to follow them or, as we will see in the next chapter, more participatory and horizontal social orders where everybody is involved in leading and following with less asymmetries of power. In essence, leadership can be a tool for domination and oppression or an emancipatory project for resistance and social justice.

Discussion Questions

1. Why can leadership be considered a social myth?
2. What type of social order do mainstream discourses of leadership support?
3. What social order would create more critical perspectives of conceptualizing and exercising leadership?
4. Can we effectively study leadership if we focus exclusively on individuals?
5. What other elements are key to understanding any leadership process?
6. Why is leadership a relational process that needs to be studied holistically?

References

Alvesson, M., & Deetz, S. (2000). *Doing critical management research.* Sage.

Alvesson, M., & Spicer, A. (2012). Critical leadership studies: The case for critical performativity. *Human Relations, 65*, 367–390.

Barker, R. (2001). The nature of leadership. *Human Relations, 54*(4), 469–494.

Bass, B. M. (1985). *Leadership and performance beyond expectations.* Free Press.

Bauman, Z. (1991). *Modernity and ambivalence.* Polity Press.

Bensimon, E. M., Birnbaum, R., & Neuman, A. (1989). *Making sense of administrative leadership.* Jossey-Bass.

Blake, R., & Mouton, J. (1964). *The managerial grid: The key to leadership excellence.* Gulf Publishing Co.

Bourdieu, P. (1989). Social space and symbolic power. *Sociological Theory, 7*(1), 14–25.

Bourdieu, P. (Ed.). (1991). *Language and symbolic power.* Harvard University Press.

Bourdieu, P., & Wacquant, L. (1996). *An invitation to reflexive sociology.* Polity.

Bruner, J. (1986). *Actual minds, possible worlds.* Harvard University Press.

Burns, J. M. (1978). *Leadership.* Harper and Row.

Chia, R. (1996). *Organizational analysis as deconstructive practice*. De Gruyter.

Collins, R. (1990). Stratification, emotional energy and the transient emotions. In T. D. Kemper (Ed.), *Research agendas in the sociology of emotions* (pp. 27–57). State University of New York Press.

Collison, D. (2014). Dichotomies, dialectics and dilemmas: New directions for critical leadership studies? *Leadership, 10(1)*, 36–55.

Cooper, R. (1983). The other: A model of human structuring. In G. Morgan (Ed.), *Beyond method: Strategies for social research* (pp. 202–218). Sage.

De Giosa, V. (2009). The cultural management of leadership. *Anales de Estudios Económicos y Empresariales, 19*, 167–191.

Deleuze, G. (1994). *Difference and repetition*. Athlone Press.

Dewey, J., & Bentley, A. F. (1949). *Knowing and the known*. Beacon Press.

Drath, W. H., & Palus, C. J. (1994). *Making common sense: Leadership as meaningmaking in a community of practice*. Center for Creative Leadership.

Elias, N. (1978). *What is sociology?* Columbia University Press.

Elias, N. (2000). *The civilizing process*. Blackwell.

Emirbayer, M. (1997). Manifesto for a relational sociology. *American Journal of Sociology, 103(2)*, 281–317.

Fairclough, N. (1992). *Discourse and social change*. Blackwell.

Fairhurst, G. T. (2011). *The power of framing: Creating the language of leadership*. Jossey-Bass.

Foucault, M. (1995). *Discipline and punish: The birth of the prison*. Vintage Books.

Galton, F. (1869). *Hereditary genius*. Appleton.

Gardner, J. W. (1990). *On leadership*. Free Press.

Gemmill, G., & Oakley, J. (1992). Leadership: An alienating social myth. *Human Relations, 45(2)*, 113–129.

Goodman, N. (1978). *Ways of worldmaking*. Hackett Publishing.

Gramsci, A. (1995). *Selections from the prison notebooks*. International Publishers.

Griffin, D. R. (1986). *Bohm, Prigogyne and the ultimate significance of time*. State University of New York Press.

Halpin, A. W., & Winer, B. J. (1957). A factorial study of the leader behavior description. In R. M. Stogdill & A. E. Coons (Eds.), *Leader behavior: Its description and measurement.* (pp. 39–51). Bureau of Business Research, Ohio State University.

Harter, N. (2006). *Clearings in the forest: On the study of leadership*. Purdue University Press.

Heifetz, R. A., & Sinder, R. M. (1988). Political leadership: Managing the public's problem solving. In R. B. Reich (Ed.), *The power of public ideas* (pp. 179–203). Ballinger.

Hernes, T. (2008). *Understanding organization as process: Theory for a tangled world*. Routledge.

Hosking, D. M. (1988). Organizing, leadership and skillful process. *Journal of Management Studies, 25(2)*, 147–166.

Hosking, D. M. (2001). Social construction as process: Some new possibilities for research and development. *Concepts & Transformation, 4(2)*, 117–132.

Hosking, D. M., & Morley, I. E. (1988). The skills of leadership. In J. G. Hunt, B. R. Baliga, H. P. Dachler, & C. A. Schriesheim (Eds.), *Emerging leadership vistas* (pp. 89–106). Lexington Books.

Husserl, E. (1960). *Cartesian meditations: An introduction to phenomenology*. Martinus Nijhoff.

Jimenez-Luque, A. (2021). Decolonial leadership for cultural resistance and social change: Challenging the social order through the struggle of identity. *Leadership*, *17*(2), 154–172.

Kegan, R. (1982). *The evolving self: Problem and process in human development.* Harvard University Press.

Knowles, H. (2007). Trade union leadership: Biography and the role of historical context. *Leadership*, *3*(2), 191–209.

Ladkin, D. (2010). *Rethinking leadership: A new look at old leadership questions.* Edward Elgar.

Luhmann, N. (1995). *Social systems.* Standford University Press.

Maalouf, A. (2009). *Las identidades asesinas.* Alianza Editorial.

Mann, R. D. (1959). A review of the relationship between personality and performance in small groups. *Psychological Bulletin*, *56*(4), 241–270.

Manz, C. C., & Sims, H. P., Jr. (1989). *SuperLeadership.* Prentice Hall Press.

Martin, P. Y., & Collinson, D. L. (2002). Over the pond and across the water: Developing the field of gendered organizations. *Gender, Work and Organization*, *9*(3), 244–265.

Marx, K. (1977). *Capital: A critique of political economy.* Vintage Books. (Original work published 1867)

Meindl, J. R., & Ehrlich, S. B. (1988). Developing a 'romance of leadership scale.' *Proceedings of the Eastern Academy of Management*, *47*, 133–135.

Melucci, A. (1995). The process of collective identity. In H. Johnston & B. Klandermans (Eds.), *Social movements and culture* (pp. 41–63). University of Minnesota Press.

Mignolo, W. (2011). *The darker side of western modernity. Global futures, decolonial options.* Duke University Press.

Pfeffer, J. (1981). Management as symbolic action: The creation and maintenance of organizational paradigms. In L. L. Cummings & B. M. Staw (Eds.), *Research in Organizational Behaviour*, *3*, 1–52.

Piaget, J. (1954). *The construction of reality in the child.* Basic Books.

Pye, A. (2005). Leadership and organizing: Sense-making in action. *Leadership*, *1*(1), 31–50.

Quijano, A. (2000). Coloniality of power, eurocentrism, and Latin America. *Nepantla: Views From South, 1*(3), 533–580.

Quijano, A. (2010). Coloniality and modernity/rationality. In W. Mignolo & A. Escobar (Eds.), *Globalization and the decolonial option* (pp. 22–32). Routledge.

Rejai, M. (1979). *Leaders of revolution.* Sage.

Rescher, N. (1996). *Process metaphysics: An introduction to process philosophy.* State University of New York Press.

Rost, J. C. (1993). *Leadership for the twenty-first century.* Praeger.

Saal, F. E., & Knight, P. A. (1988). *Industrial/organizational psychology: Science and practice.* Brooks/Cole Publishing Co.

Schein, E. (2010). *Organizational culture and leadership* (4th ed.). Jossey-Bass.

Simon, H. A. (1945). *Administrative behavior.* The Free Press.

Simondon, G. (1992). The genesis of the individual. In J. Crary & S. Winter (Eds.), *Incorporations* (pp. 296–319). Zone.

Smircich, L., & Morgan, G. (1982). Leadership: The management of meaning. *The Journal of Applied Behavioural Science, 18*(3), 257–273.

Snow, D. A., & Benford, R. D. (1988). Ideology, frame resonance, and participant mobilization. In B. Klandermans, H. Kriesi, & S. Tarrow (Eds.), *International social movement research: From structure to action* (pp. 197–217). JAI Press.

Snow, D. A., & Benford, R. D. (1992). Master frames and cycles of protest. In A. Morris & C. McClurg Mueller (Eds.), *Frontiers in social movement theory* (pp. 133–155). Yale University Press.

Snow, D. A., Rochford, E. B., Jr., Worden, S. K., & Benford, R. D. (1986). Frame alignment processes, micromobilization and movement participation. *American Sociological Review, 51*, 456–481.

Stacey, R. (2012). *Tools and techniques of leadership and management: Meeting the challenge of complexity.* Routledge.

Stogdill, R. M. (1948). Personal factors associated with leadership: A survey of the literature. *Journal of Psychology, 25*, 35–71.

Storey, J., & Salaman, G. (2009). *Managerial dilemmas.* John Wiley.

Taylor, V., & Whittier, N. (1992). Collective identity in social movement communities: Lesbian feminist mobilization. In A. D. Morris & C. McClurg Mueller (Eds.), *Frontiers in social movement theory* (pp. 104–129). Yale University Press.

Tsoukas, H., & Chia, R. (2002). On organizational becoming: Rethinking organizational change. *Organization Science, 13*(5), 567–582.

Weick, K. (1995). *Sensemaking in organizations.* Sage.

Whitehead, A. N. (1967a). *Science and modern world.* Cambridge University Press. (Original work published 1925)

Whitehead, A. N. (1967b). *Adventures of ideas.* Free Press. (Original work published 1933)

Whitehead, A. N. (1978). *Process and reality.* Free Press. (Original work published 1929)

Wilson, J. M., George, J., & Wellins, R. S. (1994). *Leadership trapeze: Strategies for leadership in team-based organizations.* Jossey-Bass.

Wood, M. (2005). The fallacy of misplaced leadership. *Journal of Management Studies, 42*(6), 1101–1121.

Zaccaro, S. J., Kemp, C., & Bader, P. (2004). Leader traits and attributes. In J. Antonakis, A. T. Cianciolo, & R. J. Sternberg (Eds.), *The nature of leadership* (pp. 101–124). Sage.

Chapter 3

Culture, Resistance, and Social Movements

Objectives

The main idea of this chapter is that challenging cultural assumptions and what is taken for granted is necessary to raise the critical consciousness of people at an individual and collective level. Processes of cultural resistance from minoritized social groups and creating a more inclusive and fair social order require broadening doxa. Leadership needs to be seen as an emancipatory project focused on creating, maintaining, and destroying culture and unfolding processes through which critical consciousness can arise. Drawing from the social movement literature can be helpful in the attempt to study leadership and social change in a more relational and holistic way than previous leadership studies that focused more on what individuals did from a psychological perspective.

Culture and Critical Consciousness

Due to cultural impositions regarding what can be thought and said and of what is legitimate and not, it is central to develop a critical consciousness that will articulate new frameworks of making sense and meaning. Doxa is more than common belief and domination because it also has the potential to give rise to common action and liberation (Bourdieu & Eagleton, 1992). Therefore, it is key for oppressed groups to understand doxa as a field for struggle and to seek broadening it with other worldviews and epistemologies going beyond the hegemonic narratives and discourses to create a new and more inclusive social order.

In our postcolonial world, the subaltern groups are dominated and manipulated by the force of the myths imposed by society's hegemonic sectors (Freire, 2013). Thus, without even being aware, oppressed people relinquish their capacity for choice and are expelled from decision-making processes. Besides, oppressed people internalize the oppressors' opinion, and eventually, they become convinced of their inferiority (Freire, 2012). As a result of this system of domination, the dominated remain unaware of the real causes of their condition, and they just naturalize them and accept them as unavoidable (Freire, 2012).

Another element of control has consisted of changing the consciousness of the oppressed instead of transforming the situation that oppresses them. As Freire (2012) states, "For the more the oppressed can be led to adapt to that situation, the more easily can they be dominated" (p. 74). Thus, individualism and "the bourgeois appetite for personal success" have been key to dismantle ideas of solidarity in terms of class (Freire, 2012, pp. 149–150). It is a strategy of "divide and you will rule" in order to preserve the status quo where the hegemonic groups of society "try to present themselves as saviors of the women and men they dehumanize and divide. This messianism, however, cannot conceal their true intention: to save themselves" (Freire, 2012, p. 145).

In the United States, the idea of social class disappeared in the 1980s as a sociopolitical category of the discourses of the Democratic Party (the same happened in Europe with the social democracy) as a result of embracing neoliberalism. As Bourdieu (1998b) argues, "Neo-classical economics recognizes only individuals, whether it is dealing with companies, trade unions or families" (p. 96). Thus, neoliberal ideology allowed a dehistoricized and desocialized political program "of methodical destruction of collectives" (Bourdieu, 1998b, pp. 95–96).

As a consequence of the process of destroying collectives and class solidarity, redistribution policies were abandoned and substituted with policies seeking to integrate minorities and women in the political system struggling against discrimination (Navarro, 2016). These policies were quite successful in the 1990s, but most of the people who benefited from them belonged to the upper middle class and not to the majority of minority groups belonging to the working class (Navarro, 2016). Thus, the identity policies without class consciousness did not change the status quo of American society's hegemonic groups. As Winant (1995) states, "Although somewhat attenuated since the 1960s with the rise of significant minority middle classes, dark skin still correlates with poverty. Class position is in many respects racially assigned in the U.S." (p. 185). In other words, discrimination in the United States is a racial process with class consequences (Winant, 1995).

Freire (2012) argued that "since the unity of the oppressed involves solidarity among them, regardless of their exact status, this unity unquestionably requires class consciousness" (p. 174). In essence, no person can resist oppression and domination if they do not trust that others will struggle with them (Federici, 2016). However, "consciousness of being an oppressed class must be preceded (or at least accompanied) by achieving consciousness of being oppressed individuals," so the subaltern need to "move from consciousness of themselves as oppressed individuals to the consciousness of an oppressed class" (Freire, 2012, p. 174).

As Freire (2013) states:

> It is sufficient to know that conscientization does not take place in abstract beings in the air but in real men and women and in social structures, to understand that it cannot remain on the level of the individual. It would not be superfluous to repeat

that conscientization, which can only be manifested in the concrete praxis (which can never be limited to the mere activity of the consciousness) is never neutral; in the same way, education can never be neutral. (pp. 130–131)

Every social or political movement "has some capacity to advance a particular agenda to protect certain interests and to veto certain threats. But no movement on its own has the potential to achieve the redistribution of wealth, power, and social priorities that would significantly improve the life chances of their constituents or sustain their deepest aspirations" (Flacks, 1995, p. 252). As a result of this void, a political party or inclusive social movement is needed to represent the common ground of demands for change and social justice as the "obvious framework for mobilizing the political resources and formulating the programmatic agenda for change" (Flacks, 1995, p. 252). To initiate this project, a leadership process needs to emerge: a critical intercultural leadership process from critical consciousness that will articulate a more holistic and inclusive framework of world-making where different cultures are valued and there are fewer asymmetries of power.

Critical Consciousness

Culture can be understood as a system for domination, but culture can also be a system for liberation and emancipation when critical consciousness arises. With critical consciousness, one focuses on achieving an in-depth understanding of the world, allowing for the perception and exposure of social and political contradictions of domination and oppression. Critical consciousness represents "things and facts as they exist empirically, in their causal and circumstantial correlations" (Vieira Pinto, as cited in Freire, 2013, p. 41). Additionally, critical consciousness also includes taking action against the oppressive elements in one's life that are illuminated by that understanding (Mustakova Possardt, 2003).

Oppressed people internalize the norms and behaviors of the oppressor and are fearful of ejecting that image because a struggle for freedom is required (Freire, 2012). The only way to initiate the struggle is to develop a consciousness, a project that transcends itself, a method toward emancipation (Vieira Pinto, as cited in Freire, 2012). Therefore, culture becomes a field for struggle and is central to transforming the world because a system of cultural domination and control involves a static perception of the world and the imposition of one worldview and one narrative upon the others.

Awakening of Critical Consciousness

The human being is a conscious body. As Freire (2013) argues:

His or her consciousness, with its "intentionality" towards the world, is always consciousness of something. It is in a permanent state of moving towards reality. Hence the condition of the human being is to be in constant relationship to the world. In this relationship, subjectivity, which takes its form in objectivity, combines with the latter to form a dialectical unity from which emerges knowledge closely linked with action. (p. 128)

This knowledge is the "logos," a critical knowledge that challenges doxa, the popular belief. Thus, some social groups begin to see themselves and their society from their perspective and not from the perspective and the narratives of the oppressors, and they become aware of their potentialities (Freire, 2013). At this moment, society is revealed as a construction, something unfinished, and not as something natural or that cannot be transformed. It becomes a challenge rather than a frustrating limitation.

The process of awakening critical consciousness has two distinct phases. In the first, the dominated unveil the system of domination and, through the praxis, commit themselves to transform it through their new framework of the world and ethics. In the second phase, once the reality of domination has already been transformed, this process must constantly be reviewed to avoid a situation where the dominated reproduce domination. In both phases, strong action is required to confront the system of domination, exclusion, and control.

Awakening critical consciousness is possible because the dehumanization suffered by the oppressed due to the oppressor's violence is not a given destiny but the result of an unjust order that also dehumanizes the oppressor (Freire, 2012). Thus, even if they do not always obtain it, the dominated always have the potential to develop critical consciousness. However, they must struggle for their humanization and the humanization of the oppressor rather than becoming a new oppressor in the process (Freire, 2012). This is the task of the oppressed: to seek their liberation and the liberation of the oppressors, because only the emancipatory power that comes from the oppressed has this potential for freeing both (Freire, 2012).

Today, social exclusion and control systems are embedded in our minds and reach consciousness to domesticate society. Thus, to confront this system, one must acquire a critical awareness of domination and oppression through the struggle. In other words, a praxis consisting of reflection and action upon the world is needed if the goal is to transform it (Freire, 2012). The first step of raising critical consciousness is when the oppressed perceives the possibility of transforming the world because it supposes a motivating force for liberation. However, to be aware of the possibility of change is not enough, and the oppressed need to get involved in organizing the struggle to start believing in themselves. Awakening critical consciousness is a combination of intellectual discovery first, followed by action. Simply stated, the process to raise critical consciousness is a praxis that combines reflection and activism (Freire, 2012). This emancipatory and critical intercultural leadership that Freire (2012) calls "revolutionary leadership" lies in dialogue because "the conviction of the oppressed that they must fight for their liberation is not a gift bestowed by the revolutionary leadership, but the result of their own conscientização" (p. 49). Therefore, it is not a monologue or a top-down process but a relational process of leadership from the bottom-up that requires the combination of reflection and action in order to transform the world. As Freire (2012) argues, "While the conviction of the necessity for struggle (without which the struggle is unfeasible) is indispensable to the revolutionary leadership (indeed, it was this conviction which constituted that leadership), it is also necessary for the oppressed" (p. 67). In other words, a critical intercultural leadership process is carried out with the subaltern, not for them, because as the result of not understanding consciousness as "an empty vessel to be filled, nor the use of banking methods of domination (propaganda, slogans—deposits) in the name of liberation," the dominated are subjects in the process of world-making (Freire, 2012, p. 79).

Consciousness neither precedes the world nor follows it; to develop critical consciousness means "being conscious of, not only as intent on objects but as turned in upon itself in a Jasperian 'split'—consciousness of consciousness" (Freire, 2012, p. 79). Once the dominated and the oppressed become conscious of their domination and oppression as a social construction, they reject mythicizing reality and, through critical thinking, start the task of demythologizing (Freire, 2012). In essence, the dominated start a process of deconstruction of narratives to be subjects of their destiny and social structures to take control of their reality. However, as Freire (2012) warns us, this reflection on the system of domination and oppression is not enough to change the status of subaltern groups since they become "subjects in expectancy," which "leads them to seek to solidify their new status" (pp. 130, 131).

In terms of consciousness, there are different phases until achieving the state of critical consciousness. First is the phase of semi-intransitivity of consciousness where people do not apprehend problems beyond their biological necessities. It is about surviving every day without a historical perspective. Thus, this phase is limited because people are impermeable to challenges outside the phase of biological needs (Freire, 2013). However, in amplifying their capacity to perceive and answer questions related to their contexts, people improve their capacity to enter dialogue with others and with the world; this is the second phase, when consciousness becomes transitive. In this phase, people are permeable, and they become historical beings concerned with problems beyond their biological necessities (Freire, 2013).

Within the second phase, there is an initial state of naïve transitivity, a state of consciousness that tends to oversimplify problems and gregariousness, have nostalgia for the past, and with a fragility of arguments prefer the practice of polemics and magical explanations rather than dialogue (Freire, 2013). These people are "still almost part of a mass, in whom the developing capacity for dialogue is still fragile and capable of distortion. If this consciousness does progress to the stage of critical transitivity, it may be deflected by sectarian irrationality into fanaticism" (Freire, 2013, p. 14). Finally, the third phase is critically transitive consciousness, which is characterized by

> depth in the interpretation of problems; by the substitution of causal principles for magical explanations; by the testing of one's "findings" and by openness to revision; by the attempt to avoid distortion when perceiving problems and to avoid preconceived notions when analyzing them; by refusing to transfer responsibility; by rejecting passive positions; by soundness of argumentation; by the practice of dialogue rather than polemics; by receptivity to the new for reasons beyond mere novelty and by the good sense not to reject the old just because it is old—by accepting what is valid in both old and new. (Freire, 2013, p. 15)

For example, while critical consciousness represents objects, facts, and their correlations as they exist empirically, naïve consciousness is superior to facts and understood according to interests. Magic consciousness, in contrast, is characterized by fatalism, the idea of a world that cannot be transformed and a destiny that cannot be resisted because it is unavoidable (Freire, 2013).

In essence, "critical consciousness is integrated with reality; naïve consciousness superimposes itself on reality; and fanatical consciousness, whose pathological naïveté leads to the irrational, adapts to reality" (Freire, 2013, p. 42).

As a consequence of these different phases of consciousness, there are different actions. Thus, while critical understanding leads to critical action, magic or naïve understanding brings us to a magic or naïve response; therefore, to reach critical consciousness, one needs a dialogical educational program that focuses on the work of social and political responsibility (Freire, 2013). Undertaking a process that implements dialogue and problem-posing will develop a critical attitude necessary to broaden doxa by introducing a different knowledge set that goes beyond the narrative imposed by the hegemonic groups in society. Thus, the internalization and naturalization of structures of domination and oppression will start to be deconstructed, and a process of building new social structures aiming to create a new society will begin to unfold.

Identity Development and Ethnogenesis

Any emancipatory process starts with an analysis of the causes of oppression to know where to focus transformative action (Freire, 2013). Within the system of domination and oppression that represent the current postcolonial world where Western culture is presented as superior to the rest, it is not enough to integrate the dominated into the system; it is necessary to organize and transform the system (Freire, 2012). In essence, against the internalization of oppressive structures of the social order that guides behaviors, dispositions, and choices, a process of ethnogenesis as a mechanism of defense against domination to deconstruct and reconstructing those oppressive structures needs to be unfolded.

The organization of this project of ethnogenesis by the oppressed needs a critical intercultural process of leadership because "authentic organization is obviously not going to be stimulated by the dominators; it is the task of the revolutionary leaders" (Freire, 2012, p. 148). It is a critically conscious organization, a critical intercultural leadership process that unfolds ethnogenesis to deconstruct internalized oppression and external structures of domination while at the same time reconstructing new structures for emancipation.

As Freire (2012) states:

> Cultural conquest leads to the cultural inauthenticity of those who are invaded; they begin to respond to the values, the standards, and the goals of the invaders. In their passion to dominate, to mold others to their patterns and their way of life, the invaders desire to know how those they have invaded apprehend reality—but only so they can dominate the latter more effectively. (p. 153)

In essence, the "invaded" have become convinced of their inferiority and have internalized the oppression. This is similar to the phenomenon of *learned helplessness* that arises when prior learning in a situation that cannot be solved undermines motivation for future responses in a similar situation and distorts the ability to change the environment (Rabow et al., 1983). According to Hiroto and Seligman (1975), "Learned helplessness is a trait-like system of expectancies that develops when responding is perceived to be futile" (p. 327). That is, dominated and oppressed groups of people feel that reality controls them, and they cannot take control of their reality; therefore, they cannot transform the world. They have recognized the superiority of the hegemonic groups in society, their values, ethics, and culture, and want to be like them (Freire, 2012). As a consequence of this cultural invasion, the oppressed need to not only be aware of the necessity of transforming the world to build a fairer society but also recognize that along with a process of reconstruction, another process of deconstruction of narratives, imaginaries, and social structures existing in the real world and their minds is also needed. In other words, doxa—the unquestionable orthodoxy that operates as the objective truth—influences the practices and perceptions of the state and social groups (fields) and the practices and perceptions of individuals (habitus). Ideologies of oppression divide the oppressed, and what is needed to reunite them is "a form of cultural action through which they come to know the why and how of their adhesion to reality—it requires de-ideologizing" (Freire, 2012, p. 173). It is the start of a process of ethnogenesis at an individual, organizational, and societal level.

Thus, to liberate themselves, take control of their destiny, and create their new reality, emergent ethnic organizations and social movements view culture as a political, economic, and an epistemological manifestation that, through a process of ethnogenesis, will create a counter-hegemonic project with a different narrative and worldview. These movements do not try to threaten the state or its sovereignty but to create political spaces within the state that allow people to form sociopolitical organizations (Hill, 1996). Ethnogenesis is about other worldviews, narratives, and frameworks because "the power to control and define the historical past is perhaps the ultimate form of hegemony" (Hill, 1996, p. 16).

Ethnogenesis Studies

Weber's (1978) definition of *ethnic identity* is understood through group affinity centered on subjective beliefs of shared common ancestry that comes from "similarities of physical type or of customs or both" or "of memories of colonization and migration" (p. 389). *Ethnomorphosis* is the historical process of ethnicity that goes from genesis, maintenance, and the disappearance of an ethnic identity (Kohl, 1998). A deeper analysis of ethnicity suggests three components: (a) the way insiders view membership; (b) the way outsiders relate to and interact with insiders; and (c) the way institutions define boundaries and classify people, how they use them, and what are the purposes behind them (Bourdieu, 1990b).

In terms of social relations, group membership feelings arise with the awareness of subconscious practices that people have in common (Bentley, 1991). These shared practices arise from dispositions called "habitus" with which people identify because of the similarity to their practices (Bourdieu, 1990b). When it comes to groups or social classes, "dispositions generate practices that in turn reinforce those same dispositions" (Hu, 2013, p. 374). Thus, people tend to gravitate toward those who physically and in terms of conduct are similar but at the same time avoid those who seem and act differently (Weber, 1978). However, even if ethnic groups establish boundaries among themselves in terms of ethnicity, nationality, class, and so on, these boundaries are still permeable, and ethnicity is dynamic (Barth, 1976). Poutignat (2008) holds that ethnicity is not an inherent quality or property of certain individuals or groups but a system of organization, a principle to divide the social world, changing according to situations and historic periods. In other words, ethnic groups are not static or bearers of culture, as an essentialist approach can suggest; they are social constructions that try to organize their social life and are subjected to constant change (Luna Penna, 2014). Other authors like Amselle and M'Bokolo (1999) support the idea of a dynamic ethnicity subjected to change but incorporate new elements from a postcolonial perspective and argue that the idea of ethnicity is a modern concept. Four principles allow one to deconstruct an ethnic group: the relation with their past, their internal composition, their external articulation, and the relations established by researchers in their fields (Amselle & M'Bokolo, 1999).

Today, the relational paradigm proposes the study of the ethnic behavior, and even without using the concept of ethnogenesis, this field includes the changes and transformations of an ethnic group that in some cases can result in the birth of a new ethnic group (Luna Penna, 2014). However, the instrumental paradigm focuses on political and economic processes that precede the origin of a new ethnic group (Obadia, 2008). As a result of these processes, ethnic movements today explore other forms of membership and solidarity, such as social class, which inspired struggles and political mobilizations for autonomy, self-determination, or independence (Gallissot et al., 2000). An example of this is the Indigenous communities in America that in order not to disappear, were capable of reinventing themselves in this new scenario of globalization. According to Hill (1996), the process of ethnogenesis is developed not only from the imposition of the hegemonic culture to dominate the Indigenous communities but also from the strategies of the oppressed to resist. In essence, it is a perspective of ethnogenesis in a political dimension and within an ethnic reaffirmation.

In South America, the study of Indigenous people included power as a key factor to understand these processes of ethnogenesis and to propose the decolonization of knowledge in different institutions, including the academy (Luna Penna, 2014). These processes of ethnogenesis, related to Indigenous communities, are characterized by a strong historical component as a result of the struggles against colonization and the emphasis on the context associated with social and identity phenomena (Luna Penna, 2014).

Today, due in part to globalization, a great number of new identities ranging from religious, political, or economic complaints have emerged all around the world. According to Bonté and Izard (2008), ethnogenesis today is understood as processes of revitalization or emergence of a collective consciousness usually by minority groups that can lean on a common language, pseudo-historical stories, or phenotypic traits. Whatever the selected criteria, one of the key elements of this contemporary conception of ethnogenesis seems to be the necessity of differentiation and opposition regarding dominant groups.

Obadia (2008) has a broader vision of this process and considers the possibility of finding a definition of the concept that combines a fundamentalist approach concerned with ethnicity and culture and an instrumentalist approach focused on social contexts. Today, globalization allows one to construct common narratives regarding identity, but this concept of identity does not have an essentialist connotation anymore, which supposes a theoretical depth to better understand the more complex ethnic identity phenomenon of the postcolonial world (Luna Penna, 2014).

Resistance Against Domination and Oppression

According to Voss (2008), "Ethnogenesis has become a powerful metaphor for the creativity of oppressed and marginalized peoples birthing a new cultural space for themselves amidst their desperate struggle to survive" (p. 36). In other words, a process of ethnogenesis "can overcome fissions and factions through rallying people against institutionalized inequalities" (Hu, 2013, p. 385).

Modernity and colonialism instrumentalized identity to divide work and power in a social hierarchy. Thus, a process of ethnogenesis driven by the hegemonic groups and their Euro-centered leadership consolidated and legitimized economic and social domination. Even after the colonial power ceased to exist, these categories imposed by the processes of modernity and colonialism still maintain their relevance and power (Tilly, 2005). Therefore, ethnic organizations and social movements situated at the lower levels of the hierarchy struggle against dominant classes seeking emancipation through a critical intercultural process of leadership, and in doing so, they make uniform different practices and material culture among members of the group (Hu, 2013).

Ethnogenesis driven from the state or hegemonic groups during colonial times and the early stages of the nation-state has been studied extensively, but not when social movements lead this process with minority political entrepreneurs (Wimmer, 2008). One way of challenging the hierarchical ordering of ethnic categories in the United States was the reverse stigmatization of hegemonic groups of society, resulting in a profound disagreement between individuals on opposite sides of the boundary (e.g., Black Power and Red Power movements). The boundary "is not a conceptual fence over which neighbors may gossip or quarrel. It becomes instead a Siegfried line across which any but the crudest communication is impossible" (Wallman, 1978, p. 212). A second proposal was to establish moral and political equality rather than superiority concerning the dominant group. The most well-known example was the civil rights movement led by Martin Luther King Jr. (Wimmer, 2008).

In all these movements, intellectual and political entrepreneurs redefined the meaning of ethnic categories, identifying culture as a field for struggle. These movements see the privilege of authenticity, they are proud of the culture of their ancestors, and they reinterpreted historical defeat and subjugation into a heroic struggle against injustice and domination. In other words, they "establish a counter culture shielded from the influence of dominant majorities and revive 'traditional' festivals and rites (from Newroz to Pow Wow), commemorate heroic acts (the occupation of Alcatraz, Rosa Parks) and leaders (Malcolm X, Mullah Mustafa Barzani)" (Wimmer, 2008, p. 1038).

In the last decades, there has been an increase in organizations and social movements emphasizing their ethnic characteristics to challenge society's hegemonic sectors while using culture as a field for struggle. Thus, culture has become a system of emancipation that involves critical consciousness and ethnogenesis to promote processes of cultural resistance and reexistence. These organizations of ethnic social movements have developed different leadership processes centered on their organizational culture to create and develop patterns of basic assumptions to cope with problems of external adaptation and internal integration that, when successful, were considered valid and taken for granted

(Schein, 2010). In conclusion, ethnic SMOs have deconstructed hegemonic narratives and frameworks and reconstructed counter-hegemonic ones to create new political, economic, social, cultural, and epistemological projects that go beyond the hegemonic canon and that seek emancipation.

Culture as a Field for Struggle

As a result of the process of critical consciousness and ethnogenesis, culture becomes a field for struggle wherein ethnic SMOs focus on how organizational culture can be used for emancipation. Ethnic social movements are distinct from social movements in general because they are based on national origin, culture, language, religion, territory, or phenotype and are enacted to promote or resist social change (Okamoto, 2013).

As noted earlier, understanding culture as a field for struggle offers the possibility for implementing not only processes of domination but also projects for emancipation. For Gramsci (1970), culture means organization, discipline, empowerment, and awareness of taking control of reality; a revolution must be preceded by an intense critique of the dominant culture and the introduction of the new one. Social movements are understood as reactions against hegemony to transform society (Gramsci, 1995). A crisis in authority and a "rupture of the equilibrium of forces" is the perfect time for a counter-hegemonic alternative to arise (Gramsci, 1995, p. 184). The crisis in hegemony occurs in a historical, social context where the class that dominated through consent begins to rely on coercion first and eventually domination (Gramsci, 1995). However, to dismantle the dominant hegemony, a new and alternative hegemony has to arise: what Gramsci (1995) called "war of position," a struggle to keep the hegemony on one side and to dismantle it on the other, and where the dominant hegemony, despite the crisis, has more power to resolve the situation due to economic, intellectual, and political power.

Another perspective that sees culture as a field of struggle is the concept of *symbolic power* described by Bourdieu (1989), which is the power granted to some social groups who have gained enough recognition to be situated in a position from where they can impose their view of the world on the rest. It is a struggle over the existence or nonexistence of other social groups, their visions, and their cultures because this power has the capacity to create groups and to transform the objective structure of society (Bourdieu, 1989).

Moreover, Adorno (1973) argues that the true sense of culture is to overcome the idea of treating everything like objects and commodities. Thus, it is central to see culture related to concepts involving politics and economics too. According to Santos (2007a), what is new in the last decades is that what is understood as cultural is also economic and political. Therefore, while it is central to consider new forms of societies in the short term, in the long term, it will be key to consider issues such as the re-foundation of the state and democracy. In essence, Santos (2007a) affirms that the state cannot be neutral; otherwise, it will benefit the dominant culture.

Social Movements and Culture

Social movements are cultural movements supported by discursive practices (Fine, 1995). Besides, their main goals are to influence and change the cultural order and perspectives of society in which they are embedded (Fine, 1995). A social movement (or social movement organization) can be understood as a space where actors interact and behave in a specific fashion: "The group provides a locus in which behaviors and forms of talk are judged to be appropriate and even encouraged" (Fine, 1995, p. 130). Besides, in a certain way, each social movement produces culture (Taylor & Whittier, 1995).

Evolution of Social Movements and Cultural Studies

A systemic view of culture "affirms the external reality of related conceptions of the world and of patterns of action" (Johnston & Klandermans, 1995, p. 6). This perspective, when applied to social movements, sees these movements as reactions to destabilized systems (Geertz, 1973). Another approach in line with this perspective views the cultural system as a factor that shapes and constrains the course of mobilization (Almond & Verba, 1963). "In this view, although movements are defined by their break with the dominant cultural code, they nevertheless are shaped by their inclusion in and modification of aspects of the dominant culture" (Johnston & Klandermans, 1995, p. 6).

However, in the last several decades, there has been a shift in cultural analysis from a systemic view to a performative tradition (Johnston & Klandermans, 1995), an approach wherein social movements are shaped by culture and also shape and reshape it. Thus, "symbols, values, meanings, icons, and beliefs are adapted and molded to suit the movement's aims and frequently are injected into the broader culture via institutionalization and routinization" (Johnston & Klandermans, 1995, p. 9).

Similarly, Swindler's (1986) concept of culture is a "tool kit" of rituals, stories, and worldviews that are used to design strategies of action. According to Swidler (1986), in times of crisis, the old cultural models are rejected, and collective mobilization starts articulating new ones implementing new ways of organization, and of "practicing unfamiliar habits until they become familiar" (p. 278). This framing perspective "cuts a middle course between a systemic view of culture and its performative aspects" and combines the focus on social processes and the creative capacity of individuals (Johnston & Klandermans, 1995, p. 8).

Moreover, other elaborations of this perspective shift their analysis to the collective arena (Snow & Benford, 1992). Thus, processes regarding frame extension and frame amplification "are for the most part treated as strategic actions of SMOs and presume systemic relations of social movement culture with the other aspects of culture" (Snow & Benford, 1992, p. 8). This type of frame analysis focuses on organizations and institutions, studying "how frames intersect with key cultural patterns and how they might be strategically used in mobilization. These processes are described using organizational documents, giving key speeches, and offering public records and media reports. New social movement groups are conscious of these processes and design strategies to construct their own collective identities: "Frame analysis at this level unites the systemic perspective of dominant cultural patterns with a performative analysis at a higher level of analysis: that of groups, organizations, and institutions" (Snow & Benford, 1992, p. 8).

New social movement theorists, especially focused on collective identity, understand social movements as a social construction that challenges political and economic institutions into the social world's limited domain (Habermas, 1987). According to Melucci (1995):

> Collective identity is a learning process that leads to the formation and maintenance of a unified empirical actor that we can call a social movement. As it passes through various stages, the collective actor develops a capacity to resolve the environment's problems and become increasingly independent and autonomously active in its relationships. The process of collective identity is thus also the ability to produce new definitions by integrating the past and the emerging elements of the present into the unity and continuity of a collective actor. (p. 49)

In other words, collective identity is a system of relations and representations that takes the form of a field that contains another system conformed by vectors in tension seeking to establish an equilibrium "between the various axes of collective action and between identification that an actor declares and the identification given by the rest of the society (adversaries, allies, third parties)" (Melucci, 1995, p. 50).

Taylor and Whittier (1992) describe collective identity as three interrelated processes:

- construction of group boundaries to differentiate the dominant group from the challenging one
- consciousness or interpretive frameworks that came up from the struggle and contribute to identifying the interests of the group
- politicization of everyday life using symbols and undertaking actions to resist and transform the dominant culture

Thus, the concept of collective identity acknowledges that the self understandings around which groups organize are critical to the transformation of hegemonic meanings and loyalties (Taylor & Whittier, 1995).

As a result of this set of relations and struggles, collective identity will adopt one form or another depending on shifts and changes within and outside the field. "Collective identity therefore patterns itself according to the presence and relative intensity of its dimensions. Some vectors may be weaker or stronger than others, and some may be entirely absent" (Melucci, 1995, p. 50). Today, identification processes are transferred from outside society when transcendent and metaphysical entities such as myths, ancestors, or the invisible hand of the market were used to its interior, through the implementation of processes of associative human action, culture and communication, social relations, and technological systems (Melucci, 1995). "As identity is progressively recognized as socially produced, notions like coherence, boundary maintenance, and recognition only describe it in static terms; but in its dynamic connotation collective identity increasingly becomes a process of construction and autonomization" (Melucci, 1995, p. 50).

For new social movements, particularly those centered on culture, "collective identity is becoming the product of conscious action and the outcome of self-reflection more than a set of given or 'structural' characteristics" (Melucci, 1995, pp. 50–51). In other words, collective action is a process of organization based on culture and experienced as an action more than a situation: It is a process of "identization" (Melucci, 1995).

As a result of the field where relationships occur, each "movement community" has access to a set of resources, and the organization to struggle for them becomes central. As Tarrow (1988) states, social movements are internally organized as communications networks consisting of both elites (movement entrepreneurs) and adherents (members). This network implements actions, cultural transmission, and the framing of movement ideology and claims (Snow et al., 1986).

Social Movements and Culture Production

The set of images and traditions created by a social movement is what Fine (1982) describes as idioculture. *Idioculture* is understood as "a system of knowledge, beliefs, behaviors, and customs shared by members of an interacting group to which members can refer and which they can employ as the basis of further interaction" (Fine, 1995, p. 128). It is a process to traditionalize shared experiences, normally through discourse, that creates cohesion among the members of a group distinguishing between insiders and outsiders (Fine 1989; Hobsbawm & Ranger, 1983). Thus, culture involves mobilizing both symbolic and material resources because the existence of an imagined community is not enough for collective action. According to Fine (1995), public support, communication, authority, social control, and material resources are central to facilitating cultural expression and mobilization.

In essence, culture can be a tool by which social movements achieve their goals while serving to express their claims and demands. "Focusing on the ways that social movements are engaged in the production of culture is one of the most promising avenues of research for scholars interested in bringing the actor back into the study of social change" (Taylor & Whittier, 1995, p. 186). Three of the most important processes of cultural production within a social movement are the creation of meaning; naming and the construction of discourses and narratives; and rituals.

Meaning

A key element involved with the process of culture production and consumption is the construction of meaning. Klandermans (1992) suggests three processes of meaning construction in a social movement: (a) public discourse; (b) persuasive communication; and (c) consciousness-raising during episodes of collective action. Public discourse affects the whole society or a particular sector within society; persuasive communication involves only specific individuals; and consciousness-raising during episodes of collective action targets participants involved in the collective action (Johnston & Klandermans, 1995). At each of these levels, the processes to create and re-create collective beliefs are unfolded in different ways: "at the first level through the diffuse networks of meaning construction, at the second level through deliberate attempts by social actors to persuade, and at the third level through discussions among participants and spectators of the collective action" (Johnston & Klandermans, 1995, p. 10).

Naming, Discourses, and Narratives

One of the goals for social movements is to resist "outside naming" and to decide "self-naming" (Chartrand, 1991, p. 2). It is a struggle for discursive space to imagine the past, the present, and the future of the communities. However, "the power of dominant groups and institutions is a limit on the self-naming of subordinate communities. Yet the latter are never without power" (Jenson, 1995, p. 108). In essence, to constitute a collective identity implies the exercise of power, "and, as in any power relation, such an act of representing a community by name has real, material consequences; it is not simply a struggle over words" (Jenson, 1995, p. 108).

This process of representing a community through naming is central for social movements to design strategies and claims, and the terrain of political discourse is the space where the struggle for constructing identities is carried out (Jenson, 1987). "It is by translating meanings into practice—often within institutions—that actors create, sustain, or change representational arrangements. The creation of meaning is, then, profoundly political" (Jenson, 1995, pp. 108–109). The struggle for constructing identities produces dominant and dominated groups. "Success in occupying space in the universe of political discourse limits the possibilities of others and may reconfigure the political opportunity structure. Thus, struggle over naming involves the exercise of power" (Jenson, 1995, p. 115).

Wuthnow (1989) understands social movements as communities of discourse centered in creating new cultural codes that challenge hegemonic perspectives. "Discourse subsumes the written as well as the verbal, the formal as well as the informal, the gestural or ritual as well as the conceptual" (Wuthnow, 1989, p. 16). Additionally, positivist discourses, such as those of science, technology, or even education, are key to maintaining the dominant narratives and worldviews (Smith, 1990). Therefore, new social movements "target not only the state but civil society, specifically institutions specializing in the transmission of cultural codes such as schools, families, religion, medicine, and the therapy industry" (Taylor & Whittier, 1995, p. 181). State institutions are central to deciding inclusion and exclusion criteria; that is why social movements create a collective identity within the movement and seek recognition of their identity by public institutions (Jenson, 1995, p. 115). "Thus, the choice of a name will configure the space available to the extent that it generates resources, identifies allies and opponents, and directs the routing of claims" (Jenson, 1995, p. 115).

Rituals

In a field for struggle, those excluded from power need to adapt to their subordinate position, creating cultural forms and expressions that challenge the dominant values and beliefs. One of these cultural forms and expressions is *rituals*, understood as "the cultural mechanisms through which collective actors express the emotions—that is, the enthusiasm, pride, anger, hatred, fear, and sorrow—that mobilize and sustain conflict" (Taylor & Whittier, 1995, p. 176). Emotions are the glue of solidarity (Collins, 1990), and rituals create moral solidarity mainly by evoking emotion (Durkheim, 1961; Hobsbawm, 1959). Rituals are what Gordon (1981) described as the "emotion culture" of a group. However, these cultural expressions of subcultures or countercultures cannot be developed openly as a result of their position of subordination and domination (Scott, 1990). Therefore, dominated groups operate in private, isolated from the control of the dominant groups of society, creating havens or free social spaces where the dominated can organize their challenge to the dominant narrative and ideologies, deconstruct old and create new meanings, construct emergent cultural forms, and transmit the culture (Fantasia & Hirsch, 1995).

Collective Action and Frames to Produce Culture

Melucci (1995) argues that "action is an interactive, constructive process within a field of possibilities and limits recognized by the actors" (p. 61). Regarding collective action, it is understood as a social construction with purpose and meaning that is not only derived from structural constraints and cannot be reduced either to leaders' discourses, militants' options, or public behavior (Melucci, 1995). Therefore, action research and research intervention that focuses on how action is constructed and aims to analyze action as it unfolds while built by actors provide a more holistic perspective of social movements (Touraine, 1978). Also, action is fundamental to develop collective frames. According to Snow and Benford (1992), *collective frames* are a discourse, a set of beliefs and meanings that seek to legitimate social movements' actions and goals. Gamson (1992) describes three components of collective action frames: injustice, agency, and identity. Injustice refers to the moral indignation; agency refers to the consciousness that through collective action it is possible to transform society; and identity refers to the process of defining the "we" versus "they" with different interests or values (Gamson, 1995). These three components are described in a similar way by Snow and Benford (1992) but are identified as (a) punctuation, or bringing attention to the injustice suffered; (b) attribution, or describing the causes and solutions for the injustice; and (c) articulation, or connecting different experiences. Klandermans (1988) suggests the concept of "consensus mobilization" to explain how social movements use communication to recruit supporters to their cause. In this view, frames are not only meaning systems but also strategic tools for recruiting participants.

As Snow et al. (1986) have suggested, collective action frames are defined throughout collective action, drawing from and modifying elements of the dominant culture, bridging, amplifying, extending, or transforming collective frames. Therefore, "collective action frames incorporate preexisting beliefs and symbols as well as oppositional values that emerge in the course of a group's struggle" (Taylor & Whittier, 1995, p. 168). The process of creating collective action frames includes elements, such as habitus (Bourdieu, 1984, 1990) or a cultural tool kit (Swindler, 1986), that are central to provide groups with a distinctive set of beliefs, values, and resources to organize their resistance.

Frame transformation unfolds when "new ideas and values ... replace old ones" and "old meanings, symbols, and so on are discarded [and] erroneous beliefs and misframings are corrected" (Taylor, 2000, p. 512). In other words, frame transformation is part of the process of ethnogenesis and supposes a "general reframing of the issues" within a social movement (Taylor, 2000, p. 512). Frame transformation is a key process to the success and sustainability of social movements because "numerous social movements have risen and fallen partly as a result of atrophy and lack of reflexivity" (Pellow & Brehm, 2015, p. 187).

Ethnic Identity, Social Movements, and Critical Interculturality

As a result of culture as a field of struggle, there has been an emergence of social movements in recent decades trying to challenge the status quo using their ethnic identity as a counterhegemonic element. Tilly (2010) defines *social movements* as a tool for ordinary people to participate in public politics and are composed of performances, displays, and campaigns to make collective claims on others. Social movements are a tool for ordinary people's participation in public politics. According to Tilly, there are three main elements in a social movement:

- campaigns: sustained, organized public effort making collective claims of target authorities
- repertoire: the employment of combinations of political action (e.g., associations and coalitions, public meetings, solemn processions, vigils, rallies, demonstrations, petition drives, statements to and in public media, pamphleteering, etc.)
- participants' concerted public representation of worthiness, unity, numbers, and commitments (WUNC) on the part of themselves and/or their constituencies

Tarrow (1994) adds to the definition the idea of culture and sees social movements as the interactions with and collective challenges to elites, authorities, groups, or cultural codes carried out by people with common purposes and solidarity. These social movements, in negotiating a common understanding of their motivations and the problems they try to address, construct collective action frames (Snow & Benford, 1988). These frames seek social change when they bring new ideas and values that replace old ones, correcting or discarding them in a process of general reframing (Taylor, 2000). Besides, new social movement theorists particularly focus on collective identity and see social movements as a social construction, a process based on culture and action that aims to challenge political and economic institutions.

One particularity of emergent ethnic SMOs is that their essence is centered on culture, language, or religion, and they create social change through a process of critical interculturality. According to Walsh (2010), interculturality can be used as a project built from the bottom-up and aims to transform physical and mental structures, institutions, and social relations of domination while creating new ones for emancipation. Additionally, interculturality is a pedagogic tool that (a) challenges domination and asymmetric relations of power; (b) makes visible different ways of being, knowing, and organizing; and (c) creates the conditions for an effective and true intercultural dialogue (Walsh, 2010). In essence, interculturality is the project led by ethnic organizations and social movements that will foster the transition from a postcolonial world to an intercultural society using culture in general and organizational culture in particular as a field for struggle and liberation.

Today, we have "entered an epoch in which mainstream politics not only are failing but cannot be restored in the traditional ways. Government based on representation through political parties and capable of steering national economies is now obsolete" (Flacks, 1995, p. 263). Globalization has threatened the modern notion of nation-state, and while politics has remained at a local-national level, power has fled to a global sphere (Bauman, 2006). As a result of this lack of power, national political parties cannot find solutions to global problems, and "the fate of democracy and the chances for social justice will depend on the movements' capacity to take ongoing responsibility for the social future" (Flacks, 1995, p. 263). In essence, for these social movements to be effective and transform society, organizations will be needed in general and an organizational culture that will raise critical consciousness and unfold ethnogenesis in particular.

Conclusion

Social movements use culture as a resource for resistance and to challenge dominant social orders. Leadership in social movements goes beyond the leader-centered and individualistic approaches since they focus on the movement and processes of collective identity and action. Leadership is key to creating, maintaining, and destroying culture and unfolding processes through which critical consciousness can arise. Therefore, leadership can be a means for liberation and emancipation that influences the identity of the people empowering them within an organization or society. In the next chapter, we will see how leadership and culture within organizations can be used as a resource to either control and dominate or liberate and emancipate.

Discussion Questions

1. How can non-mainstream discourses of leadership contribute to challenge the status quo?
2. Is social change possible using mainstream leadership approaches, or do we need to change how we conceptualize and exercise leadership?
3. Why is raising critical consciousness central to social change?
4. How do social movements use culture as a resource for social change?

References

Almond, G. A., & Verba, S. (1963). *The civic culture: Political attitudes and democracy in five nations*. Princeton University Press.

Amselle, J. L., & M'Bokolo, E. (1999). *Au cœur de l'ethnie: Ethnies, tribalisme et État en Afrique*. La découverte.

Barth, F. (1976). *Los grupos étnicos y sus fronteras: La organización social de las diferencias culturales*. Fondo de cultura económica.

Bauman, Z. (2006). *Liquid times: Living in an age of uncertainty*. Polity.

Bentley, G. C. (1991). Response to Yelvington. *Comparative Studies in Society and History, 33*, 169–175.

Bonté, P., & Izard, M. (2008). *Dictionnaire de l'ethnologie et de l'anthropologie*. Presses universitaires de France.

Bourdieu, P. (1984). *Distinction: A social critique of the judgment of taste*. Harvard University Press.

Bourdieu, P. (1989). Social space and symbolic power. *Sociological Theory, 7*(1), 14–25.

Bourdieu, P. (1990). *The logic of practice*. Stanford University Press.

Bourdieu, P. (1998). Neo-liberalism, the utopia (becoming a reality) of unlimited exploitation. In P. Bourdieu (Ed.), *Acts of resistance: Against the tyranny of the market* (pp. 94–105). The New Press.

Bourdieu, P., & Eagleton, T. (1992). Doxa and the common life. *New Left Review, 191*, 111–121.

Chartrand, P. (1991). Aboriginal self-government: The two sides of legitimacy. In S. D. Phillips (Ed.), *How Ottawa spends 1993–1994: A more democratic Canada?* (pp. 231–256). Carleton University Press.

Collins, R. (1990). Stratification, emotional energy and the transient emotions. In T. O. Kemper (Ed.), *Research agendas in the sociology of emotion* (pp. 27–57). University of New York Press.

de Sousa Santos, B. (2007). *La reinvención del estado y el estado plurinacional.* Revista OSAL-CLACSO.

Durkheim, E. (1961). *The elementary forms of the religious life.* Free Press.

Fantasia, R., & Hirsch, E. L. (1995). Culture in rebellion: The appropriation and transformation of the veil in the Algerian revolution. In H. Johnston & B. Klandermans (Eds.), *Social movements and culture* (pp. 114–159). University of Minnesota Press.

Federici, S. (2016). No puedes resistir a la opresión si no tienes confianza en que otros lo harán contigo. *Desinformémonos.* Retrieved September 1, 2021, from https://desinformemonos.org/no-puedes-resistir-a-la-opresion-si-no-tienes-confianza-en-que-otros-lo-haran-contigo-silvia-federici/

Fine, G. A. (1981). Friends, impression management, and preadolescent behavior. In S. R. Asher & J. M. Gottman (Eds.), *The development of children's friendships* (pp. 29–53). Cambridge University Press.

Fine, G. A. (1982). The Manson family as a folk group: Small groups and folklore. *Journal of the Folklore Institute, 19*, 47–60.

Fine, G. A. (1995). Public narration and group culture: Discerning discourse in social movements. In H. Johnston & B. Klandermans (Eds.), *Social movements and culture* (pp. 127–143). University of Minnesota Press.

Flacks, R. (1995). Think globally, act politically: Some notes toward new movement strategy. In M. Darnovsky, B. Epstein, & R. Flacks (Eds.), *Cultural politics and social movements* (pp. 251–263). Temple University Press.

Freire, P. (2012). *Pedagogy of the oppressed.* Bloomsbury.

Freire, P. (2013). *Education for critical consciousness.* Bloomsbury.

Gallissot, R., Kilani, M., & Rivera, A. (2000). *L'imbroglio ethnique en quatorze mots clés.* Sofedis.

Gamson, W. A. (1992). The social psychology of collective action. In A. Morris & C. McClurg Mueller (Eds.), *Frontiers in social movement theory* (pp. 53–76). Yale University Press.

Geertz, C. (1973). *The interpretation of cultures.* Basic Books.

Gordon, S. (1981). The sociology of sentiments and emotion. In M. Rosenberg & R. H. Turner, (Eds.), *Social psychology: Sociological perspectives* (pp. 562–592). Basic Books.

Gramsci, A. (1995). *Selections from the Prison Notebooks.* International Publishers.

Habermas, J. (1987). *The theory of communicative action: Vol. 2. Lifeworld and system: A critique of functionalist reason.* Beacon.

Hill, D. J. (1996). *History, power, and identity: Ethnogenesis in the Americas, 1492–1992.* University of Iowa Press.

Hiroto, D., & Seligman, M. (1975). Generality of learned helplessness in man. *Journal of Personality and Social Psychology, 31*, 311.

Hobsbawm, E. J. (1959). *Primitive rebels.* Norton.

Hobsbawm, E. J., & Ranger, T. (Eds.). (1983). *The invention of tradition.* Cambridge University Press.

Hu, D. (2013). Approaches to the archaeology of ethnogenesis: Past and emergent perspectives. *Journal of Archeological Research, 21*, 371–402.

Jenson, J. (1987). Changing discourse, changing agendas: Political rights and reproductive rights in France. In M. F. Katzenstein & C. McClurg Mueller (Eds.), *The women's movement of the United States and Western Europe* (pp. 64–88). Temple University Press.

Jenson, J. (1995). What's in a name? Nationalist movements and public discourse. In H. Johnston & B. Klandermans (Eds.), *Social movements and culture* (pp. 107–126). University of Minnesota Press.

Johnston, H., & Klandermans, B. (1995). The cultural analysis of social movements. In H. Johnston & B. Klandermans (Eds.), *Social movements and culture* (pp. 3–24). University of Minnesota Press.

Klandermans, B. (1988). The formation and mobilization of consensus. In B. Klandermans, H. Kriesi, & S. Tarrow (Eds.), *International social movement* (vol. 1, pp. 173–196). JAI Press.

Klandermans, B. (1992). The social construction of protest and multiorganizational fields. In A. Morris & C. McClurg Mueller (Eds.), *Frontiers in social movement theory* (pp. 77–103). Yale University Press.

Kohl, P. (1998). Nationalism and archaeology: On the constructions of nations and the reconstructions of the remote past. *Annual Review of Anthropology, 27*, 223–246.

Luna Penna, G. (2014). Trayectoria crítica del concepto de entnogénesis. *Logos: Revista de Lingüística, Filosofía y Literatura, 24*(2), 167–179.

Melucci, A. (1995). The process of collective identity. In H. Johnston & B. Klandermans (Eds.), *Social movements and culture* (pp. 41–63). University of Minnesota Press.

Mustakova-Possardt, E. (2003). *Critical consciousness: A study of morality in global, historical context.* Greenwood Publishing Group.

Navarro, V. (2016, October 18). De lo que no se informa y/o se conoce sobre las elecciones en EEUU. *Diario Público.* Retrieved September 1, 2021, from http://blogs.publico.es/vicenc-navarro/2016/10/18/de-lo-que-no-se-informa-yo-se-conocesobre-las-elecciones-en-eeuu/

Obadia, L. (2008). Cartographie critique des usages et significations attribués au concept d'ethnogénèse dans les Globalization Studies. *Parcours Anthropologiques, 6*, 7–27.

Okamoto, D. (2013). Ethnic movements. In *The Wiley-Blackwell encyclopedia of social & political movements.* Retrieved September 1, 2021, from https://onlinelibrary.wiley.com/doi/10.1002/9780470674871.wbespm278

Pellow, N. P., & Brehm, H. N. (2015). From the new ecological paradigm to total liberation: The emergence of a social movement frame. *The Sociological Quarterly, 56*(1), 185–212.

Poutignat, P., & Streiff-Fénart, J. (2008). *Théories de l'ethnicité.* Presses universitaires de France.

Rabow, J., Berkman, S. L., & Kessler, R. (1983). The culture of poverty and learned helplessness: A social psychological perspective. *Sociological Inquiry, 53*, 419–434.

Schein, E. (2010). *Organizational culture and leadership* (4th ed.). Jossey-Bass.

Scott, J. (1990). *Domination and the arts of resistance.* Yale University Press.

Smith, D. (1990). *The conceptual practices of power.* Northeastern University Press.

Snow, D. A., & Benford, R. D. (1988). Ideology, frame resonance, and participant mobilization. In B. Klandermans, H. Kriesi, & S. Tarrow (Eds.), *International social movement research: From structure to action* (pp. 197–217). JAI Press.

Snow, D. A., & Benford, R. D. (1992). Master frames and cycles of protest. In A. Morris & C. McClurg Mueller (Eds.), *Frontiers in social movement theory* (pp. 133–155). Yale University Press.

Swindler, A. (1986). Culture in action: Symbols and strategies. *American Sociological Review*, *51*, 273–286.

Tarrow, S. (1988). National politics and collective action: Recent theory and research in western Europe and the United States. *Annual Review of Sociology*, *17*, 421–440.

Tarrow, S. (1994). *Power in movement: Social movements, collective action, and politics*. Cambridge University Press.

Taylor, D. (2000). The rise of the environmental justice paradigm: Injustice framing and the social construction of environmental discourses. *American Behavioral Scientist*, *43*, 508–580.

Tilly, C. (2005). *Identities, boundaries, and social ties*. Paradigm Publishers.

Tilly, C. (2010). *Los movimientos sociales: 1768–2008*. Ed. Crítica.

Touraine, A. (1978). *La voix et le regard*. Seuil.

Voss, B. (2008). *The archaeology of ethnogenesis: Race and sexuality in colonial San Francisco*. University of California Press.

Wallman, S. (1978). The boundaries of race: Processes of ethnicity in England. *Journal of the Royal Anthropology Institute*, *13*(2), 200–217.

Walsh, C. (2010). Interculturalidad crítica y educación intercultural. In J. Viaña, L. Tapia, & C. Walsh (Eds.), *Construyendo interculturalidad crítica* (pp. 75–96). Instituto Internacional de Integración.

Weber, M. (1978). *Economy and society: An outline of interpretive sociology*. University of California Press.

Wimmer, A. (2008). Elementary strategies of ethnic boundary making. *Ethnic and Racial Studies*, *31*(6), 1025–1055.

Winant, H. (1995). Race: Theory, culture, and politics in the United States today. In M. Darnovsky, B. Epstein, & R. Flacks (Eds.), *Cultural politics and social movements* (pp. 174–188). Temple University Press.

Wuthnow, R. (1989). *Communities of discourses: Ideology and social structure in the reformation, the Enlightenment, and European socialism*. Harvard University Press.

Chapter 4

Organizational Culture and Change
A Work of Deconstruction and Reconstruction

Objectives

The main idea of this chapter is that although culture influences leadership, at the same time leadership creates, maintains, and destroys culture. Thus, leadership is central in creating and legitimizing social orders. Culture is fluid and not static, and there are three main levels of culture that we need to be aware of if we want social change: artifacts, beliefs and values, and assumptions. If we want to change the culture of a society or organization, we must remember all the levels are interconnected and interdependent. Therefore, we need to go to the deepest level, the assumptions. Changing assumptions creates anxiety, and this is why changing culture can be very challenging and find resistance.

Social movements are cultural movements that aim to have influence and change the cultural order and perspectives of their societies (Fine, 1995). To be more sustainable, they create organizations and structures that produce culture (Taylor & Whittier, 1995). Regarding ethnic identity–based organizations, they not only create culture but also destroy manifestations of a hegemonic culture that hinder their processes of emancipation, and in the process, they increase critical consciousness, which is not only about awareness and theory but also about praxis. Ethnic SMOs raise critical consciousness while they unfold ethnogenesis processes to deconstruct social structures of domination and reconstruct social structures of emancipation within their organizations and societies.

Culture and Organizations

According to Hofstede et al. (2010), organization is needed to answer two questions:

1. Which person has the power to decide what?
2. What are the rules and procedures implemented to attain the desired goals?

"The answer to the first question is influenced by cultural norms of power distance; the answer to the second question, by cultural norms about uncertainty avoidance" (Hofstede et al., 2010, p. 302).

An organization is the result of a group of people working together for a common purpose. Etzioni (1975) distinguishes between three types of organizations in every society: (a) coercive organizations, where authority is arbitrary and absolute and the individual must obey the rules because they are subjected to physical or economic consequences; (b) utilitarian organizations, where authority is a negotiated relationship and the individual provides their work for a salary and accepts the rules of the organization; and (c) normative organizations, where authority depends on personal consent and the individual is committed because their goals are the same as the organization.

Organizational Culture

Since the early 1980s, several scholars have contended that "the 'excellence' of an organization is contained in the common ways by which its members have learned to think, feel, and act," and corporate culture is understood as "a soft, holistic concept with, however, presumed hard consequences" (Hofstede et al., 2010, p. 47).

Organizational cultures are different than national cultures because an organization is a social system with different characteristics than a nation. Basically, although members of a national culture were born within it, the organization's members were not: They "had certain influence in their decision to join it, are involved in it only during working hours, and will one day leave it" (Hofstede et al., 2010, p. 47). Thus, even if the national culture, or macro culture, has an influence, "research results regarding national cultures and their dimensions proved to be only partly useful for the understanding of organizational cultures" (Hofstede et al., 2010, p. 47).

According to Schein (2010), there is no standard definition of organizational culture, but scholars of corporate culture agree that it is:

*   holistic: The whole is more than the sum of the parts.
*   historically determined: It reflects the history of the organization.
*   related to the cultural domains anthropologists study, such as rituals and symbols
*   socially constructed: It was created and preserved by the group of people who form the organization.
*   soft, although Waterman and Peters (1995) state that "soft is hard."
*   difficult to change, although there is no agreement on how difficult.

As noted earlier, Hofstede et al. (2010) defined culture as "the collective programing of the mind that distinguishes the members of one group or category of people from others" (p. 5).

Consequently, organizational culture can be understood as "the collective programming of the mind that distinguishes the members of one organization from others" (Hofstede et al., 2010, p. 343). However, the organizational culture is internalized by the members of the organization, the stakeholders, and everyone who interacts with the organization because culture is about interactions and relationships.

Schein (2010) affirms that organizational culture is

> a pattern of shared basic assumptions learned by a group as it solved its problems of external adaptation and internal integration, which has worked well enough to be considered valid and, therefore, to be taught to new members as the correct way to perceive, think and feel in relation to those problems. (p. 18)

Thus, organizational culture becomes a field for struggle and liberation when ethnic SMOs can invent, discover, or develop basic assumptions that challenge the hegemonic culture and what is allowed to be said and thought. Because "the development of a worldview with its shared understanding of group identity, purpose, and direction are products of the unique story, personal interactions, and environmental circumstances of the group" (Smircich, 1983, p. 56), for any social group it is central to create and maintain its frameworks of meaning to make sense of the world.

Moreover, an organization's culture does not necessarily require homogeneity to hold together the members of an organization. Heterogenous and diverse members of an organization can develop a sense of belonging by articulating a "common frame of reference or a shared recognition of relevant issues" (Feldman, 1991, p. 154). For Martin (2002), the cultural observer has to attend to aspects of working life to seek "an in-depth understanding of the patterns of meanings that link these manifestations together, sometimes in harmony, sometimes in bitter conflicts between groups, and sometimes in webs of ambiguity, paradox and contradiction" (p. 58). From Bourdieu's (1993) perspective, culture is seen as "a system of schemes of perception, expression and historically constituted and socially conditioned thinking" (p. 233) that consecrates a social order and is achieved only when this system becomes natural (i.e., a habitus) after the objective structures of society are embodied in the categories of perception of individuals and groups of people.

In this study, culture is about the stream and flow of relationships, interactions, interconnections, disagreements, and struggles at an internal and external level among cultures and subcultures that configure the cultures in an organization. In short, culture is not static but fluid because it is constantly evolving within a field where, through struggle, it is decided what each (sub)culture can do and how others interpret it.

Levels of Culture Within an Organization

Schein differentiates three levels of culture from the most superficial to the deepest: (1) artifacts, (2) espoused beliefs and values, and (3) assumptions. Thus, to understand the essence of a culture, it is central to decipher the pattern of basic assumptions; otherwise, it would be impossible to understand the meaning of the artifacts and their connection to espoused values.

Artifacts

Artifacts represent what is visible to a group or organization. For example, among the artifacts, we find architecture, language, artistic creations, style (e.g., clothes, manners, emotional displays), myths and stories portraying the organization, rituals and ceremonies, documents describing values and ethics, and technology and products (Schein, 2010). For Martin (2002), artifacts are not necessarily superficial, and it depends on how people interpret their meaning; that is, they are interconnected with espoused beliefs and values and assumptions, so it is not about the cultural manifestation by itself but how people interpret it. "The depth of a researcher's analysis of these interpretations—that is, the patterns of meaning underlying a collection of cultural manifestations—can (and I argue should) approach the depth of understanding that Schein terms 'basic assumptions'" (Martin, 2002, p. 47).

The symbols that these artifacts represent "make it possible for there to be a consensus on the meaning of the social world, a consensus which contributes fundamentally to the reproduction of the social order" (Bourdieu, 1991, p. 166). Thus, artifacts and symbols construct society by providing people with a social being and recognizing it in a public manner. Therefore, artifacts and symbols are political and embedded in relations of power because they represent a space where general social relations can be represented and negotiated (Bourdieu, 1994).

Espoused Beliefs and Values

Cultures cannot prove that their beliefs or values are superior to others. However, if these moral and ethical systems are reinforced to each other, they will eventually be taken for granted. Gradually, "the group learns that certain beliefs and values, as initially promulgated by prophets, founders, and leaders, 'work' in the sense of reducing uncertainty in critical areas of the group's functioning" (Schein, 2010, p. 26). Thus, if beliefs and values keep comforting the group, they will become indisputable and embodied in the organization's philosophy as the resource to deal with uncertainty or turbulences. For Martin (2002), "Because espoused values are an attempt to create an impression on an audience, usually portraying the organization in an attractive light, they tend to be highly abstract and somewhat platitudinous" (p. 89).

Delegates or leaders base universal value on themselves and "monopolize the notions of God, Truth, Wisdom, People, Message, Freedom, etc. They make them synonyms. What of? Of themselves. 'I am the Truth.'" (Bourdieu, 1991, p. 210). They become sacred and establish a division between them and ordinary people. However, if the narratives, values, and explanations of a habitus suggested by leaders do not make sense, the dispositions, knowledge, and values of the supporters will change, and they will not give them their support anymore.

Two central elements regarding espoused beliefs and values are the processes of internalization and identification. *Internalization* occurs when the members of an organization perceive the leader's proposals as desirable and support them, while *identification* consists of imitating the leader's behavior to please or be like them (Yukl, 1994). Besides, *social identification* is understood as a process of influence that involves the definition of self at a group or collective level, becoming one of the member's different social identities (Ashforth & Mael, 1989).

From a Bourdieusian perspective, countries, communities, and organizations can have collective habitus, understood as shared beliefs and perspectives on the world, common values, and shared dispositions to believe and behave in particular ways. This habitus is orchestrated in a certain way by creating the conditions under which the social order comes to be viewed as natural and inevitable and other alternatives as unthinkable. However, to create these conditions, power and capital are needed (Webb et al., 2002). A powerful mechanism used by a community or the state to internalize a specific social order or vision of the world is to establish what constitutes acceptable behavior and how deviance should be punished. Perhaps the most effective way to orchestrate this collective habitus "is by ensuring that it is seen by the people it governs as being 'the voice of the people,' which gives it legitimate authority to rule us, and even to exercise violence against us" (Webb et al., 2002, p. 93).

Basic Underlying Assumptions

Basic assumptions are "theories-in-use" that guide behavior and inform group members how to perceive, think, and feel (Argyris & Schön, 1996). When a solution to a problem works repeatedly, it is taken for granted and considered natural, becoming a basic assumption for the group (Kluckhohn & Strodtbeck, 1961).

Like doxa, what can be said or thought, a basic assumption is not discussed, because it is taken for granted. As a result, changing basic assumptions is extremely difficult. Additionally, the challenging of basic assumptions destabilizes our view of the world and releases anxiety, unfolding a psychological process that ultimately can distort, deny, project, or even falsify to ourselves what is happening around us to avoid that anxiety (Schein, 2010). This level of culture provides its members with a sense of identity and establishes the values that produce self-esteem (Hatch & Schultz, 2004). In essence, it is through culture that people learn how to behave toward each other and feel about themselves (Schein, 2010).

Assumptions about "human nature" are central to perpetuating systems of oppression and control because when people are treated consistently based on specific basic assumptions, they will eventually behave according to them to get stability and predictability (McGregor, 1960). However, this domination process based on exclusion and injustice can also be a system of emancipation centered on inclusion and justice.

For Bourdieu (1989), "Habitus is both a system of schemes of production of practices and a system of perception and appreciation of practices" (p. 19). The unconscious is the process that both emerges out of and naturalizes the agendas, strategies, goals, values, and desires of the habitus. In other words, we incorporate the habitus within the self when we suspend disbelief and believe without thinking, without critical consciousness (Bourdieu, 1990).

Organizational Culture from an Academic Approach

There are three main academic perspectives in researching organizational culture: integration, differentiation, and fragmentation (Martin, 1992). From each perspective, one views culture differently, but at the same time, all three approaches can be complementary from a holistic and relational perspective. This is how culture is understood in this study.

The focus of integration studies is on a pattern of consistent interpretations of the different cultural manifestations and looking for consensus and clarity within an organization (Martin, 1992). Culture is "an area of meaning carved out of a vast mass of meaninglessness, a small clearing of lucidity in a formless, dark, always ominous jungle" (Berger, 1967, p. 23). In essence, there is no ambiguity, and it is argued that ambiguity is not part of culture.

Cultures are "an explanation of what causes them to cohere in the first place" (Helms-Mills & Mills, 2000, p. 57). From this perspective, cultural change is an organization-wide cultural transformation, and even if conflict and ambiguity occur during this process, it is seen as the substitution of a strong culture by another (Martin et al., 2004). Thus, dissent is understood as an anomaly, and it is not considered a subculture or counterculture within the organization. The focus is not on diversity and variety but homogeneity and a unified culture as desirable (Martin et al., 2004).

On the other hand, differentiation studies consider that consensus uniquely can occur within subcultural boundaries, and only subcultures can show clarity even if their relations are ambiguous (Martin et al., 2004). Thus, they propose to go beyond the superficial representation of culture as a whole and go deeper to understand subcultures and their relationships. In addition to cognitive and symbolic elements of culture, differentiation scholars suggest considering material manifestations and environmental influences and looking for inconsistencies between what is said and what is done, between the formal and the informal aspects, and, above all, between the different interpretations of each group within an organization (Martin et al., 2004). Differentiation scholars contend that when cultural change happens "within one or more subcultures, alterations tend to be incremental, and innovations are triggered primarily by pressures from an organization's environment" (Martin et al., 2004, p. 15). Therefore, organizational culture is not unitary and can be understood as an overlapping set of subcultures within an organization's permeable boundaries that are affected by environmental influences (Martin et al., 2004).

Those taking the fragmentation perspective interpret cultural manifestations as multiple and complex, accepting contradictions and confusion within culture. Besides, there is no consensus organization-wide or within subcultures, because consensus among individuals is fluid and changes depending on the issues and affinities. Thus, "the essence of any culture is pervasive ambiguity" (Martin et al., 2004, p. 16), which can include irony, paradox, contradictions, and multiple meanings because "change is a constant flux, rather than an intermittent interruption in an otherwise stable state" (p. 17). For fragmentation scholars, any research on culture that does not acknowledge ambiguity is an incomplete and oversimplified representation of the fluxes and complexities that characterize any organization today (Martin et al., 2004).

Combining Integration, Differentiation, and Fragmentation

When an organization is studied in depth, elements from the different academic approaches arise. For example:

> Some issues, values, and objectives will be seen to generate organization-wide consensus, consistency, and clarity (an integration view). At the same time, other aspects of

an organization's culture will coalesce into subcultures that hold conflicting opinions about what is important, what should happen, and why (a differentiation view). Finally, some problems and issues will be ambiguous, in a state of constant flux, generating multiple, plausible interpretations (a fragmentation view). (Martin et al., 2004, p. 31)

From a perspective of critical theory, "a strongly unified culture is an oppressive hegemony that successfully controls employees, in some cases even giving them a false consciousness that approves of their own oppression" (Martin et al., 2004, p. 21). Thus, what is understood as an organization's culture from an integration perspective is what has imposed on the other subcultures: a hegemonic subculture that dominates the rest of subcultures. A culture that "unifies (the medium of communication) is also the culture which separates (the instrument of distinction) and which legitimates distinctions by forcing all other cultures (designated as sub-cultures) to define themselves by their distance from the dominant culture" (Bourdieu, 1991, p. 167).

In differentiation studies, a critical theorist focuses on vertical differentiation between "advantaged and disadvantaged subcultures, drawing attention to the organizational life of non-managerial employees. This focus on labor versus management highlights conflicts of interest (as well as other subcultural differences associated with demographic markers such as sex or race)" (Martin et al., 2004, p. 22). However, it can still be a static way of approaching culture within an organization. Social reality and cultures are fluid because they are the result of a relationship between objective and subjective structures, and they exist twice:

> In things and in minds, in fields and in habitus, outside and inside of agents … the world encompasses me … but I comprehend it … precisely because it comprehends me. It is because the world has produced me, because it produces the categories of thought that I apply to it, that it appears to me as self-evident. (Bourdieu, 1994, pp. 127–128)

Therefore, in my study, I propose a conversation among the three perspectives of approaching organizational culture because culture is understood as a field for struggle where different groups relate to imposing their views within the organization and at an external level with other cultures. Thus, the organization's culture can be either the imposition of a subculture to the rest of the subcultures or a "culture" that results from the consensus of an intercultural dialogue. That is, a culture can be integrative, differentiated, and fragmented at the same time, but the key issue is how and in which terms the culture of the organization is created: top-down domination and/or bottom-up consensus.

Using all three perspectives results in a more complex understanding of organizational culture because a three-perspective framework is a meta-theory that allows the research to move "to a higher level of abstraction" (Martin, 2004, p. 32). Today, as a result of globalization, the internet, and the transportation revolution, boundaries around culture are more permeable and fluid than ever, and it seems more accurate to understand the research on culture as "an open conversation rather than a struggle for intellectual dominance" (Martin et al., 2004, p. 42). Additionally, organizational culture scholars have usually focused on individuals or groups, ignoring larger organizational contexts, such as the social, political, and legal (Barbour, 1999).

Barbour (1999) suggests a perspective of anthropology to broaden the scope and comparison among cultures and better understand the interconnectedness of components within a system and how humans create cultural frameworks to give meaning to their lives. Therefore, in my study, culture is understood as relationships and interactions considering "cultural boundaries as moveable, fluctuating, permeable, and blurred" (Martin et al., 2004, p. 40). As a political project within a field for struggle, it would also be necessary to consider the social, political, and legal perspectives.

Organizational Culture and Social Movements Organizations

Normally, social movements are organized through organizations with coordinating roles designed to carry out the necessary to survive and achieve its goals. Within these SMOs, culture can be understood as a mechanism of social domination and control and a tool to manipulate members to make them perceive, think, and feel in specific ways (Van Maanen & Kunda, 1989). Simply stated, this is just another way for those in power to mask their manipulation and control of others (Martin, 1992). However, through a process of critical intercultural leadership, organizational culture can also be a tool for liberation and social emancipation. "The challenge for organizations is to maintain the delicate balance between making organizational membership fulfilling, and intensely controlling thoughts and actions" (O'Reilly & Chatman, 1996, p. 192). In essence, organizations can either empower or disempower, and in terms of empowerment, culture can be the tool for enactment through raising critical consciousness and unfolding a process of deconstruction and reconstruction of social structures and identities. According to Martin (2002), "By conceptualizing the boundaries of a culture as permeable, moveable, and fluctuating, we allow for intercultural penetration and cultural change" (p. 340). Thus, redefining cultural boundaries from a perspective of ethnogenesis offers a new perspective of approaching the study of culture.

When people exist in relationships with each other in collectivities (e.g., within an organization with a structure arranged in space where people work together), they create cultures. Thus, as an aspect of a collectivity, "culture can be defined as patterns of interpretation composed of the meanings associated with various cultural manifestations, such as stories, rituals, formal and informal practices, jargon, and physical arrangements" (Martin, 2002, p. 330). According to this definition, culture is seen as a system of constructed ideas instead of the physical presence of individuals within a boundary; the construction, deconstruction, and reconstruction of these ideas will define whether the culture of the organization seeks domination or emancipation. Therefore, it is vital to better understand how culture is created, embedded and transmitted, evolves, changes, and can be destroyed within organizations in general and particularly within an ethnic organization that is part of a bigger social movement that challenges the dominant culture, intending to replicate processes of critical intercultural leadership in other spaces and contexts.

Macrocultures, Cultures, and Subcultures

Schein (2010) argues that cultures emerge from three sources:

- beliefs, values, and assumptions brought by founders of organizations
- learning experiences of group members during their time at the organization
- new beliefs, values, and assumptions brought by new members

However, organizational cultures are developed within one or more macrocultures, and the processes a group adopts are the result of both: the preferences of founders and leaders and the macroculture in which the organization exists (Schein, 2010). While national cultures are part of the "mental software" acquired during the first 10 or so years of our lives, the organizational culture is learned when we enter a work organization and, therefore, is more superficial (Hofstede et al., 2010). Thus, understanding culture at any specific level requires a certain understanding of all other levels: national, ethnic, occupational, organizational, and microsystems (Schein, 2010).

An organization can be seen as a set of subcultures interacting within a bigger context, what would be the organization's culture or, at a largest level, a subculture as a whole. An example would be a Native American organization struggling against the hegemonic culture of a country understood as an organization (hegemonic White culture in the United States). These subcultures develop assumptions about the organization and external actors and contexts. Thus, to be effective, an organization needs to align and harmonize its different subcultures and the microcultures that can emerge from multicultural teams in the current period of globalization (Schein, 2010).

Subcultures appear when managers and leaders in charge of an organization's divisions want a certain grade of autonomy. Besides, as the number of people in an organization increases, the most common solution is to create additional layers in the hierarchy, contributing to the creation of levels within an organization that fosters the emergence of new subcultures (Schein, 2010). Thus, it is central to encourage a dialogue among different subcultures that will develop in the long term a common language, goals, and decision-making procedures (Schein, 2010).

From a Bourdieusian perspective, it is central to understand that "the description of objective regularities (structures, laws, systems) do not tell us how people use—inhabit, negotiate, or elude—those objective regularities" (Webb et al., 2002, p. 36). In other words, subcultures also emerge from the intentionality and agency of the members of an organization or, from a Foucauldian approach, as a consequence of their processes of resistance against power.

How Culture Emerges in New Groups

When a group first meets, the main issues at an organizational level are related to their mission and goals. In an individual sphere, the group members are also concerned about their personal survival and how they are going to fit within this new group (Schein, 2010). Although each member brings their own cultural approach, the group starts without a specific culture.

When all members within an organization witness the same behavior and responses of other individuals, an emotional environment emerges, which confirms they belong to a group (Schein, 2010). Shared emotional responses normally occur the first few hours of group life when the members of a new group are struggling with issues of inclusion, identity, or authority and people are concerned about their own safety and profit rather than doing good for the group (Schein, 2010). At this stage, the members of the group are still acting at an individual level and looking out for their safety, so it is difficult to find consensus on what to do, and the group is very dependent on the leader to avoid anxiety. Gradually, as the group deals with different events, a sense of unity arises, and norms start to be created unconsciously, unless attention is drawn to it (Schein, 2010). In other words, norms are formed when a person takes a position within a group and the rest react by accepting it (either in silence or strongly approving it) or rejecting it (Schein, 2010, p. 208).

For Bourdieu, capital is central to impose a vision or what is considered legitimate within a community. Thus, capital is a social relation within a system of exchange and is extended "to all the goods, material and symbolic, without distinction, that present themselves as rare and worthy of being sought after in a particular social formation" (Harker et al., 1990, p. 1). The position a person has within a field—understood as a social site where people and institutions engage in specific activities—and the amount of capital they possess will designate what is "authentic" capital (Bourdieu, 2000). Therefore, the person with the better position within the field and with the most capital will have the capacity to manage regulatory and coercive discourses within the field. In essence, considering the relations within the field and the habitus, "'interpersonal' relations are never, except in appearance, individual-to-individual relationships and that the truth of the interaction is never entirely contained in the interaction" (Bourdieu, 1977, p. 81).

In terms of processes of social influence, Shamir and colleagues (1993) describe two main concepts:

- *social identification*: when the supporters identify themselves with the group and they feel proud to be part of it
- *internalization*: when the leader's vision reflects values and concepts of the supporters and they start seeing their work role as inseparably connected to their self-concept

Another term connected with social influence is *social contagion*, which was coined by Meindl (1990) and is focused on processes of social influence among the supporters themselves and not centered on the leaders. Social contagion is understood as the spontaneous development of emotions and behaviors among groups of people who reject their inhibitions—basically, established social norms or fear—and start acting in different ways. These behaviors are imitated by others and feed upon themselves, resulting in collective actions that individual people would probably not do, such as mob, riot, loot, or burn cars. When the group gets a sense of ownership that influences decision-making processes, the importance of the leader diminishes gradually. From then on, leadership is not seen as being embodied in a leader who knows what to do but as a shared set of activities within an organization (Schein, 2010).

Culture Formation in Organizations

Groups and organizations face two main problems: "(1) survival in and adaptation to the external environment, and (2) integration of the internal processes to ensure the capacity to continue to survive and adapt" (Schein, 2010, p. 73). When it comes to the formation of assumptions, there are two basic mechanisms that are connected with these archetypical problems: "(1) positive problem solving to cope with external survival issues, and (2) anxiety avoidance to cope with internal integration issues" (Schein, 2010, p. 215). Thus, assumptions are consolidated when norms and behaviors have been used successfully to navigate external survival issues and avoid anxiety while coping with internal integration challenges (Schein, 2010).

Therefore, to understand the evolution of a culture within an organization, it is important to identify the challenges that any group faces—at internal and external levels—from its origin, during maturity, and through the decline. Simply stated, group growth and culture formation are two sides of the same coin, and they unfold as a result of shared experiences, transmission of knowledge, and communication.

Shared Experiences of the Group

Groups are created with criteria of inclusion and exclusion. With new organizations, the founders and leaders establish the criteria, but as the group starts to interact, these criteria can be broadened or narrowed (Schein, 2010). Thus, members of the organization make sense and meaning of the world together against the internal and external environments and gradually configure their organizational culture. It is a process of reaching consensus to build a shared social reality, a leadership process that involves leaders, supporters, environment, culture, context, and specific purposes.

When it comes to the group's shared experiences, Bourdieu uses a concept called "misrecognition," which is key for the function of symbolic violence. According to Bourdieu (2000):

> The agent engaged in practice knows the world … too well, without objectifying distance, takes it for granted, precisely because he is caught up in it, bound up with it; he inhabits it like garment … he feels at home in the world because the world is also in him, in the form of the habitus. (pp. 142–143)

In other words, even if agents are subjected to forms of violence, they do not perceive it like this, because the situation seems to be the natural order of things. Thus, through misrecognition, leaders or managers can appear to be acting in a disinterested manner for the field and its values (Webb et al., 2002).

Transmission of Knowledge and Communication

A common language is needed to achieve any kind of consensus and to have efficient communication. If the members of an organization come from the same culture, the common language will already be present. However, as the group evolves, they create words with special meanings that only the group understands, making communication for outsiders more difficult (Schein, 2010).

Within most organizations, there is a process of accumulating knowledge that is constantly learned and shared by the different members. This knowledge is passed on from one member to another and can be represented through language, dress, demeanor, technology, rituals, and ceremonies (Barbour, 1999). Language is the channel of transmission for cultural knowledge within an organization, and each contains specific terms, phrases, ideas, or concepts. This language can not only be symbolic and deal with the spiritual but also can be materialistic and manage the physical (Barbour, 1999).

Since the struggle to impose on others a particular view of the world is symbolic, language is both the battleground and the weapon. This is what Bourdieu refers to when he writes about language and symbolic power. Language becomes powerful when it is used in particular ways or by particular groups and institutions, and it is "both a 'structuring structure' (it provides the means for understanding the world) and a 'structured structure' (it is the medium by which these understandings are communicated)" (Webb et al., 2002, p. 95). Thus, when leaders or managers control "legitimate language" (i.e., the structures and the media of meaning-making and understanding), this results in ensuring that citizens of a state or members of an organization will accept their right to rule them.

According to Bourdieu (1991), language has an oracle effect. He argues:

> If I, Pierre Bourdieu, a single and isolated individual, speak only for myself, say 'you must do this or that, overthrow the government or refuse Pershing missiles,' who will follow me? But if I am placed in statutory conditions such that I may appear as speaking 'in the name of the masses' … that changes everything. (p. 212)

Language, then, is one of the most effective instruments for embodying the structures and relations of the objective structures within the individual's sense-making apparatus to constitute the practical reason of the habitus (Bourdieu, 1991).

How Actors Create, Embed, and Transmit Organizational Culture

Founders of an organization define the basic mission of their organization according to their philosophy and other members' influence. Organizations are the result of planning and design, and rarely do they form accidentally (Schein, 2010). Thus, in terms of adapting to external influences and coping with issues of internal integration, the leader implements their ideas and solutions that, if successful and alleviate anxiety, will become norms and eventually assumptions.

As Barbour (1999) argues, actors in an organization are varied and involve key people who can be in contact with the leader and influence others to create values and norms in the organization. A leader's function within an organization "involves relationships in the transmission of cultural knowledge and in the social relationships with others in the work culture" (Barbour, 1999, p. 56). There is a communal aspect of work derived from the organization's value system and which is based on the "need to rely on others in the performance of work or in the need to exchange the products of work" (Barbour, 1999, p. 56). In essence, work within an organization involves members from within the community and from outside the community, and both networks contribute to shaping the organization's culture.

During this process, members other than the leader of the group can propose their ideas and solutions. However, leaders have certain advantages in the initial stages because—in addition to their power and bigger impact as a consequence of their position—they normally have well-articulated theories about how the group and the organization should work (Schein, 2010). However, if the leaders/founders do not have ideas and solutions or their ideas do not work, the group will become anxious, and others can emerge as leaders, empowered by the group looking to avoid anxiety within the organization (Schein, 2010). Also, if the environment changes and those assumptions that used to work start to fail, the organization will need to change part of its culture, which will be extremely difficult due to how founders and leaders have been embedding and transmitting their assumptions to the different members of the organization (Schein, 2010). The habitus not only coordinates practices but also requires practices of coordination since the agents adjust themselves within the field and "since undertakings of collective mobilization cannot succeed without a minimum of concordance between the habitus of the mobilizing agents (e.g., prophet, party leader, etc.) and the dispositions of those whose aspirations and world-view they express" (Bourdieu, 1977, p. 81).

To understand how authorized spokespersons (e.g., party or union boss) constitute and institute their power, it is not enough to analyze their specific interests or structural affinities that link them with whom they represent; one must study "the logic of the process of institution, ordinarily perceived and described as a process of delegation, in which the representative receives from the group the power of creating the group" (Bourdieu, 1991, p. 248). According to Bourdieu (1991),

> The mystery of ministry is at its peak when the group can exist only by delegating power to a spokesperson who will bring it into existence by speaking for it, that is, on its behalf and in its place. The circle is then complete: the group is created by the person who speaks in its name, thus appearing as the source of the power that he exerts over those who are its real source. (p. 249)

The paradox is that isolated agents who want to position themselves as a group to be heard in the political field cannot do it "unless they dispossess themselves and hand over their power to a political apparatus: they must always risk political dispossession in order to escape from political dispossession" (Bourdieu, 1991, p. 249). In essence, a group or a social class only exists and has force in the political field when representatives with the power to set the agenda are authorized to speak in its name, like, for example, "the Party is the working class," or "the Pope is the Church" (Bourdieu, 1991, p. 250).

To create, embed, and transmit culture, it is necessary to have power. Thus, narratives and discourses that support dominant practices are going to be amplified, repeated, reproduced, and remembered if the actors involved have power to construct an official history that will eventually configure the shape of the society, and this process of cultural construction will be seen as both natural and inevitable (Webb et al., 2002, pp. 90–91). For example, the systems of organization that a state develops with national laws and policies, bureaucratic procedures to operationalize these, and educational institutions where people are trained how to think are the tools by which "the state molds mental structures and imposes common principles of vision and division" (Bourdieu, 1974, p. 7).

Returning to the organizational culture literature, another explanation of how leaders embed and transmit culture is through charisma, understood as the "magical" ability to capture the subordinates' attention and to communicate assumptions and values in a clear and meaningful way (Bennis & Nanus, 1985; Conger, 1989; Leavitt, 1986). However, not all leaders of organizations have this mysterious gift, and they embed and transmit culture using different primary and secondary mechanisms.

Primary Embedding Mechanisms

These mechanisms are visible artifacts of the organizational culture that create the "climate" of the organization (Ashkanasy et al., 2000; Schneider, 1990). One of the most effective mechanisms for leaders to transmit culture is showing what they pay attention to: what they notice and comment on; which questions they ask; what they measure, control, and reward; or, in general, what they deal with daily (Schein, 2010). Through these elements, it is possible to understand their priorities, goals, and assumptions.

When Bourdieu (1990) analyzes the cultural production of art, he concludes that something becomes art when it is named as such by legitimized persons, or gatekeepers. This is the same process that occurs when imposing what counts as good taste: It is basically decided by *cultural arbitrary*, understood as the difference between cultural power relations constructed by dominant groups that, after being inscribed in the habitus of the community, appear universal. In other words, something becomes culture because it is in the interest of some dominant person or institution, and among these dominant persons or institutions are the government, the education system, major cultural institutions, and important gatekeepers.

Another important situation in the transmission of culture is when organizations face a crisis, particularly crises that arise around major external survival issues (Schein, 2010). Leaders of organizations are generally aware that their behavior is central to communicate assumptions and values to other members of the organization because informal messages are the more powerful mechanisms to teach and communicate (Schein, 2010). How leaders react and deal with the crisis reveals organizational assumptions "and creates new norms, values, and working procedures. Crises are especially significant in culture creation and transmission because the heightened emotional involvement during such periods increases the intensity of learning" (Schein, 2010, p. 243). Basically, with any crisis within an organization, anxiety increases, and to reduce the anxiety, it may be necessary to change cultural elements and learn new others. "If people share intense emotional experiences and collectively learn how to reduce anxiety, they are more likely to remember what they have learned and to ritually repeat that behavior to avoid anxiety" (Schein, 2010, p. 243).

People tend to accept the authority of a government or state, and "the question of the legitimacy of the state, and of the order it institutes, does not arise except in crisis situations" (Bourdieu, 1994, p. 15). For Bourdieu, because the state can engender a collective habitus, a shared identity, and a set of dispositions, it can convince its population that it was there for them. However, if the state neglects public needs, it will no longer be seen as the most effective actor to take care of the population. "The social world is riddled with calls to order that function as such only for those who are predisposed to heeding them as they awaken deeply buried corporeal dispositions, outside the channels of consciousness and calculation" (Bourdieu, 1994, p. 14).

Secondary Embedding Mechanisms

These are mechanisms of articulation and reinforcement and only work if they are consistent with the primary mechanisms. If so, they create organizational ideologies and contribute to formalizing what has been previously informally learned (Schein, 2010). "In a young organization, design, structure, architecture, rituals, stories, and formal statements are cultural reinforcers, not culture creators. Once an organization has matured and stabilized, these same mechanisms come to be constraints on future leaders" (Schein, 2010, p. 250).

Routines and bureaucracy in an organization lend structure and predictability and, as formal structures do, create a predictable life within the organization that serves to reduce ambiguity and anxiety. Additionally, the creation of systems, procedures, and routines contributes to reinforcing the leaders' message when they can formalize the process of "paying attention" (Schein, 2010). These symbolic ways of formalizing assumptions are key artifacts to observe but are difficult to decipher.

The final mechanism of articulation and reinforcement is the formal statement. In this context, a *formal statement* is the attempt by leaders to state their values or assumptions explicitly (Schein, 2010). However, these statements normally emphasize a small part of the leader's assumption or ideology, particularly the one that can be made public. That is why formal statements are not considered a way of defining an organization's culture (Schein, 2010).

According to Bourdieu (1977), "The structures constitutive of a particular type of environment (e.g. the material conditions of existence characteristic of a class condition) produce habitus" (p. 72)—that is, structured structures that function as structuring structures. Thus, the day-to-day material conditions turn you, against your own inclinations, into a specific person with particular dispositions and values and make you feel "like a fish in water" (Bourdieu, 1994, p. 127).

How Culture Changes

Cultural change requires leaders to offer the impression of competence, articulate an ideology, clearly communicate convictions, be a role model, have confidence, and motivate the supporters (Trice & Beyer, 1993). Cultural innovation leaders also need to be dramatic and expressive with their vision and require a source of additional power to implement new ideas and to deal with possible resistance (Yukl, 1994).

It is easier to change the culture at an individual level than at a group level because changing the culture of a group means that "all interpersonal relationships have to be renegotiated. However, if new tasks or a new environment force such a renegotiation, there is a good chance that undesirable aspects of the old culture will be cleaned up" (Hofstede et al., 2010, p. 375). For a process of cultural innovation and change, two roles are needed (Witte, 1973):

- machtpromotor: an expert in making the right diagnosis of the organizational culture and subcultures. This is necessary because organizations from the top are very different than from the middle or bottom, where the actual work is done.
- fachpromotor: a power holder who preferably has charisma to convince the members of the organization that change is needed, in particular with all the resisters

Tichy and Devana (1987) propose four approaches for leaders to increase awareness for culture change within an organization: (a) encouraging objective critiques and dissenting opinions; (b) performing external evaluations of the organization's strengths and weaknesses; (c) traveling and visiting other organizations to learn; and (d) measuring performance against competitors. Thus, having the support of key actors who acknowledge the necessity for change within the organization is central to facilitate the process because culture within organizations changes with the introduction of new values and the example of top managers. However, this theory also recognizes that "only when the new values are absorbed into unconscious assumptions will the culture actually change, giving employees a controlling role as well" (Tichy & Devana, 1987, p. 185). For a vision to be successful, it requries more than a leader because the vision evolves throughout time and results from a participative process that includes key actors who have to support the new ideas and changes. Moreover, Bennis and Nanus (1985) argue that rarely does the leader conceive a vision from nowhere; rather, the vision results from formal and informal networking with people within the organization and with outsiders.

Forces for stability and change coexist within an organization, but change is produced when "assumptions are symbolically challenged within the interpretation process and this starts a chain of effects" (Schein, 2010, p. 191). In other words, it is a double process of deconstruction first and reconstruction later because, as Martin (1992) states, a postmodern organization that deconstructs and then reconstructs would support diversity, plurality, and ambiguity. This double process to change the culture within an organization requires persistence and consistency. Process change is about "instituting new procedures, eliminating controls or establishing new controls, implementing or discontinuing automation, and short-circuiting communications or introducing new communication links" (Hofstede et al., 2010, p. 375). At an individual level, personnel changes mean new policies regarding hiring and promoting employees. Human resource managers unconsciously maintain their model when it comes to hiring for the organization, and they are key to changing culture by hiring individuals that will fit within the new culture and not the old one (Hofstede et al., 2010). Additionally, new symbols are central because they are easily visible: a new "name, logo, uniforms, slogans, and portraits on the wall—all that belongs to the fashionable area of corporate identity" (Hofstede et al., 2010, p. 376). However, symbols represent the surface of a culture; that is why if they do not have the support of fundamental changes at the deeper levels of the culture of the organization, they will not be sustainable in the long term (Hofstede et al., 2010).

Changing the culture within an organization is complicated, and structural changes such as closing and opening departments, merging or splitting activities, or moving people can facilitate the process (Hofstede et al., 2010). External crises of survival can also influence the process of change due to the discredit of their leaders, and they have a positive effect when challenging assumptions. Organizations going through survival crises discover in their responses deep assumptions that need to be transformed to adjust to the new situation. Thus, new senior managers can start leading and fostering changes within the organization that, if successful, will eventually become assumptions and will change the culture of the organization (Schein, 2010).

From a Bourdieusian perspective, because the categories of perception of the social world result from incorporating the objective structures of the social space, people are inclined to accept the social world and take it for granted instead of rebelling against that social order and struggling to impose a different worldview. However, since some cultural fields and institutions are alienated and marginalized, members of those fields can keep a strong commitment to the field's inalienable ideals and values through their habitus from where they can initiate processes of resistance. Besides, the indeterminacy of the objects of the social world and a certain degree of agency and reflexivity applied to those objects offers an "Archimedean point" for political action (Bourdieu, 1991, p. 235). The categories that make possible the order of the world are central for the political struggle, "a struggle which is inseparably theoretical and practical, over the power of preserving or transforming the social world by preserving or transforming the categories of perception of that world" (Bourdieu, 1991, p. 236). Thus, this objective element of uncertainty provides a base for symbolic struggles to impose a legitimate vision of the world. These symbolic struggles can adopt two different forms: (a) collective actions of representation that aim to display specific realities (e.g., demonstrations that make visible the group); and (b) individual actions of representation, which include all the strategies of presentation of self to manipulate one's self-image and particularly the image of one's position in social space (Bourdieu, 1989). Additionally, the symbolic struggle adopts the form of transformation of categories of perception and appreciation of the social world—essentially, the words and names that construct social reality as much as they express it, or what Bourdieu (1989) calls the "struggle over the legitimate exercise" or "theory effect" (p. 21).

In the struggle for the production and imposition of the legitimate vision of the social world, not all projects of world-making have the same importance, "and holders of large amounts of symbolic capital, the nobiles (etymologically, those who are well-known and recognized), are in a position to impose the scale of values most favorable to their products" (Bourdieu, 1989, p. 21). World-making consists of "carrying out a decomposition, an analysis, and a composition, a synthesis, often by the use of labels" (Bourdieu, 1989, p. 22), and to carry out this process, symbolic power—the power that through words preserves or transforms objective principles of union and separation—and social classifications is needed. Besides, as any form of performative discourse, symbolic power depends on the possession of symbolic capital, which is understood as "the power granted to those who have obtained sufficient recognition to be in a position to impose recognition," and to be symbolically efficient, "on the degree to which the vision proposed is founded in reality" (Bourdieu, 1989, p. 23).

Symbolic power creates "reality" with words because it "is a power of consecration or revelation, the power to consecrate or to reveal things that are already there," and the "'theory effect' is all the more powerful the more adequate the theory is" (Bourdieu, 1989, p. 23). As Bourdieu (1989) states:

> In fact, as a constellation which, according to Nelson Goodman (1978), begins to exist only when it is selected and designated as such, a group, a class, a gender, a region or a nation begins to exist as such, for those who belong to it as well as for the others, only when it is distinguished, according to one principle or another, from other groups, that is, through knowledge and recognition (connaissance et reconnaissance). (p. 23)

Although changing culture is a difficult process, for ethnic SMOs, this process can be a key tool to create alternative spaces and push back the assumptions and values of what was imposed by the dominant culture. Thus, it is about understanding existing cultures, and how culture is created, evolves, and can be destroyed, and how leadership influences all these processes. "This dynamic view also reflects a more functional point of view in that we are trying to understand not only what culture is but also what functions culture serves for a given group, occupation, nations, and so on" (Schein, 2010, p. 74). If the function of a social order is to "provide meaning to its members, to create psychological safety through the rules of interaction that protect face and self-esteem, and to define personal boundaries and the interactional rules for love and intimacy" (Schein, 2010, p. 154), what happens when the social order has been designed by a dominant culture for a dominant culture? In a scenario like this, subcultures and countercultures need to focus on culture as a field for struggle and a tool for emancipation, mastering the art of creating, changing, deconstructing, and destroying when necessary. Thus, culture can be either a system of domination resulting from modernity and colonialism and implemented through a process of Eurocentric leadership or a project that can be effective in transit from our current postcolonial world to an intercultural society with minimum asymmetries of power where different narratives and worldviews can coexist.

Toward an Intercultural Society

Eurocentrism was imposed as a global hegemon during colonization and imagined modernity and rationality as exclusively European products and experiences. Additionally, intersubjective and cultural relations between Western Europe and the rest of the world were codified in new categories: East-West, primitive-civilized, magic/mythic-scientific, irrational-rational, traditional-modern, Europe and not Europe (Quijano, 2000).

As a result of a dualism that excludes and that does not see difference as complementary, the European culture is seen as the only rational one. It is the only one that can contain "subjects." The rest are not rational; they cannot be or harbor subjects. This false dilemma presents other cultures as different and unequal and inferior by nature (Quijano, 2000). There are subjects and objects; there is one model of person (White upper-middle-class Christian man) and one region (Western world) as the house of enunciation, while the rest are just enunciated and are denied enunciation (Mignolo, 2011). As a consequence of these relationships, every relation of communication, interchange of knowledge, and modes of producing knowledge between cultures is blocked. It is a colonial epistemology, not dialogic, that does not allow any other form of knowledge to enter into dialogue (Mignolo, 2011).

Social orders proposed by both the "right" and the "left" are reactionary because they develop forms of action that negate freedom: The former imagines a "well-behaved" present and is willing to continue in that way, while the latter imagines a predetermined future that they already know (Freire, 2012). In other words, it is their own truth and not the truth of the people struggling to build their future. Besides, it is not "the truth of men and women who fight side by side and learn together how to build this future—which is not something given to be received by people, but is rather something to be created by them" (Freire, 2012, p. 39). Thus, an intercultural society is a society where there are no owners of the discourses and the narratives and where the people take control of their realities, naming and transforming the world from their cultural perspectives and worldviews. As Freire (2012) argues, "Who are better prepared than the oppressed to understand the terrible significance of an oppressive society? Who suffer the effects of oppression more than the oppressed?" (p. 44).

Their emancipation will be gained by themselves through reflection (intellectuality) and action (praxis), through a critical intercultural leadership process that goes from critical consciousness to ethnogenesis.

Therefore, what is needed first is a leadership process of social movements from below separated from the bonds existing between rationality/modernity and coloniality aiming to destroy the framework and social order of coloniality. "Critiques of modernity, in short, are blind to the (epistemic and cultural) colonial difference that becomes the focus of modernity/coloniality" (Escobar, 2010, p. 40). As a consequence of this lack of perspective, epistemological decolonization is key in any leadership process.

As Quijano (2010) states, "Epistemological decolonization is needed to clear the way for new intercultural communication, for an interchange of experiences and meanings, as the basis of another rationality which may legitimately pretend to some universality" (p. 31). This "thinking from the excluded other" or "thinking otherwise" is not just a question of changing the content of the conversation but changing the very terms of it (Escobar, 2010). It is a new intercultural model of leadership understood as a process from the borders and the margins and, with their people, an emancipatory and critical leadership process.

Today's social movements are more radical, complex, and inclusive than former movements (Hunter, 1995). They are radical because they seek a holistic transformation of society that stems from structural changes to deconstruct social imaginaries and frameworks instead of proposing cosmetic political reforms. Additionally, while former social movements used to think that taking over power was enough to transform the system of domination and oppression, new movements are aware of a broader and comprehensive struggle in different fields, such as the objective and subjective social structures that conform the social order of the world (Hunter, 1995). In essence, "radical new social movements seek to change the rules of the game, 'not just the distribution of relative advantages in a given organization.' Indeed, only by changing those rules can their ends be achieved" (Hunter, 1995, p. 331).

These new movements aim to build an intercultural society that overcomes the postcolonial world of domination and oppression that many marginalized groups experience. Because in the current society, both objective and subjective social structures do not allow diversity, and a new society not built on Eurocentric frameworks of domination is needed. This should be a new society where different cultures can coexist and interact without being objectified, where there is a dialogue and not a monologue among cultures, where there are even relations of power among groups, and where the difference is valued and appreciated (Viaña, 2010). Interculturality means processes of construction of different knowledges, different political practices, different social power, a different society, and different ways of thinking and acting regarding modernity/coloniality through political praxis. It is a thought, a praxis, a power, and a paradigm of and from the difference that goes beyond the dominant forms while challenging them (Walsh, 2007). In a postcolonial society where culture is a system of domination, exclusion, and control, an intercultural society seeks for emancipation to overcome the objectification of culture. Here, culture is understood as economy and politics, including different worldviews and projects beyond the Western world canon (Santos, 2007). In this scenario, the debate about the refoundation of the idea of nation-state and the liberal concept of democracy is promoted to create more inclusive forms of territorial, political, and economic systems of organization from the bottom-up.

To build an intercultural society, there is a need for a new model of critical intercultural leadership as a social movement. This leadership process could produce a new intercultural matrix that substitutes the hegemonic matrix to reduce the asymmetries of power between cultures and decolonize our minds to value difference and overcome the obstacles that hinder social and cognitive justice. One would understand this new model as a process that goes beyond current political projects and seeks to include the difference within the hegemonic worldview because it would (a) have a broader doxa (or more than one doxa) than simply the hegemonic doxa; (b) value cultural and epistemic differences; (c) design a pluriversal world resulting from a true and efficient dialogue between cultures; and (d) constantly review the creation of internal and external structures and institutions to avoid reproducing asymmetries of power between cultures and new mechanisms of domination and oppression.

Therefore, it is central to understand how a critical intercultural leadership process shapes the culture of an organization that resists within a hegemonic culture and the frameworks articulated to make sense and meaning of reality to resist. Thus, this study could shed light on leadership processes from a postcolonial world to an intercultural society. Besides, it is vital to discover the strategies implemented in an ethnic organization to raise critical consciousness and unfold ethnogenesis and whether, to do so, there are necessary conditions (and how they can be created). Any sustained leadership process that aims to transform society needs to be concerned with social structures, both mental and physical, and particularly how these structures are deconstructed and reconstructed in an ethnic organization through a process of critical intercultural leadership. Finally, what differentiates a critical intercultural leadership process from the Eurocentric leadership is developing processes of constant revision of the existing structures to avoid the creation of new asymmetries of power and structures of domination and oppression between cultures. In other words, it is a process without an end. There needs to be willingness to change a hierarchical system for more horizontal structures and institutions where a true and effective dialogue can be unfolded, and it is not about changing the subjects at the top of the hierarchy and reproducing a new monologue from a different cultural perspective.

Conclusion

If we want to change the culture of a society or organization, we need to go to the deepest level, the assumptions. Changing assumptions requires an initial leadership work of regulating anxiety since cultural assumptions are connected with the identity of the people and who they are. Situations of crisis at a social and/or organizational level are key moments to change a culture and facilitate these transformation processes. Additionally, power is critical for creating change, and framing through words and cultural artifacts are effective leadership tools for changing a culture. To create an inclusive organizational culture and social order requires formal and informal leaders to work from the bottom-up so that everybody is heard and valued. In the next chapter we will see a case study focusing on the macro context of an organization that uses the organizational culture to raise critical consciousness and unfold a process of ethnogenesis for its members.

Discussion Questions

1. What are the main mechanisms to create a culture within an organization?
2. Why is it critical to challenge cultural assumptions if we want to change the culture of an organization?
3. How are leadership, organizational culture, and social change interconnected?
4. What would an intercultural society with a fair social order look like?

References

Argyris, C., & Schon, D. A. (1996). *Organizational learning II.* Addison-Wesley.

Ashforth, B. E., & Mael, F. (1989). Social identity theory and the organization. *Academy of Management Review, 14,* 20–39.

Ashkanasy, N. M., Wilderom, C. P. M., & Peterson, M. F. (Eds.). (2000). *Handbook of organizational culture and climate.* Sage.

Barbour, J. D. (1999). Out of the field, into the field and back again: Understanding administrative theory development from a naturalistic perspective. In L. T. Fenwick (Ed.), *The seventh yearbook of the national council of professors of educational administration* (pp. 46–64). Technomic.

Bennis, W. G., & Nanus, B. (1985). *Leaders: The strategies for taking charge.* Harper & Row.

Berger, P. (1967). *The sacred canopy.* Doubleday.

Bourdieu, P. (1977). *Outline of a theory of practice.* Cambridge University Press.

Bourdieu, P. (1989). Social space and symbolic power. *Sociological Theory, 7*(1), 14–25.

Bourdieu, P. (1990). *The logic of practice.* Stanford University Press.

Bourdieu, P. (Ed.). (1991). *Language and symbolic power.* Harvard University Press.

Bourdieu, P. (1993). *The field of cultural production.* Columbia University Press.

Bourdieu, P. (1994). Rethinking the state: Genesis and structure of the bureaucratic field. *Sociological Theory, 12*(1), 1–18.

Bourdieu, P. (2000). *Pascalian meditations.* Polity Press.

Bourdieu, P., & Wacquant, L. (1996). *An invitation to reflexive sociology.* Polity.

Conger, J. A. (1989). *The charismatic leader.* Jossey-Bass.

de Sousa Santos, B. (2007). *La reinvención del estado y el estado plurinacional.* Revista OSAL-CLACSO.

Etzioni, A. (1975). *A comparative analysis of complex organizations.* Free Press.

Feldman, M. (1991). The meanings of ambiguity: Learning from stories and metaphors. In P. Frost, L. Moore, M. Louis, C. Lundberg, & J. Martin (Eds.), *Reframing organizational culture* (pp. 145–156). Sage.

Fine, G. A. (1995). Public narration and group culture: Discerning discourse in social movements. In H. Johnston & B. Klandermans (Eds.), *Social movements and culture* (pp. 127–143). University of Minnesota Press.

Freire, P. (2012). *Pedagogy of the oppressed*. Bloomsbury.

Goodman, N. (1978). *Ways of worldmaking*. Hackett Publishing.

Harker, R., Mahar, C., & Wilkes, C. (1990). *An introduction to the work of Pierre Bourdieu*. Macmillan.

Hatch, M. J., & Schultz, M. (Eds.). (2004). *Organizational identity: A reader*. Oxford University Press.

Helms Mills, J., & Mills, A. (2000). Rules, sensemaking, formative contexts, and discourses in the gendering of organizational culture. In N. Ashkanasy, C. Wilderom, & M. Peterson (Eds.), *Handbook of organizational culture & climate* (pp. 55–70). Sage.

Hofstede, G., Hofstede, G. J., & Minkov, M. (2010). *Cultures and organizations: Software of the mind*. McGraw Hill.

Hunter, A. (1995). Rethinking revolution in light of the new social movements. In M. Darnovsky, B. Epstein, & R. Flacks (Eds.), *Cultural politics and social movements* (pp. 320–343). Temple University Press.

Kluckhohn, F. R., & Strodtbeck, F. L. (1961). *Variations in value orientations*. Harper & Row.

Leavitt, H. J. (1986). *Corporate pathfinders*. Dow Jones-Irwin.

Martin, J. (1992). *Cultures in organizations: Three perspectives*. Oxford University Press.

Martin, J. (2002). *Organizational culture: Mapping the terrain*. Sage.

Martin, J., Frost, J. P., & O'Neill, O. A. (2004). *Organizational culture: Beyond struggles for intellectual dominance* [Paper No. 1864]. Stanford Graduate School of Business. https://doi.org/10.4135/9781848608030.n26

Meindl, J. R. (1990). On leadership: An alternative to the conventional wisdom. In B. M. Staw & L. L. Cummings (Eds.), *Research in organizational behavior* (vol. 12, pp. 159–203). JAI Press.

Mignolo, W. (2011). *The darker side of western modernity. Global futures, decolonial options*. Duke University Press.

O'Reilly, C., & Chatman, J. A. (1996). Culture as social control: Corporations, cults and commitment. *Research in Organizational Behavior, 18,* 157–200.

Quijano, A. (2000). Coloniality of power, eurocentrism, and Latin America. *Nepantla: Views from South, 1*(3), 533–580.

Quijano, A. (2010). Coloniality and modernity/rationality. In W. Mignolo & A. Escobar (Eds.), *Globalization and the decolonial option* (pp. 22–32). Routledge.

Schein, E. (2010). *Organizational culture and leadership* (4th ed.). Jossey-Bass.

Schneider, B. (Ed.). (1990). *Organizational climate and culture*. Jossey-Bass.

Shamir, B., House, R. J., & Arthur, M. B. (1993). The motivational effects of charismatic leadership: A self-concept based theory. *Organization Science, 4,* 1–17.

Smircich, L. (1983). Concepts of culture and organizational analysis. *Administrative Science Quarterly, 28,* 339–358.

Taylor, V., & Whittier, N. (1995). Analytical approaches to social movement culture: The culture of the women's movement. In H. Johnston & B. Klandermans (Eds.), *Social movements and culture* (pp. 163–187). University of Minnesota Press.

Tichy, N. M., & Devanna, M. A. (1987). *The transformational leader.* John Wiley.

Trice, H. M., & Beyer, J. M. (1993). *The cultures of work organizations.* Prentice Hall.

Van Maanen, J., & Kunda, G. (1989). Real feelings: Emotional expression and organizational culture. In B. Staw (Ed.), *Research in organizational behavior* (vol. 11, pp. 43–103). JAI Press.

Viaña, J. (2010). Reconceptualizando la interculturalidad. In J. Viaña, L. Tapia, & C. Walsh (Eds.), *Construyendo interculturalidad crítica* (pp. 9–16). Instituto Internacional de Integración.

Walsh, C. (2007). Interculturalidad y colonialidad del poder: Un pensamiento y posicionamiento otro desde la diferencia colonial. In S. Castro-Gómez & R. Grosfoguel (Eds.), *El giro decolonial: Reflexiones para una diversidad epistémica más allá del capitalismo* (pp. 47–62). Siglo del Hombre.

Waterman, R. H., & Peters, T. (1995). *In search of excellence: Lessons from America's best-run companies.* HarperCollins.

Webb, J., Schirato, T., & Danaher, G. (2002). *Understanding Bourdieu.* Sage.

Witte, E. (1973). *Organisation für innovationsentscheidungen: Das promotoren-modell.* Verlag Otto Schwarz & Co.

Yukl, G. (1994). *Leadership and organizations* (3rd ed.). Prentice Hall.

Chapter 5

A Case Study of the Macro Context of the Organization
History, External Relationships, and Current Challenges

Objectives

After the theoretical framework introduced in the previous chapters, this chapter describes the case study of a critical intercultural leadership process that creates an organizational culture that raises critical consciousness and unfolds ethnogenesis at a Native American organization[1]. This chapter describes the macro context and is presented in three different sections with corresponding themes and subthemes that emerged from data analysis to better represent the culture of the organization created by a critical intercultural leadership process: (a) history and background; (b) external formal and informal relationships; and (c) current challenges.

---

1   The research was conducted at the organization's main building and other locations in a midsize city of the Northwest where the organization developed activities in areas such as the City's Public Montessori, Cannon Park, or Riverfront Park. This organization is a Native American–owned small business led by women that delivers health services from a Native American cultural perspective in the area. In addition to observing and gathering artifacts for 6 months, I interviewed 34 employees of the organization working in different positions (leaders and supporters) and services (medical, pharmacy, dental, behavioral health, children and youth, and patient services) who were selected according to their accurate knowledge of the critical intercultural leadership process that emerges within the organization. It is important to clarify that the selected quotes in this chapter are representative of the "general" thinking of the members of the organization because the quotes chosen describe the main patterns that emerged through the analysis of data. In other words, these quotes are not just one person's opinion but a person's opinion that implies an existing pattern resulting from data analysis and that better summarizes the critical intercultural leadership and culture of the organization.

History and Background

According to the civil and human rights coalition The Leadership Conference (2016), Native Americans in the United States suffer from many of the same social and economic problems as other subordinated groups in the country that experience long-term bias and discrimination, including, for example, disproportionately high rates of poverty, infant mortality, unemployment, and low high school completion rates. Besides, Native people suffer from the three typologies of violence defined by Galtung (1990): direct, structural, and cultural violence.

Direct violence represents all those behaviors that threaten life itself and/or reduce the capacity of human beings to meet their basic human needs (e.g., killing, bullying, sexual assault, emotional manipulation, etc.). For example, according to research from the Centers for Disease Control and Prevention (CDC, 2018) on 47 states between 1999 and 2011, Native Americans were even more likely than African Americans to be killed in the hands of law enforcement. In terms of structural violence, this type of violence is understood as the systematic ways certain social groups have more difficulties enjoying equal access to opportunities, goods, and services to fulfill their basic human needs (e.g., unfair legal structures or lack of access to education or health care). Finally, cultural violence represents the existence of social norms that naturalize direct and structural types of violence and that are seen as "right" or "fair" (e.g., stereotypes and cultural assumptions about lack of intelligence, laziness, or inclination to violent behavior of some social groups).

To address these political, social, and economic problems with subordinated groups in general and the Native American population in particular, it is vital to focus on all three types of violence holistically and comprehensively. Thus, when it comes to Native American communities, the emphasis needs to be put on issues such as

- raising awareness about the killing, bullying, sexual assault, and emotional manipulation exercised upon Native people;
- transforming the social structures that situate the Native population at a subordinated position within a social hierarchy with big asymmetries of power and limit their access to good education, job opportunities, and health care; and
- debunking myths and deconstructing cultural assumptions about lack of intellect, laziness, or "primitive" behavior, that naturalize a system where racism, sexism, classism, and a cultural epistemicide overlap and are interdependent.

While referring throughout my study to subordinated cultures in general and the Native American culture, it is important to clarify that the Native population is not homogeneous. Today in the United States, there are 567 tribes legally recognized by the Bureau of Indian Affairs (BIA), which share common cultural elements and present many differences. Additionally, there are differences between Native communities living within reservations and Native populations living in urban areas.

According to a report by the Urban Indian Health Commission published in 2007, more than one million American Indians and Alaska Natives had left reservations and other rural areas during the three previous decades and moved to metropolitan regions. This change of lifestyle has had a big impact on the health of this population, who for many are invisible although they represent nearly 67% of the nation's 4.1 million self-identified American Indians and Alaska Natives (Urban Indian Health Commission Report, 2007). In the 1980s, within that context of lack of health services for "invisible" urban Native people of the area who were dying due to substance abuse and suicide on the one side and a system of cultural violence that portrayed Native people as primitive and situated them at the lowest levels of the social hierarchy of power on the other, a group of 15 urban Native Americans from different tribes living in the city decided to found the organization.

Foundation and Evolution: The "Dream" Comes True

By the end of the 1980s, this group of 15 Native Americans, identifying that their people were dying systematically as a result of not having access to basic health services in the city and that their cultures were disappearing as a consequence of a process of epistemicide initiated during colonialism to destroy any other knowledge and epistemology that went beyond the Western canon, felt it necessary to create the organization to address these two main issues. Thus, the organization was founded in 1989 to enhance lives and promote cultural appreciation and resistance for Native Americans in the city as a part of the Pan-Indian movement that originated a few decades before in the country struggling against assimilation and Imperialism. The organization started with a treatment section for drugs and alcohol abuse (two leading causes of death among Native people in the 1980s) and just one employee on the payroll. The founders also decided to continue organizing leadership camps, as they had done in 1987 and 1988, focused on the young urban Native Americans to give meaning to their lives and to encourage them to be proud of their cultural traditions and worldviews while training them as future Native leaders who would serve the urban Native community of the city and struggle for social justice and cultural resistance.

As one of the founders of the original project remembers when talking about the reasons that were central to the creation of the organization[2]:

> Only one out of every four kids were getting to high school. And of those one in four kids that got to high school, only one was going to graduate. And those are the super-achievers that were also going to go to college. But there's a lot of suicide, substance abuse. … All that was happening in between. And they said, "There's got to be some way that we can make a difference!" So, we formed [the organization]. (L33)

---

2   At the end of every quote there will appear a code to identity the person who is talking. The codes follow this system: The letter "L" is used for the positional leaders of the organization (CEO, COO, CFO, clinic director, and human resources director), followed by a random number from 1–34 (L22, L11, etc.). The letter "S" is used for the rest of employees or supporters of the organization, including directors of the different services (medical, dental, pharmacy, behavioral health, children and youth, and patient services), followed also by a random number from 1– 34 that has not been used for the leaders before (S15, S1, etc.). With this coding system, the reader will be able to track what the different positional leaders and supporters are saying and how often they are talking.

One of the main problems that the founders faced when starting the organization was finding the resources:

> We passed the hat. Literally, a baseball cap. And 15 Indians we came up with just a little over a hundred bucks to open a bank account. Then, we found out that the incorporation cost was $150. So, one of the members had an old Pinto car, bright orange, and we took it up to Cusick Pow Wow and raffled it off. We got enough money to get the incorporation money, and then [two people] wrote a grant. A federal and unprecedented. And never happened that anyone you talk to that you write your first grant you get it funded. And not only get funded, but it was a three-year federal grant. (L33)

The founders felt the responsibility and obligation of creating the organization to help the youth and the future generations of urban Native Americans. During the interviews conducted, the founders talked about how Native Americans today are not dying systematically due to direct violence, as was the case during the last centuries, but from structural violence. More specifically, the main cause for Native deaths today is the lack of access to education and health care resulting in a pattern of lack of employment, depression, substance abuse, and suicide among young people (HHS, 2016).

Since the inception of the project, the founders have been very community-oriented from the bottom up, listening to the community needs and identifying the best way to help them make their lives better. Initially, the community was understood as the urban Native population from the city experiencing drug and alcohol addiction. However, when the urban Native patients started to bring their relatives and friends from the reservation and even non-Natives to the organization, the founders decided to broaden the concept of "community" and serve everyone.

After a few years, in 1995, the Indian health clinic that provided services closed, and the urban Native community started to ask the leaders of the organization to create a clinic, although these leaders did not have previous experience with health clinics and even less with the Indian Health Service (IHS) system, which is the agency within the Department of Health and Human Services responsible for providing federal health services to American Indians and Alaska Natives. The provision of health services to federally recognized tribes grew out of the special government-to-government relationship between the federal government and Indian tribes. The IHS is the principal federal health care provider and health advocate for Indian people, and its goal is to raise their health status to the highest possible level. However, it seems that two problems emerge with the services the IHS provides: (a) Poor funding results in low quality of service, and (b) most of the budget is implemented in the reservations while just a small part goes to the health centers for urban Indians. As one employee of the organization noted:

> I grew up in the IHS system. It's a real crappy substandard subhuman way to treat Natives, and it starts from birth if you have to go to IHS. Their standard of care is ridiculously low, and it has caused a lot of deaths. (S18)

Another employee stated:

> The IHS services get lousy. I have been to my reservation recently, and the two clinics are substandard care. The only reason why I am living here and doing what I am doing, I had to move home because I couldn't get health care out here. (S16)

Finally, after 4 years of petitions from the city's urban Native community asking for a health clinic, the founders of the organization decided to create a clinic to provide basic health treatment to urban Indians in the area due to the low quality of IHS and the underfunded health centers for urban Indians. Since its foundation in 1999, the leadership of the organization have been focused on quality service and holistic medicine, as the mission statement claims: "Our Mission is to provide quality services that promote wellness and balance of mind, body, and spirit for individuals, staff, families and communities." However, the challenge of transitioning from just a treatment service of substance abuse to a health clinic was huge, and as one of the founders remembers, they encountered different barriers:

> The most underfunded piece of the Indian health is the urban. We get 1% of the funding. The tribes and the Indian Health Clinics get 99% of the funding. So, I mean, we just made it happen. We all did two jobs. We save, save, save. When we built this building, we had 900,000 dollars in savings. (L22)

According to the founders, this long-term and sustainable method of saving, buying, and building was the "Indian way" that seems to be the opposite of a Western mindset of immediate reward, economic debt, and overexploitation of natural resources without considering future generations. One of the organization leaders said, "There was like no grand design. Nobody rode in on their white horse and saved us" (L22). In other words, the urban Native community in the city needed to take control of their reality and destiny as active subjects instead of waiting to be saved. Besides, it was a leadership process based on organization, work, and sustainability, not vertical heroic leadership or movement. In addition, to consolidate the organization, a lot of sacrifice and work was needed:

> People didn't get big bonuses at Christmas, and I personally worked for 11 years with no benefits, with no healthcare, no savings, or 401(k)s. So now here I am [mature age]. I look at my 401(k) on my retirement, and there's this over a decade gap of no retirement. But, you know, I was willing to do that. (L22)

Gradually, the organization grew, going from a treatment service where there was one employee, to 15 people working when they opened the health clinic with basic services in 1999, and up to the 57 employees they have on the payroll today. Currently, the organization specializes in medical services (providing comprehensive care to Native and non-Native people), dental services (providing exams, cleanings, fluoride varnish, fillings, extractions, etc.), pharmacy (exclusively for their patients who can see the provider and get their prescriptions filled at the same visit), behavioral health (offering chemical dependency assessments, chemical dependency outpatient, aftercare/relapse prevention program, etc.), and children and youth (organizing leadership camps, summer programs, and community wellness programs).

The secret for growing was the "Indian way": A lot of work, sacrifices, quality services, and saving, along with good audits that attracted more money from loans and particularly from donations.

> The biggest change is that we are more prosperous like any business that started small with two people and then 10 and now 57 people. But prosperity didn't come because we had a casino or we had a benefactor. Prosperity for us came just in a very old-fashioned way that Native people have done for hundreds, thousands of years. You know that you're frugal with your resources, you're not crazy. We didn't pay ourselves big salaries, so that's the biggest change. Now we have salary scales, people. … We're the best paid behavioral health people in town, but that wasn't how it used to be. (L22)

With the growth of the organization, the providers working at the different services started to see more patients than before, but the organization has been able to keep its focus on the quality service and holistic medicine described in its mission statement. For example, the organization still offers patients longer visits with the providers than average Western clinics do. At the health clinic, the patients are encouraged to talk about personal issues to facilitate the understanding of the providers who can practice a more efficient and holistic approach to medicine. In addition, since its foundation in 1989, the organization has been aware of its role not just as a health provider but also as an SMO that contributes to creating a culture of social and cognitive justice in the region:

> From my standpoint, it seems like they've not only grown in size and able to handle more patients, but it seems too that they're working on trying to leave a lasting legacy. It's a lot of people that are here now being almost founders, and I think they're either trying to leave administrative policy or culture and instill that in newcomers to keep our values as well as just keep [the organization] standing and keeping growing. (S5)

Today, the organization can be considered much more than a business and a nonprofit in the field of health care as a result of the social justice motivations that originated its foundation (i.e., trying to address the systematic deaths of young urban Native as a consequence of substance abuse) and the particular characteristics of SMOs related to organizing collective actions of protests and campaigns to struggle for cultural resistance. This is why, although SMOs are mostly volunteer-run and this is not the case in this study, to better understand the leadership process that emerges within the organization and the collective actions that they organize, the theoretical framework of this book combines literature from the organization studies and the social movements discipline looking at this health clinic as an organization and an SMO.

Characteristics: A Diverse Organization as a Holistic Process

The first characteristic that one can observe when entering the organization is that it is a space of diversity that honors, recognizes, and embraces other people's cultures within a regional context where most of the population is White. On the payroll of the organization, there are people from 17 different tribes (Bad River Chippewa, Blackfeet, Chippewa Cree, Cheyenne,

Coeur d'Alene, Colville, Gros Ventre, Hopi, Native Village of Kotzebue/Inupiaq, Mandan, Navajo, Nooksack, Pine Ridge Sioux, Rosebud Sioux, Spokane, Turtle Mountain Chippewa, and Yakama) and from seven different countries (England, Canada, India, Kenya, Mexico, Vietnam, and United States) representing five different continents (Africa, North America, South America, Asia, and Europe). As one founder stated: "We're inclusive and we have probably the most diverse staff in all of the [city], eastern [Northwest]" (L33). In addition to diversity in terms of ethnicities and nationalities, the organization is also characterized because it is a business led by Native women working within a field of health dominated by White men and struggling for cognitive and social justice in a social context of racism, patriarchy, and sexism.

Two other central ideas that better characterize the organization and described in the vision and "sacred hospitality" statements are a holistic perspective for life in general and medicine in particular and a community-centered approach with a short-term focus on health care and a long-term perspective of activism and social justice. According to the vision statement on their website, the organization has a vision of community that promotes balance and harmony in the pursuit of:

- Drug and alcohol free lifestyles
- Spiritual, cultural, and traditional Native values
- Wellness and balance of mind, body, and spirit for each person
- Respect and integration of all healing paths to wellness for self and others
- Lifestyles that encourage and are supportive of prosperity
- Education and awareness

> By creating a circle of care using one team and one voice, individuals, staff, families, and agencies will utilize skills, leadership, cultural and spiritual consciousness to give back to his or her community by living as Warriors, nurturers, scholars, and community activists.

While the vision statement of the organization was designed along with the mission statement in 2008, the practice of Sacred Hospitality was introduced more recently in 2014. According to the organization's website, Sacred Hospitality is understood as

> an intentionally created practice where our compassion meets the needs of our patients, staff, and community; where they are welcomed, cherished, and respected as human beings; where stories are shared and valued; and where healing of the body, mind, and spirit can happen.

Theirs is a holistic approach to medicine and, at the same time, a process of raising awareness and empowering the community, facilitating collective action, and resisting to maintain their cultural traditions. It is a deep and complex concept that implies a general process articulated with different subprocesses. As one of the leaders of the organization noted:

Our characteristics are strength, wisdom, perseverance, and resistance. There's a lot of depth. It looks superficial on the outside, but there's a lot of depth. It looks like clear, clean water on top of the lake, but then there's so much movement going on under. You're not seeing it, but it's happening, and it's awesome. It's like this awesome thing. (L2)

Since it is a very community-oriented organization and the needs of the community change over the years, the organization is also characterized by a high degree of flexibility to serve the generational changes better than the community experiences (e.g., the evolution from substance abuse as the main cause of death among Native population in the 1980s and 1990s to the epidemic of diabetes today). Additionally, since its foundation in 1989, the organization has been dependent on government funds and donations that, according to the administration's political ideology at the moment, can represent more or less budget and resources to provide the different services to the community.

Therefore, due to an environment of economic dependence and political uncertainty, the organization has developed flexible structures and a capacity to adjust to different scenarios and make the most of the resources they have at any given period:

There's always things in flux, like plans. And I think in order to be successful here, you definitely need to be able to adapt. That's probably one of the key elements of success here, I think, is adaptability, just because of its size. And we seem to kind of be growing rapidly. And just to best serve our Mission, too. I think it's a pretty important characteristic. Personally and organizationally. (S6)

Another strategy to cope with the uncertainty that can generate different changes within the political administration in general or within the health care system in particular is to develop foresight and always think ahead to be ready when problems appear. The leadership of the organization can understand the organization and its structures as a holistic process, and they are aware of the multiple elements, relations, and possible combinations in any process and therefore the need to try to think ahead of different future scenarios for better adjustment. As an employee argues when talking about vision and leadership:

It's very empowering that we never just shoot for the status quo, which I see a lot in Native culture. We are like, "All right, here's our plateau, we're going to get you just to right here," which is functional. Hopefully, we make that functional. But always around here, whether we like it or not, we're always shooting for that next one. And our leadership will not let us be status quo. It's like we're always going to be a step above. That's where we're aiming. We're not aiming for the bottom tier. And that's one thing I like, and I think that's one thing that especially our youth need to see. (S10)

Moreover, the organization is characterized by its passion, creativity, optimism, and humor. According to one of the founders, "We are culturally based and mostly that means we have humor, food, laughter, and self-care" (L22). Through optimism and humor, employees cope with the multiple challenges they have been encountering since its foundation, including the challenges any fledgling business faces as well as the barriers they have been facing for being a

Native business led by women in a predominantly White and patriarchal society that exercises violence against subordinated social groups such as Native American people and women.

The Employees: A Combination of Openness, Empathy, and Awareness

Today, the organization has 57 employees and there are plans to increase the number of services provided and the staff within the following five years. Most of the staff are young professionals between the ages of 25 and 45, and there is a gap of age regarding the founders, who are all around 60. When it comes to the age of the leadership, there is much variety, going from founders over 60 years old to leaders around 30 years old. Approximately 65% of the 57 employees on the organization's payroll are women (those numbers jump to 80% of the leadership and 100% of the founders who are currently working at the organization).

These employees are characterized by their openness to new cultures and socioeconomic differences in terms of personal and collective characteristics. The organization represents in itself one of the most diverse spaces of the city, and a majority of the patients belong to the most impoverished social sectors of the area:

> You have to be open to the different cultures because we have Vietnamese, we have Russian, we have Caucasians, we have Blacks, we have Natives, and I think you have to be open to that. And also to the poverty in the community and the challenges they face. (S1)

Also, to adjust to different types of cultures and people, employees need to have an openness to embrace flow and change because every patient is different and has a unique socioeconomic background:

> You need to be able to adapt and understand the patients you're working with. I think that has to do with every department, behavioral health, all the way to medical. All the people we serve have different ethnicities and backgrounds. You have to look at that and different aspects when you come from different places. (S5)

It seems that this openness of the employees is the base from where empathy to think about the context of the patient is developed. As opposed to Western medicine that only focuses on the health issues without considering the social context, employees have a holistic perspective of medicine, and when they treat their patients, they are aware that those suffering from health issues are situated within historical and social contexts of racism, classism, and sexism that cannot be denied. Thus, the organization provides holistic health because they not only care about the disease or the outcome but also about the social, mental, and spiritual state of the patient:

> A lot of people come in, and they're not happy. We haven't been in their shoes, so when they come in, and they're difficult, you have to realize some of that difficulty stems from their lifestyle and poverty and their drug use, and their mental health.

I think you have to remind yourself through that throughout the day, especially at the front desk. They get damned every day, bam bam bam! (S1)

This empathy seems to result in responsibility and commitment too. For example, one of the leaders stated:

Working with our most vulnerable people … if they're sick, they get cranky. If they have behavioral health issues, they don't understand what you're saying. So, just be compassionate. Just put yourself in their shoes and understand that you're probably the only thing that is keeping them out of the hospital or from a mental health institution. Just try and bear with them. (L11)

Two central elements in enhancing the development of empathy and a sense of responsibility are awareness and knowledge. This is why the leadership of the organization emphasizes transmitting the history and culture of their people to the different employees. One of the founders had this to say about new employees:

They need to know like oral history. They need to know the historical context of why they work here. They need to know about trauma. They need to know the truth about what happened to Native people. We're sitting in this building today as a direct result of historical trauma. The genocide and how it shows up now. They killed almost most of us, so we better be on-board all hands-on deck to save what is rest of us. (L22)

It is a process of raising awareness among those employees who are not familiar with the story of Native people in the community, the region, and the country, either because they are non-Native or because they are urban Native who have been disconnected from their cultural traditions and practices. One non-Native leader explicitly noted:

Some of my White colleagues don't necessarily understand why the Native population has a different set of needs than the White population. I've worked on reservations in Alaska in the past, and one sees what happens to Indigenous Natives sometimes not getting a fair shake. So, understanding the history of where folks come from would be really helpful for most new employees. (S25)

This leader concluded that as a result of colonialism and how the United States was built,

most of this population has in their families experienced drug abuse, alcohol abuse, suicide, homicide, child abuse. In my family, nobody experienced any of that. I don't know about your family, but the majority of the dominant culture, I think, doesn't have that experience, and I think the majority of the Indigenous culture does have that. So, one needs to be aware that we're just different. (S25)

Thus, non-Native employees and also Native staff who were disconnected from their cultural traditions and practices have the opportunity of learning and/or relearning about Native culture and raising their awareness when it comes to issues of social justice involving Native communities in the United Staes in general and in Northwest in particular.

External Formal and Informal Relationships

There is a general consensus among the organization's employees on discrimination, White privilege, and strained cultural relationships existing in the city and the United States between the dominant White culture and subordinated cultures in general and with Native American people in particular.

Non-Native members of the organization are aware of the history of the United States and the impact that all the abuses and violations of human rights have had on Native American people and their Native patients.

> We totally screwed the Native American population. There's a fair amount of cultural injury that came from that, and there's a lot of post-traumatic stress. It's as if your reason for being was to work or whatever your reason for being is, and somebody just took it away and said, "Screw it you can't work anymore." And their way of life was functioning quite well in the 1500s. Everybody was doing something. There was a purpose for being, and over the subsequent 400 years, their reason for being was taken away. (S25)

However, while to the non-Native employees, it may seem that the situation for the Native American population in the United States has improved overall, Native employees consider that they are still living in a scenario of domination and oppression, one that is less overt and more subtle:

> I think there's genocide still happening in this country. And slavery in the prison system. We're being taught in our school system that stuff was over with and done for and not happening because it was ancient history. I feel like the fact that this stuff is still happening right now is really conflicting because the people that are suffering from those things can't pretend that those things are happening. They're happening. It's affecting our lives. Affecting our cultures. And we're not taking ownership. There's a lot of ownership that's not been taken or taught about what's still happening in our country. (S10)

While for the Native members of the organization, the past is still present and the current context is still one of domination and oppression, for White employees, the past is over, and even if they are aware that Native people are suffering from traumas that originated in the past, they are more optimistic and seem to think that the situation has improved substantially. When talking about the evolution of cultural relations in the United States, one non-Native employee said: "It's a journey and we're far from completion of the journey, but I think we've done pretty well" (S25).

Traditional cultures, in general, conceptualize time more circularly or understand it as a spiral, meaning that to project the community into the future, it is necessary to look at the past while living deeply and growing collectively in the present. Conversely, the Western world conceives a more linear concept of time, where the past seems to be over, the present has little relevance, and the emphasis is mainly on a future that does not exist (Little Bear, 2000). Therefore, the different forms of understanding the concept of time for different cultures may seem to explain why Native employees consider that the relations between their culture and the dominant one are still based on colonialism and genocide, whereas for the non-Native employees, those terms belong to the past and are not applicable anymore.

According to the employees, there is a general lack of knowledge regarding the Native American culture and particularly the "invisible" urban Native population in the United States. For example, as one Native employee who used to live in a big city noted:

> I feel like a lot of times that people don't even know Native Americans still exist, and that's like a big culture shock growing up in a suburb of [big city] which was pretty much [a big city], right? I mean, so a huge city. I was probably the only Native American student, and some of the students thought I still lived in a teepee. Then, if I didn't live in a teepee, they didn't know I even existed. (S16)

And regarding the city, although the presence of Native populations is very important in this region because the area is situated in the land of the Indigenous peoples of the Northwest Plateau, the lack of knowledge about Native people is also very generalized. As one of the founders stated:

> Relations in the U.S. are strained. Very not respectful and not integrated. And I feel the same in [the city]. We've been here 28 years, and people still ask me what do you do there? And I thought that's the definition of White privilege that you don't know where the resources are for every single person and every kind of person in the city. It's true, police officers asking me what do you guys do here? Or we go to the ER, and the ER docs go, do you have real doctors there? (L22)

In the same line of argument, another of the founders stated, "I think there's a lot of lack of understanding, and it's privilege. If it doesn't affect me it's not my problem" (L33). One of the leaders had this to say about the marginalization and erasure of Native people in American society today:

> We're the forgotten. We have all of our celebrations, our cultural events, and things like that. We choose not to let anybody forget us, but I see us as being forgotten, or maybe not even forgotten, but just put aside. I just see this as somebody that we were put aside on our little reservations and hopefully never seen or heard of again. (L11)

One proposed cause of these misinterpretation and lack of knowledge is an education system and a "White curriculum" that situate Native culture and Native people in museums as a manifestation of the past and objects without agency, which make invisible the contemporary cultural manifestations and processes of cultural resistance:

> I feel like learning starts traditionally in the United States in the classroom K–12, and I feel like a lot of the history books written are written not from an Indigenous perspective. When they treat topics of Native American history or more contemporary issues that we face, they are sort of glossed over, and they sort of depict us

as being ancient versus here today, and I feel like we have to become the teachers of our culture. We're tasked with that. (S14)

Another common concern that emerged through the conversations with the staff was the political climate under Trump's administration that, according to their views, promoted more overt racism in the United States than in previous years and empowered far-right groups to stop being "politically correct" and start showing through public demonstrations and rallies their political ideologies of White supremacism:

I think when you turn on the TV, and you see the Black Lives Matter movement and things like that, I think that's pretty indicative of the cultural climate. With the current administration, it's more overt than it has been since the '60s–'70s. Just like it was last night at [baseball stadium] where they unleashed that banner that said, "Racism is just as American as baseball." (S14)

One leader criticized multiculturalism in the United States because "difference" is celebrated but always in a position of subordination regarding the dominant culture contributing to maintaining the status quo:

I think there's a lot of talk about embracing culture, about celebrating culture, but I think what we say and what we do are two completely different things. Because I think we might not be aware of our own prejudices, and our own biases, and things like that. And when we look at viewing other cultures, I think it comes from a place of the viewpoint of looking at somebody else's culture as, maybe it's on purpose, maybe it's not on purpose, that it's inferior or less than your own. And so, you know yourself, but when you learn about others, it becomes it's less than. (L8)

One supporter argued that American multiculturalism was struggling in terms of inclusion: "My experience living here is that it's just like it's not a melting pot, it's more like a tossed salad. Let's put it like this. In the same bowl but they are not really mixing well" (S14). Another employee was criticizing the current social divisions in the United States society as a result of colonialism and advocated for a "class solidarity" that unites all subordinated cultures and social groups regardless of their race, ethnicity, gender, or social class:

If we were able to switch over to looking at our similarities when it comes to economics … if the poor got together, the way we were founded, no matter what color, there would be a lot more movement. But the way that we are divided so much in our minds, it's just hard to stop. (S10)

This employee was proposing at a macro level what the organization represents at a micro level: a general movement, a SMO that tries to overcome the social divisions that a hegemonic system imposed through a colonial matrix of power to justify and legitimate their domination and oppression based on categories of race, class, or gender, which situated a few people (basically rich, White men) at the top of the social hierarchy while most of the population remained subordinated.

A Sanctuary to Balance Asymmetries of Power and Decolonize

When it comes to these "strained" social relations between cultures in the United States, one of the key elements that emerge from data analysis is the existence of asymmetries of power in a divided society. Within this context of domination, oppression, and social divisions where the hegemonic culture is at the top of the social hierarchy, the organization represents an answer to counterbalance those asymmetries of power, providing an independent platform and channeling a collective action. As one of the founders explained:

> Any system you work in, whether it's education, government, even health care … If I were to work in those systems, I would never have power. I would have to always acquiesce to the power and control of the colonizer because they own every system in this country. I get that. So, I just had conversations with people, and we're like, "We can do this ourselves, we can make systems that maybe from the outside look like their system so if it's palatable enough they'll give us money or … but underneath really like nurture the spirit or the core of it." We know that it's safe here to be an Indian organization even though we do work that is dominant society work, if that makes sense. (L22)

The organization is a safe space where Native people can be who they really are. As another of the founders noted, "We have worked to be accepted for who we are and what we do based on who we are and what we do, and not on expectations" (L33). Therefore, the organization becomes a sanctuary for subordinated cultures in general and Native people in particular where they can be who they want to be and live their lives how they want to live them.

> [The city] being that it's not such a diverse city, the diverse population that we do have really finds comfort in coming to [the organization] because we are diverse staff, because they're staff that looks like them. Who might come from the same country they do, or might talk like them, or have the same language, and go through the same struggles, the same background, and probably celebrate the same holidays or family traditions, and things like that. (L8)

It is a sanctuary where people can feel comfortable and safe and, at the same time, can feel empowered through frameworks of collective action. Besides, it is an organization where, daily, one encounters and can "practice" diversity, social justice, and cultural resistance. As an employee stated:

> [The organization] allowed you more of a practice of interculturality and social justice, like maybe enlightenment. You know, working for a nonprofit, at the end of the day, it's not just about making money for the organization but also the benefit for the society and patient care for the group that we serve. So, I think it allows us to practice that, which is why I'm here. (S6)

The leadership of the organization seems to be very aware of the difference between paternalism and "assistentialism" on one side and critical consciousness and empowerment on the other. Thus, leaders of the organization emphasize practicing holistic medicine and patient-centered care where the patients take an active role in their health and work closely with the providers. *Patient-centered care* aims to convince patients to take control of reality in their own hands by taking charge of their health and lives instead of being passive and dependent.

> People who have a hard time here are what you call "codependents." They want to do things for other people, and we're very clear that's not what we're doing here. I mean, it really isn't the best way to undo colonization. To be free is to be independent. We teach people to be autonomous, healthy, independent, to live on their own, and to take care of their own health and their mental health. So, it's been a challenge sometimes because I think some professions like social work, medicine, or counseling have an unhealthy part that teaches people to be codependents and take care of other people. ... That is not our culture. (L22)

The organization is a space for decolonization of minds of both Native and non-Native employees and is also a project that aims to deconstruct social structures of domination and oppression. Within the organization, social justice issues are present every day, and, for example, White members of the organization can perceive even more their privilege and try to use it to advocate for and amplify the voice of people from the subordinated cultures with whom they work. As one White employee said:

> I feel that as I've learned more about Native culture here, I feel like I'm able to actually empower the Native besides the Native people individually. For example, going to dentist associations and organizations, I can bring a voice for them that often contrasts with normal private practice or something like that. ... And just bring the concerns that a lot of Native people have for their sake or lack of care or need for better care or better accesses as it needs to the attention of saying the state legislature or something like that. I think it's a great opportunity, like I said, to empower those around me about Native concerns. (S4)

Decolonization is not just an endeavor of subordinated cultures but also of allies belonging to the dominant culture who need to be aware of their privilege and use it to advocate for a transformation of a system of domination and oppression that hinders the potential of human development of all those who are not at the top of the social hierarchy.

Raising Awareness and Educating Hegemonic Institutions

Although allies from the hegemonic culture are necessary since they are part of the problem—and therefore part of the solution—Native people at the organization are not voiceless. They exercise their voice and agency to raise awareness of and educate about Native culture and traditions to a predominantly White community in the city and their main institutions, such as the city council or the police department.

The leadership of the organization works on improving relationships with the city council and the police department to raise awareness among them about Native people's presence in the area:

> [The organization] has always worked to have a good relationship and to improve that with the city. It's been an ongoing process. I started with the [organization] in 1999, and I have watched the improvement in the relationships with the city, and I think [the founder and CEO] does a wonderful job of educating people about Native culture and people of color. (S1)

At the same time, they try to educate those institutions about the political, economic, and social struggles of Native population in the city and the region.

> One key is education. Going out and educating people. [The founder and CEO] has sent people to the hospital to meet our clientele and invite them over to see the clinic and see what we do, the fire department, the ambulance, the police. ... We've had people from senators and their staff comes over to be introduced. Yeah, it's amazing. (S1)

Regarding the police department, it seems that their relationship with the organization has improved through the years, even if there still may be a history of police abuse and violence with Native people. For example, one employee explained:

> If you have kids or relatives that are identifiably Indian and Native relatives or whatever, I always tell them that "if the police say stop, you stop. You stop." I said, "You don't have to tell them anything else, you can call me, but at least stop and identify yourself and don't put your hands in your pockets for God's sake." But you tell them that even here in [Northwest city], you do because in [Northwest County] if a person of color drives through [Northwest County], you don't want to go one mile over the speed limit because you will get a ticket. These are really the laws of the country. (S15)

The following anecdotes combines the humor that characterizes the organization with the certain sadness inherited from historical genocide and abuses and exemplifies the strained relations between law enforcement and Native communities today:

> Our police came in uniform to meet with [the founder and CEO], and we had one patient run to the bathroom, one patient turned around and went out the door, one patient refused to come through. ... It was just like that, but also it can be traumatic for kids. I saw a little kid and when she saw a policeman started crying because she said, "That's when my uncle died and they came into the house and they took me away and blah, blah, blah, and all this ..." That's your memory of the policeman. (S15)

Thus, the leadership of the organization tries to improve the relationships between the urban Native community of the area and the police department, organizing different events with them, like roundtables or workshops, or just inviting the police department to participate in social gatherings, like the summer camp graduation. Through a more fluid and constant relation and presence of the police department in activities organized by the leadership of the organization, the police officers get to know the urban Native community, their traditions and cultural practices, on one side, and the Native population of the area has the opportunity to express their concerns and to share their historical traumas resulting from decades of violence exercised by the military and the police in order to raise awareness among police officers and also for healing and reconciliation.

> I think the relationship with the [Northwest city] Police Department was like they did our summer camp for our kids, which was positive. And then [the founder and CEO] hosted a focus group, a public forum for them to come in, and it was sort of a hot seat for them because it was the community being able to ask these hard questions. And I commend all of them for coming in and putting themselves in a spot like that, but I don't know the extent of the relation, working relationship, just that they have made themselves an appearance with [the organization]. (S14)

Although the relationship is not perfect and has its setbacks, it seems that, due to the initiative of the leadership of the organization to establish a fluid communication, today the police department sees the organization as a liaison with the Native communities of the area.

> I think for good or bad, I think they see us representing Natives in the community, so whenever they have a Native issue, they come and talk to [the founder and CEO], and that's good, and that's right. I mean, she will always say I do not represent … she will always tell them I don't represent the Natives here in this community, I represent [the organization] myself. (S20)

When it comes to the city council, the relationship between them and the organization appears to be neither fluid nor good. According to one of the leaders, communication is almost nonexistent:

> City council, mayor … those guys they all want to talk to you when they need something. That's what I always feel like. I always feel like it's always about what their needs are and never about what our needs are. And they don't want to talk to you unless they need something. I don't really see any of them here. (L11)

Finally, at a federal level, the organization is dependent on IHS funding and tries to get grants and have some sort of influence on the government decisions, sending people to Washington, DC, occasionally to advocate for the cause of urban Native population in the area. As one of the employees put it:

> On the federal level, we're pretty dependent on IHS for funding in terms of grants to help us. So we're always doing some outreach. Like we have an outreach right now for postcards to our governors and senators to try to raise awareness for the importance of a grant that helps subsidize some of our positions here. So, I think we're in pretty good communication. I think people do visits to the capital and discuss legislation that can affect our funding and things like that. (S6)

In order for any ethnic organization within the United States to survive, it is central to learn to navigate between cultures and systems, and the leadership of the organization must know how the political and health systems work and how to navigate them to get funds for the sustainability of the organization while keeping their independence.

Current Challenges

Among the challenges that the organization faces today, one main problem appears to be related to funding to sustain the organization and to be able to grow while continually providing high-quality services to the community. The historical dynamic of the city's governmental institutions for funding does not prioritize activities related to culture and ethnic minorities:

> The funding for cultural activities it's not as big as it should be with the city council, and that's what we're kind of fighting against. They allocate something that they get from businesses, but it goes to more like sports activities. Kind of non-kind of cultural things, or trying to work to divert some of that money to more cultural activities. Not just for us, but for people who are trying to grow these things. I think it starts with those things at the city council, and it's not really supported. (S9)

Moreover, with the current political climate, the funding is in jeopardy because the funders perceive uncertainty and do not know what to do and to say to the organization's leadership. Therefore, not only is the organization's ability to grow under threat but also its sustainability and the provision of some basic services. For example, one of the founders noted:

> Resources are always a challenge, and right now, even more with the [Trump] administration where everything is up in the air, and we don't know. Under the Affordable Care Act, we were just starting to make money where we could put stuff aside and start looking at expansions and stuff, but that might end. We don't know. (L33)

And this uncertainty is not only affecting the organization's leadership and staff but above all impacting the patients:

> The uncertainty in the Affordable Care Act is like, "Where is healthcare going, you know?" And you see that in patients as well, like, "Well, am I going to pay more for my coverage next year? Am I going to have coverage next year? Am I going to be able to afford my medications? Am I going to be able to come here anymore?" That's probably one of the greatest challenges to see where we're heading. And I think the uncertainty creates anxiety in the public, and we can see that in patients. A general anxiety starts to step up a little bit. (S6)

Another main challenge that emerged with the interviews is the dissonance between what the founders think and what some leaders and supporters believe when it comes to implementing the mission. For example, for one of the founders, the mission seems to be very clear for all staff:

> Our Mission statement is over every single desk, every single workstation. We talk about it in staff retreats. We talk about it in staff meetings. All staff meetings. And

you walk to the building, you see Sacred Hospitality. Sacred Hospitality is the coin fairy, is a Mission that for everyone our commitment to your health, whether it be mental, physical ... (L33)

However, for some of the young leaders, practicing the mission does not appear as obvious, and perhaps more work is needed:

With all the employees, we do obviously orientation. All staff meetings, things like that. We try to reiterate what we're here for and what we do. Probably do better at that. We've asked staff to post that on their office space so they can have a reminder of what our work is here, but I think as an agency, I think we would be even stronger if we were really focused on instilling that, and it'd be a dream if we could just have everybody on staff be able to recite it word for word and know what each of those words really means. We're nowhere near that, and that's part of the administration to set that tone, and that's part of the things we have to walk and talk about. Because if the administration can't recite the Mission statement word for word, we can't expect the staff to do it either. (L8)

Additionally, for another leader:

I think, at times, we lose sight of it. At times we say it but don't enact it. I will contend that there are times that leadership are the farthest ones away from the Mission, and that's unfortunate, but I think it comes from their own injury or history that they can't get beyond that. I don't know that we're really good about sharing that. I think sometimes there's just the verbal, you know, here's our Mission, read the Mission, but I don't think we always enculturate that. (S25)

Interestingly, although the organization has experienced rapid growth since its foundation, it seems that another of the main challenges is their poor visibility and the lack of knowledge regarding their existence and the services they provide within the community. One of the founders, when asked what they would like the community to know about the organization, said:

That we are here. Even after almost 30 years, people don't have a clue that [the organization] exists. So, I would have them know who we are, that we serve everyone, and we have a complete palette of services available. (L33)

One leader of the organization also complained that although the community could have heard about them, there is still a lack of knowledge regarding what the organization offers and the quality of the services they provide:

First of all, many people don't even know what we do still. They don't know that we're a health facility that we have all these great services here. I'd like them just to know what we do, number one. Number two, I want them to know that we have qualified and very good talent here. This is not the reservation where people go because they cannot get a job anywhere else. Does that make sense? I want them to know that we're a very viable organization. And then our Mission, obviously. We want them to know what we are about. (L11)

Yet another leader mentioned that misunderstanding and added the lack of awareness about the full health package of the organization, which is one of its strengths:

> The biggest misconception about the [organization] is that we only serve Native people. But we serve everyone. And we have a unique infrastructure to help provide a wide range of services for them. It's not just a one thing get out of it. It's a complete wellness package that we offer here. You're not going to come here just for a doctor's appointment. We're here for being healthy, for Dental, and Pharmacy, and prevention, and wellness, and healthy eating, and exercising, and diabetes care. (L8)

Among the staff, a common idea that emerged with the interviews regarding why the organization is not well-known within the community is the apparent misinterpretation of the organization's name. For several organization members, the name (a Native-related name) brings confusion among the community and, in particular, with non-Native people who think they cannot be treated there. Thus, one employee was very critical of the name:

> I think, the name, it's deceiving. I think probably the clinic would rebrand this, but it is not up to me to decide. One of the things that I get from my patients is, "Oh, I thought you guys only see Native Americans because the name is [a Native-related name], right?" (S3)

In the same line of argument, another employee stated:

> Even from family and friends. They say: "So only Native people can go there, right?" And I'm like, "No. It's open to the whole community." And that's something we actually need to work on, to get that message out a little bit better, you know. (S20)

Finally, another of the main challenges that the organization currently faces and has been facing since its foundation is an environment of stress and pressure, which has impacted turnover within the organization for the last years. For example, due to the uncertainty that sometimes can produce the lack of funding and the political instability, staff and patients can be impacted by stress and anxiety. Additionally, members of the organization deal with patients who are suffering personal dramas, and dealing with these situations and testimonies daily can be very hard and emotionally eroding. In addition, the organization promotes many programs and events to reach out to the community, and for some employees, this can be too much added workload. According to one member of the organization, as a consequence of this context of stress, pressure, and high workload, not everybody can work there: "It can be a stressful job; people relying on you and being able to affect their life can weigh heavily on you. That's not for everyone" (S4). Thus, it seems that a lot of passion, commitment, and resilience are needed to work at the organization, and sometimes employees just need a break from the organization before coming back. For example, it seems common for employees of the organization to take a break, leave, and return after working for a while in another organization. As a leader argues, "Sometimes it is good to leave and to bring back new ideas" (L8), a practice that seems to be very common at the organization and is called by the members of the organization "stealing shamelessly."

Everybody should do something that they're in love with, and if you're not in love with what you're doing here, then this probably isn't the best place for you. Anybody who's ever worked here has always been, and always will be, part of [the organization] family. But sometimes you have to go away and come back. We have a rule here where everybody gets to come back to [the organization] at least three times, and people do. (L8)

Among the negative impacts of a high turnover, several employees agreed that one negative consequence is a lack of stability for the patients who see different people going and coming every time they visit the organization.

I've seen a lot of people come and go, come and go like providers and medical assistants. And that has always created much turbulence because my goal is to provide a safe space. When I say safe, I'm talking about a constant and stable environment where a patient will meet the same person throughout, and they would feel more comfortable, kind of like a home. Does that make sense? (S3)

Moreover, for many employees, the turnover is perceived as a personal struggle because of the strong sense of family within the organization and the close relationships among staff:

We have had a lot of turnover. We have lost a lot of people. A lot of people. We have had a lot of turnover. Lots of people have gone. From my perspective, I see that, and that's been a struggle. I think a little bit because we have gotten from here to here, and we are trying to figure out how to do this and still maintain all those qualities that make it a comfortable place to work and help people. And then, the high number of people that have gone ... but we were part of the family, and now they have moved on. (S15)

Another negative consequence of the high turnover is that it implies an organizational struggle due to the amount of time and money invested in training people who, eventually, will leave the organization.

Since I've been, we've gone through so many people. And like once we get some great people to stay, it's awesome. But I don't know. I feel bad for [member of the organization] and some of the people who have to train constantly. Like it's just a lot of extra work for them. (S23)

However, although the leadership of the organization is aware of the negative consequences of a high turnover for the organization, it seems that they also understand this process as a certain way of filtering those employees who are fit to work in a stressful environment and are committed to the mission and vision from those who are not.

Conclusion

Relations with external actors and the structural and systemic context influence the leadership work of sense- and meaning-making and identity formation that emerges in any organization.

Additionally, power relations between the organization and its members regarding external actors and the context need to be acknowledged since leadership does not emerge in a vacuum and has implicit power relations. Leadership work unfolded with a critical intercultural leadership process is central for organizational and social change based on raising the critical consciousness of the organization members and deconstructing and reconstructing organizational and social structures of oppression. In the next chapter, we will see a case study focusing on the micro context of an organization that uses the organizational culture to raise critical consciousness and unfold a process of ethnogenesis for its members.

Discussion Questions

1. What differentiates a Eurocentric leadership process from a critical intercultural leadership process?
2. How does a critical intercultural leadership process shape an organization's culture that resists within a hegemonic culture?
3. How are the frameworks designed to make sense and meaning of a process of resistance and identity formation within the organization?
4. What are the main strategies at a macro level to raise critical consciousness and unfold ethnogenesis?

References

Centers for Disease Control and Prevention. (2018). Retrieved September 1, 2021, from https://www.cdc.gov/

Galtung, J. (1990). Cultural violence. *Journal of Peace Research*, *27*(3), 291–305.

US Department of Health and Human Services (HHS). Profile: American Indian/Alaska Native. (2016). Retrieved September 1, 2021, from http://minorityhealth.hhs.gov/omh/browse.aspx?lvl=3&lvlid=62

Urban Indian Health Commission. (2007). *Invisible tribes: Urban Indians and their health in a changing world*. Retrieved September 1, 2021, from https://www2.census.gov/cac/nac/meetings/2015-10-13/invisible-tribes.pdf

Chapter 6

A Case Study of the Micro Context of the Organization
Internal Relationships, Understandings, and Meanings

Objectives

After viewing the macro context of the organization in the previous chapter, this chapter describes the case study of a critical intercultural leadership process that creates an organizational culture that raises critical consciousness and unfolds ethnogenesis at the organization introduced in the previous chapter[1]. This chapter describes the micro context and is presented in two different sections with corresponding themes and subthemes that emerged from data analysis to better represent the culture of the organization created by a critical intercultural leadership process: (a) internal and informal relationships and (b) tacit and explicit understandings and meanings.

---

1 The research was conducted at the organization's main building and other locations in a midsize city of the Northwest where the organization developed activities in areas such as the City's Public Montessori, Cannon Park, or Riverfront Park. This organization is a Native American–owned small business led by women that delivers health services from a Native American cultural perspective in the area. In addition to observing and gathering artifacts for 6 months, I interviewed 34 employees of the organization working in different positions (leaders and supporters) and services (medical, pharmacy, dental, behavioral health, children and youth, and patient services) who were selected according to their accurate knowledge of the critical intercultural leadership process that emerges within the organization. It is important to clarify that the selected quotes in this chapter are representative of the "general" thinking of the members of the organization because the quotes chosen describe the main patterns that emerged through the analysis of data. In other words, these quotes are not just one person's opinion but a person's opinion that implies an existing pattern resulting from data analysis and that better summarizes the critical intercultural leadership and culture of the organization.

Formal and Informal Internal Relationships

Formal and informal relationships within the organization represent a variety of different encounters, interactions, miscegenation, power, and resistances that are influenced and shaped by different elements. Among the main ones, there are (a) the diversity of the staff; (b) the encouragement for creativity and the fluidity of the organizational structures; (c) the commitment of the organization to social justice and cultural resistance; and (d) the particularities of the leadership process that emerges within the organization.

Diversity of the Staff

The organization under discussion is a Native American organization led by women with 57 employees on the payroll belonging to 17 tribes and with people from seven different nationalities representing five different continents. It is probably one of the most diverse places in the city, a predominantly White area in the Northwest. As one leader noted[2]:

> I remember when I first came here and I was like, "Wow, this is fun, there are a lot of people of different cultures here!" That was refreshing because, as you've come to appreciate, [Northwest city] at large is pretty uni-cultural. There's pockets of everything, but the dominance, by far, is White Americans. (S25)

Formal and informal relations that unfold daily within the organization are strongly influenced by this diversity. This diversity of Native and non-Native perspectives creates the constant feeling of navigating between cultures, and the strong sense of family that arises among the very diverse staff acts as a sort of glue for the employees regardless their culture, race, ethnicity, class, or gender.

Native and Non-Native Cultural Perspectives

Within a space where people from different cultural backgrounds and worldviews work together, it seems inevitable that cultural differences, shocks, and conflicts emerge. As one leader noted:

> We see a lot of cultural conflicts. It's not just Natives that work here. We have Vietnamese and Kenyans. We have different cultures that we're trying to intermix, and a lot of my time is a lot of miscommunication in personnel, coaching in here with a lot of the departments or staff coming in here and like, "So and so said this" or "So and so said that." I go, "Okay, let's take a step back and see what the miscommunications was." Because 99% of the time, it is a miscommunication issue or a

---

2   At the end of every quote there will appear a code to identity the person who is talking. The codes follow this system: The letter "L" is used for the positional leaders of the organization (CEO, COO, CFO, clinic director, and human resources director), followed by a random number from 1–34 (L22, L11, etc.). The letter "S" is used for the rest of employees or supporters of the organization, including directors of the different services (medical, dental, pharmacy, behavioral health, children and youth, and patient services), followed also by a random number from 1– 34 that has not been used for the leaders before (S15, S1, etc.). With this coding system, the reader will be able to track what the different positional leaders and supporters are saying and how often they are talking.

cultural exchange that somebody is not getting. I say, "Let's talk about that. Here's the space to talk about it and you guys aren't forced to be friends, but you do need to understand each other at some point because you are serving the same patients!" We have that constant. (L2)

One of the most visible aspects of the organization's diversity is the relationship between Native and non-Native people and their different cultural perspectives. For example, an interesting concept that emerged from the data analysis in terms of differences between Native and non-Native staff is the degree of respect that each group of employees has for elders and ancestors. As one Native leader explained:

Culturally, you follow the elders. Elders have the most knowledge. Elders have the most life experience. But there are also elders that teach and mentor those people within the organization, or even within the community, that have shown and demonstrated trust and bond relationship and rapport in the American Indian community. (L2)

This concept of respecting the elders appears to be much stronger among Native employees than with non-Native employees and seems connected with a mentality of mentorship in life in general and particularly within the organization. Thus, the leadership within the organization promotes and encourages the mentoring of other employees, patients, and youth. As an employee stated:

[The founder and CEO] is a great mentor, and she believes in empowering her staff. She believes in mentoring the young ones to follow up and assume her position when she's gone. For instance, her daughter, and [the director of Human resources]. I've watched them be mentored to come up, and she talks about it all the time: mentoring our Native kids to educate and to take over and to keep doing that. (S1)

Everybody is mentored at the organization regardless of whether they are Native or non-Native:

Being White, I wasn't exposed to any culture growing up. I was just surrounded by White people, and so my sister is African American and Native American, and she had a horrendous time here. I got some exposure to her experience, but working with these kids, working with Native American kids, or working with the Latino kids ... I have mentors that can teach me. Because I don't know everything. You know? And I love that. (S32)

Today, around 30% of the employees on the payroll participated in past editions of the leadership and summer camps as children. This statistic shows that the leadership's main focus is on empowering urban Native youths and proves that the system of teaching and forming future leaders for the community has been effective and sustainable until now. As one of the leaders who was part of the leadership and summer camps as a child described:

I think working here, I have become prouder and feel more celebrated and hopeful. Before I came here, there wasn't really a place that had a bunch of professionals who were like, "Hey, you're awesome as you are. Come join us." That kind of thing. And when I came here and then saw these people who are movers and shakers in the community, who are doing awesome things, who've asked me to sit at the same table as they have … I didn't have to sit at the kids' table. (L8)

This culture of mentorship at the organization is reproduced generation after generation, particularly with the young people who were once mentored and now work there and feel the obligation to mentor others. Interestingly, although Native and non-Native employees stated during the interviews that they were mentored at a certain point and consider it a very positive practice, only Native American interviewees explicitly expressed a sense of responsibility and duty to mentor future generations. This does not mean that non-Native employees do not mentor in their lives or within the organization, as mentorship is a very widespread practice in the United States, particularly in businesses and colleges. However, there seems to be a deeper level of commitment to mentoring others among Native employees than non-Native employees who, despite making references to the importance of being mentored within the organization, did not talk explicitly about mentoring others. As one young Native leader stated:

I obviously want to be able to offer the same opportunities for other people after me, and I want to make a community, a workforce, and a place like that for other people. And in order for that to happen, I have to be part of the conversation. I have to have a conversation at work. I have to have it outside of work. Talking about fairness, and equality, and cultural competency when it comes to certain things. And [the organization] has taught me how to have that conversation and taught me how to really be who I am and stand my ground. And to share with others my gift. (L8)

Another difference between Native and non-Native employees and perspectives within the organization emerges regarding the practice of medicine. On the one hand, there is a Native approach that focuses on the long term and implements a holistic perspective. On the other hand, there is a Western model that centers on the short term and exclusively emphasizing the outcome.

Our providers, the more and more they work in medicine, the more and more they get upset and jaded because they're saying, "I'm only treating the outcome, I'm not treating the cause." You see them kind of like, "Well, I'm the provider and I am just going to treat the outcome and that's how medicine is running right now." And in an Indian organization, you really have to take a cue from the tribe and the tribal leadership on where your health efforts are going to go, and that's the challenge I often observe in the work setting with our providers. They know they're doing outcome, and they really, really are passionate and Mission-driven and want to make people healthy, but at the same time, they know they're going to have to treat chronic disease if our prevention efforts or our wellness efforts aren't interjected during that lifespan of the family. (L2)

While the cultural differences noted before (the degree of respect for elders and the commitment to mentoring) do not imply a conflict within the organization, differences in the understanding regarding the practice of medicine of some non-Native providers seem to contradict the basic principles of holistic medicine stated by the mission and vision statements of the organization and can result in a negative environment. Therefore, this different approach to medicine represents a concern for the leadership when it comes to hiring new employees: Candidates may meet the professional requirements to work at the organization but may have a rigid Western mindset regarding medicine that will make it difficult to provide health care from a holistic perspective. Thus, the Department of Human Resources becomes central in deciding who can work at the organization and preserve the organizational culture and the mission and vision statements. As one leader noted when describing the hiring process:

> At first, I'm like, "Oh, they just need to be oriented and blah-blah-blah." Now I say, "Oh no, you have to do a lot of cultural norming with them!" And even with our seasoned senior providers, you still have to do a lot of cultural norming with them and also coaching. And sometimes you just ask a question back to them and let them guide them, but they got to make their own mistakes and their own miscommunications, so they learn from that. You can't be like a helicopter administrator down there trying to figure it out. So, I think, for the most part, the organization it's very traditional of a Western concept, but it's non-traditional in how we practice that. (L2)

When it comes to solving these conflicts among employees, instead of a more "Western" procedure (e.g., complaining to the board or human resources), the system implemented at the organization is to "call a circle." The circle is described in the book of policy and procedures of the organization as "circle management," and although it may sound like a managerial concept, its origin comes from the traditional tribal circles where people used to plan, argue, make decisions, and have conversations about different issues face-to-face in a circle.

> You're not working at Deaconess or Sacred Heart hospital anymore [hospitals in the Northwest city]. This is really a life shift for them. They need to know how we started and why, and this isn't their private practice. If they are unhappy, they don't go to the board and bitch about it. That's a very White corporate way of doing business that goes up and down the chain. No, this is "sit right here and work this out; let's work it out in your circle." (L22)

For Native American people within the organization, this system appears to be very natural, and they seem to be very comfortable calling circles to address personal and organizational issues because they are familiar with this cultural practice. However, for non-Native employees, it seems to be a very uncomfortable and sometimes even traumatic procedure because it does not provide confidentiality: "Some staff who first came here when they were in their first circles were just freaked out. Especially health care workers" (L22). Notwithstanding, as non-Native employees get more awareness about Native culture, most of them end up being comfortable with the circle and eventually prefer to call a circle instead of complaining to human resources or asking for confidential evaluations.

> Some staff who used to freak out with the circles later said, "Oh, I want to call a circle on that," because they realized the power of it. I hate doing things like evaluations.

Evaluations are absolutely worthless. What does that teach someone? How about a circle with all your coworkers? Yeah, why don't you hear it from them what you're fabulous at? What you could work on? Or what you're not fabulous at? Don't you think you're going to remember that more than a little piece of paper that I didn't sign? (L22)

Non-Native members of the organization who learn to navigate between different cultural practices such as the circle gradually get more awareness about Native history and worldviews that improve their work and interactions with patients. They start to see medicine more holistically and understand the need for context and connection of different elements such as the history, the culture, or the socioeconomic status of the patient to provide health care. As one non-Native employee noted:

In Dental specifically, a lot of Native American experiences have been terrible. Kind of, we deal with a lot more anxiety. There's always the general anxiety because everybody kind of has a dental anxiety. But coming from someone who doesn't have a Native background to somebody who is Native, I feel like that's a lot more negative. Their experiences were a lot more negative as children. Not saying that there's not negative experiences for everybody, but like being everybody put on a bus and brought to the dentist like cattle, whereas I didn't grow up like that. (S5)

In general, this awareness and knowledge of Native American history and culture helps non-Native employees understand the cultural context of their patients and develop empathy toward them.

We try to relate to their ethnic or cultural backgrounds. Different socioeconomic backgrounds. We have homelessness, we have people with mental health issues and minorities. People who are impoverished. So, trying to relate to what conditions they might encounter or what they have endured in their life or try to have an understanding. (S6)

However, not all employees learn to navigate between cultures and develop a better understanding of Native culture and medicine. When new employees do not agree with the organizational culture and mindset of the organization, it is very clear to the leadership that these people need to leave. For example, as noted before regarding cultural and training differences that emerge when it comes to resolving personal conflicts with the native practice of circles instead of complaining to human resources, one leader said:

It's really a training exercise to teach people to resolve their conflict one-on-one. It's kind of aversion therapy because people don't want to go back in the circle. I think it's so in corporate America where is that at. Everybody goes to HR, but here that is not [the human resources director's] job to babysit you on the job. You have a problem with your coworker, then work it out or go work at the bank. I don't care. (L22)

The same leader continued:

> I don't care what you do at [Northwest city's] Mental Health. I don't care what you did at Sacred Heart Hospital. You're at [the organization] now. But that's part of the colonization too. People drag their old stuff in, or "We don't like this … up there it was better." I'm like, "I don't care. I do it like this and it works for our community." (L22)

Certain lines in the sand cannot be crossed, such as the concept of holistic and long-term medicine, the circle management, and the mission and vision statements, which I believe represent a decolonial framework or core of values and cultural assumptions that cannot be adjusted, modified, or changed. The rest of the principles, values, or beliefs can be discussed, modified, or changed through the dialogue among cultures. However, there is a core that guarantees the decolonial mindset and the organization's autonomy that appears to give the organization its particular identity.

Navigating Between Cultures

As a result of a workplace where there are employees and patients from different tribes, nationalities, ethnicities, classes, gender identities, professional mindsets, and types of training, members of the organization are obliged to learn how to navigate between different cultures in order to offer quality services. One leader compared the diversity within the organization with a former job and expressed the necessity to navigate between cultures there:

> We are navigating between cultures here every single day. I worked as [former job] for 20 years prior, and I didn't. I was in a private practice, and I wasn't having to navigate it so much. But yeah, it's constantly here, and I actually like it. I really do. I feel like it keeps me on my toes. (L11)

Notwithstanding, there is a noticeable difference between Native and non-Native employees (in particular, those individuals belonging to the hegemonic White culture). The Native employees appear to be more used to navigating between cultures as a result of having done so since they were born, whereas the non-Native employees appear to need more effort when it comes to relating with other cultures. According to one of the founders:

> I'm a biracial person. I have privilege because of my skin color till I open up my mouth because my brain isn't really biracial, although I do understand them. I think the old days in a lot of Native language mix-blooded people will call the interpreter. People that could explain both sides, and a lot of times, I see that as my role. And I think it irritates White people, and sometimes it irritates Indians, so I just say, "Hey, this is what they mean." (L22)

Conversely, for non-Native people, the process is not as smooth, and they need to actively learn how to navigate between cultures:

> One of the things about making myself more accustomed to the Native American culture is to acknowledge that I know nothing about them. Very quickly, I became

very aware that for me to be able to take care of them, I need to understand where they're coming from. I need to understand the history. I need to be aware of what their needs are. I have colleagues here that are Native Americans. And I started asking questions. (S4)

One of the strategies that the leadership of the organization implements to facilitate the process of navigating between cultures is to share information and knowledge about Native issues in every meeting or event that they organize:

I think learning to navigate for me is first to learn. [The organization] did a great job of kind of sharing what Native culture meant to them as well as a lot of history that they have gone through, whether it be positive and proud or kind of negative experiences that we're trying to overcome. I think by learning that knowledge and having kind of, I suppose, first- or second-hand knowledge on kind of these experiences, say domestic violence or alcoholism, or something like that, it just allows me to be more empathetic to individuals' situations or even to broad situations such as the Dakota Access Pipeline or something. (S4)

This learning process is necessary not only for non-Native employees but also for Native employees who are not very aware of their culture and, in particular, urban Native people who can be disconnected from their cultural roots due to processes of cultural assimilation into the Western culture. As one Native employee argued:

When I first came, even though myself I am Native, I was very much an urban Native. I had never been on the reservation. I'm an enrolled [Indian tribe], but I never lived on the reservation, so I was very White. I did have to learn to navigate between cultures then and get educated. So, they've done a great job. (S1)

The leadership of the organization facilitates navigating between cultures sharing information and knowledge regarding their culture, history, and political struggles and offers the employees and community spaces for interacting and dialogue. For example, there is a monthly "all staff meeting" where all employees meet to discuss the situation of the organization, general policies, and designs to follow; weekly "directors meetings" where the directors of every service provided by the clinic update the leadership and each other to coordinate their work; weekly "departments meetings" where members of each department inform each other about their tasks and share ideas to improve the services they provide; and "Employee Appreciation Day" on Fridays to share and get to know each other in a more informal way. Besides, there are different events organized every week outside the office where the employees can participate, and in general, the whole building is a big space to interact when working, walking, having lunch, or resting.

Generally, individuals belonging to the White hegemonic culture in the United States do not need to know about other cultures due to a system that bestows White people with the "privilege" of living in a society designed by and for them. However, when it comes to working at the organization, they will encounter diversity when interacting with Native colleagues and patients, and they will feel the need to learn and know about subordinated cultures and social groups. According to one employee, these "formal" spaces of interaction in the organization were central to meeting with different cultures and being empowered in terms of learning to navigate between cultures:

> Providing the environment for me to meet with other people and to meet with the Native American community. I think that by itself is empowerment. Several community events like the Pow Wow and the fun run and things like that have been the building blocks where I have been able to tap into meeting people in the community. A lot of questions are how I met with people and asked those questions, and I feel more empowered that way. (S3)

Moreover, as one leader argued, besides the formal spaces, employees can always interact with each other, creating informal spaces within work and also outside work:

> I call it setting the sacred space; it could happen anywhere. It could happen in my office, it could happen privately, [or] it could happen in a group depending on the situation. It could happen to all staff. You set the sacred space, and you set the tone, and that's different than where you want to see elsewhere. I call it studying the sacred space and having those conversations and making sure it's safe. (L2)

Navigating between cultures means learning from the cultural backgrounds not only of the different organization members but also the community in general and the patients in particular. As one employee argued:

> We get time to talk to our patients, whereas not a lot of places get that. It's not a run-in, run-out experience, and that's gotten for me it's made me kind of relax a little bit with getting involved in their lives. I talk to people a lot more. I know a lot more where they're coming from as opposed to "Oh, they're going to be 20 minutes late. Too bad." I was like, "Why are they going to be 10 minutes late? What's happening? There's probably something happening." We're not rushed through, and that's been my experience at most other offices, and here it's not, which has been nice for me. (S5)

Relations between employees—and between employees and patients—are valued and, as opposed to a more Western approach that presents a rigid organizational system based on an industrial concept of society centered on productivity, the organization represents a more relational and fluid way of organizing while still being able to provide high-quality standards for the treatment of patients.

Sense of Family as the Glue of the Organization

Despite all the cultural differences, conflicts that may emerge, and difficulties employees face in constantly navigating between cultures, the general mentality that seems to predominate and act as the glue that keeps the organization together is that of a "family," where differences are accepted and valued as strengths. Thus, all employees seem to be aware of being part of the organization family, and they understand this sense of belonging that unites them and goes beyond any possible argument or conflict.

One of the employees had this to say regarding the organization:

> I guess it's more of like a sense of family. I like that feeling. There's familiar, but then you're learning new things from the other people who are here. I like all the events that we offer to the community members and our youth, and our teenagers. I like that we do that. Not a lot of work innovations do stuff like that, and I think that we're unique in that we do that and keep up with it and something that we do every year. (S27)

Another employee shared a similar sentiment:

> There is a lot of diversified Natives that we have, but we all look at them because of who we are and where we come from, and we want to make sure that we can help them to do whatever they want, but we'll do a White, Yellow, Black, Red, indifferent. It doesn't matter; they all need help, and I think it's from all of us being Native and being so closely connected to our family and our family ties that we are able to do this successfully and continue doing it without burning out. (S18)

In addition, another employee described how important the sense of belonging to a community that protects and cares about you is as both a professional and a person:

> I really appreciate the fact that we are all here together. And I think that's been one of the best parts about this. It is just like learning so much about the Native American culture and having that sense of like family and community. You can get up and go to work every day and just know that you have people around that care. And they care about what they do and what you do at work. (S21)

And another employee coined the term "urban reservation" for depicting the organization when stating:

> I think the [organization] sort of like is a pillar in the community, and I think you feel like you are family. I left the "res" to come here, and you sort of make up your own reservation with the people you work with, and they become your family, and it's Natives helping Natives, it's Natives helping other non-Natives, and it's non-Natives helping … you know what I mean? It's just that melting pot, and I think I am trying to process that while protecting it. (S14)

For one of the leaders, the organization is not just a community or family but a home because it represents the place where people can be who they really are and be celebrated and honored:

> Just being Native in a non-diverse place, being gay in a very conservative city … it's nice because you can be what you want here, and celebrated. This is a place of diversity to the max, and in [Northwest city], it's hard to find places like that. That's why I'm really thankful and so blessed to be able to call [the organization] my home and to be able to really be myself here and to be celebrated, and that feels really good. (L8)

However, just like with every family, there are arguments. Although the relationship between employees and departments is good, there are strong personalities within the organization that occasionally can lead to personal and/or departmental conflicts. From the data analysis of the observations and interviews, it emerged that some employees considered that the medical department did not understand medicine in a fully holistic way; others had the perception of existing preferences from the leadership of the organization for some services over others; and other members of the staff experienced a slight feeling of frustration when implementing the idea of sacred hospitality for the employees and not just for the patients.

For example, regarding the criticism of the medical department and their difficulties in understanding medicine in a more holistic way, one employee noted:

> We have different perspectives on how we're going to treat clients. And that affects the function of the program. I know behavioral health. About having fun, relaxing … and compared to the medical side, there's a difference in that mentality. There's different things that the team helps out with that no one else probably would help out with. And I think that part of it contributes to the whole foundation of what the [organization] is. Because it's not about treating, providing medical service. It's not just, you know, doing counseling sessions, but there's an underlying piece behind that, as you know, relaxing, having fun, talking. And participating in events and having that time to do those things. (S10)

When it comes to the rivalries between departments, one employee said, "We used to think behavioral health was kind of favored but I don't think so, but they were there the longest. They were at the beginning, and we were added on" (S1). And a leader stated that although hierarchies between departments did not exist, there could be differences in terms of some services making more money or being more strategic:

> My guess is that Medical makes the money for this place. I think if you ask [the CFO], she would say Medical floats the other things that we do because we get a lot of money. Thus, it's important that Medical function well to generate that money. (S25)

When it comes to implementing the concept of sacred hospitality, it seems that although it is gaining more clarity among the staff, it is not clear enough yet, and there is a certain degree of confusion around how to define the concept and the best procedure to implement it. As one employee explained:

> I think as a family, you don't always treat the ones that you're closest to the best. You treat your guests way better. I think that that's what needs to shift for all of us. I value you and treat each other almost like guests, but as closely and as nicely as we would … but I think we're getting better. I think for a little while, this term, "Sacred Hospitality," would almost make you cringe because it really wasn't all mindset yet. And I think we're getting better at that. (S10)

It appears that discussions and arguments are common in the organization, but what differentiates this organization from others is that these conflicts are not necessarily understood as negative or destructive, because the organization seems to view differences and conflicts as opportunities that, when channeled positively, can result in resilience and social change. One leader noted:

> Sometimes there's a lot of disagreements, and sometimes there's some side remarks or whatever kind of thing. But one of the things I learned from [the CEO] was that she said this building wasn't built in quiet rooms. There was shouting. There was yelling. There was passion behind people's samplings. And because of some of that passion work we had, we're now sitting in the building that was once a conversation. And when you want to really impact change, affect change, and really help people, it's not a quiet process. (L8)

One founder summarized this mentality, arguing: "It's a little brutal at times, but it is what it is. We come from a matriarchal society, and decisions are made, and discussions are had, and sometimes very loudly" (L33). Similarly, as with the example of how non-Native employees felt very uncomfortable with the circle of management and having face-to-face confrontations, it seems that issues regarding differences, arguments, and conflicts have a negative connotation in the Western worldview and are systematically avoided, erased, or hidden behind politically correct behavior, whereas Native cultures feel more comfortable with differences, arguments, and conflicts as part of a diverse and fluid reality and believe that they can be used as catalysts for social change.

Encouragement for Creativity and Fluidity of Organizational Structures

Regardless of the differences between Native and non-Native people and other cultural differences in terms of nationality, class, gender, or position, another characteristic differentiates certain groups within the organization. On one side, there are those employees who appear to feel more comfortable with having the freedom to be creative and enjoy being encouraged to think outside the box, and on the other side, there are staff members who prefer more direction and planning to develop their tasks. It also appears that some employees are better at navigating fluid structures that are constantly changing and evolving while others feel more comfortable with static and rigid structures that offer them more stability to develop their work.

Overall, both groups work well together and maintain a positive and professional relationship, but it seems that the group advocating for creativity and fluid structures is the one with more power and influence to impose their vision upon the organization. For example, one of the leaders was arguing about the need to find providers with creativity and imagination focused on developing quality relationships instead of just high productivity and efficiency:

> Finding a provider who wants to think outside the box and who presents ideas and creative challenges that are exciting would be wonderful to have it here. I think creativity is what's exciting about helping to find a practitioner. I feel that here at

[the organization], it's not about how many patients do I have to see in a day or how long their appointment is. It's about who do I get to work with, how do I get to work with them, and what ways do we get to help impact the community in creative ways. (L2)

Thus, the freedom that exists within the organization to develop that creativity can represent a struggle for some employees and an opportunity for others:

If you think we're doing something wrong, let's improve it. And for me, there's always the freedom of trying to improve it. It freaks people out when you have that much freedom and creativity. Some of them just don't do well because they want the structure, and you're like, "Oh well, go ahead and do it," and it just boggles their mind. "What do you mean, go ahead and do it?" And for me, I'm like, "Okay …" Some people that I directly supervise need to be coached a lot, and then some people just do it because they love it, they love the creativity. (L2)

And the same leader, when referring to the fluid structures at the organization, said:

Here there's a structure, but it's not as strict as corporations would like it. We take on the title like a corporation, but I feel like it's fluid, like horizontal. And then there's some staff that don't get that, so then you have this cultural block, like, "Well, you guys aren't following the chart" or "You're not following the structure I'm used to." Then, they have issues and anxiety and worries, and you're like, "Okay … well, that's a Western model. Can we have this conversation again?" Honestly, I feel like I have the Western concept model or White privilege model or the White male privileged discussion one to five times a week. (L2)

Besides a Native worldview that is not as embedded in an industrial mindset as the Western culture when it comes to understanding organizations, there are other factors that appear to explain the fluidity of the structures of the organization. One of them seems to be related to the evolving context in terms of community needs; a second would be the political environment and the changes of political parties governing at different levels; and a third seems to be related to the rapid growth of the organization in the last years. Thus, to cope with and adjust to all the changes and uncertainties derived from the community, the politics, and the growth, the organization has created fluid and flexible structures that will contribute more efficiently to a better adjustment and survival of the organization. In terms of the evolution of the community needs, one leader stated:

The needs of the community have changed. Diabetes has gone down, but hypertension has increased. Anxiety and stress have increased, but smoking has gone down. So just things like that. And how [the organization] evolved with that is listening, being an agency that really listens to the community. What do you really need from us, and let the community say, and take that with truth, and then go back and rearrange the public to make it work. (L2)

Regarding the political environment, another leader pointed out the necessity for flexible structures to adjust to rapid political changes that have a big impact on the organization:

> We always have to look at our lawmakers, our legislative, and our policymakers. I feel like we're always having to keep our eye on that externally. Every time a new president comes in, every time a new house representative, senator, congressperson, commissioner, city councilperson. I feel like that is one of the things we are always keeping our eye on as an administrator. I don't know about the other employees in the building, but you're always keeping your eye on that to make sure the policy changes. What's Plan A, B, and C for the viability and sustainability of building as a whole? (L8)

Moreover, the organization's growth has influenced developing fluid structures, particularly in terms of keeping an efficient degree of coordination between the different services offered.

> We've grown rapidly. I've worked here for a while, but we went from four exam rooms to this huge clinic. We all are under one roof now. So, having even just combining Medical with Behavioral health in the same building has been a challenge. Trying to figure out how to navigate the patients to the right channel. Getting the right paperwork done. Making sure they get the services they need. It's really been like getting to know the other programs and how they operate when you're all under one roof. (S24)

When asked how the organizational structures of the organization could be described, one leader summarized the capacity to be fluid and adjust: "Just go with the flow. Figure things out. We try and do everything we can within our power, if that makes sense. Just trying to give the best you can with what you have" (L11).

Besides coping and adjusting to the evolution of the needs of the community, the change of the political environment, and the rapid growth that the organization experienced since the health clinic was created in 1999, fluid and flexible structures contribute to good coordination among departments, which is a cornerstone for providing holistic medicine. As one of the employees described:

> We do have medical. We do have dental. We do have prevention, and insurance, and all that. A patient can really come here and get all of their needs met. And if I don't know something, I can run and find it somewhere, you know. (S13)

Within the organization's main building, you can have medical, dental, behavioral health, pharmacy, and children and youth services. Having these services under the same roof is very useful for patients who, for the majority, belong to the most impoverished social sectors of society and, for example, may not have a car, may have problems with personal mobility, or may live far away from the city. Additionally, it seems that the fluidity of structures has another positive effect on involving all the different services and departments to work together and garner feedback from each other.

> I think respect and professionalism exist through every department, but particularly having them together there is almost like a synergy, and what may normally be a

barrier between your medical clinic and a pharmacist, which usually may just be physical, doesn't exist here. We can go over and discuss and decide what the best care is. Bring more than just one mind and get to know how that person does take care of their patients and provide outside perspectives. I think that exists between Medical and Pharmacy, Dental and Pharmacy, Dental and Medical, Dental and Behavioral health. ... I think just that lack of almost logistics, physical barriers, makes one person's care go that much further. (S4)

However, although there is good coordination and feedback between departments as a result of fluid structures, some issues of communication have emerged as a consequence of the organization reaching a certain size. As one of the leaders described:

Because of the size, we don't see everybody all the time. We do have our weekly meetings so we can stay in touch with communications. We have our weekly, what's it called, directors meetings. And we have medical meetings, and then all of the teams have their own special little meetings for each other. We all try and communicate. We still fail in the ... we could always do better when we communicate. I feel like we're always working on ways to get better at it. We haven't found the perfect model yet. (S3)

And these issues regarding communication seem to take on a new dimension when it comes to the relationship between "boomers" and "millennials" who have different ways of using technology and social media. As one young leader who strongly advocates for the use of technology noted:

We have a workforce with different generations, and different styles, and the incorporation of technology into the practice. Some people like to embrace that, and some people don't. Some people like it more traditional, whereas some were really looking for different, creative ways that they've never seen before. You have these different languages coming together, and it's hard to find a happy medium. Now it's about technology and access for everyone. How do you create a document that 20 or 30 people can see at once rather than making something that only a select few can see when you tell people you have a voice at the table? You have to be able to back that up, and some technology can help you do that. Incorporating technology, and not being afraid of it, and not thinking of it as a setback, but more as a helpful tool [is important]. (L8)

Certainly, technology and social media can improve communication within the organization and contribute to developing more horizontal decision-making processes. Technology can also have a big impact in shaping or changing the culture of an organization, and it seems that, so far, the founders who are still working at the organization—despite being aware of this conflict with millennials and having made the decision to increase the use of social media to improve the external relations and visibility of the organization—are not willing to implement the use of excessive technology at an internal level, because they feel more comfortable with "classic" procedures that have been implemented successfully.

Commitment with Social Justice and Cultural Resistance

As a consequence of interacting between different cultures in the spaces that the organization provides, facing issues of injustice and cultural struggles daily, and the continuous encouragement of the leadership to share information and knowledge regarding those struggles for cognitive and social justice, awareness and critical consciousness raise among the employees. From gathering and analyzing artifacts, I discovered one central strategy implemented by the leadership at the organization to raise awareness and empower urban Native people begins with showing a very clean and well-conserved space full of beautiful Native artwork where highly qualified Native American professionals work.

> I think it's empowering as an employee or a patient to walk through those doors and to see a lot of different Natives specializing in a lot of different areas of medicine, social services, administration. I know when I started with them, I was just like blown away. I am like, "Wow these tribal members from different tribes all coming here for the greater good of [the organization] of [Northwest city's] community and our people!" And I am also a patient there, so sitting there as a patient and the way it's designed like with the artwork and with the Sacred Hospitality, you feel you come to a place where you are going to be understood. (S14)

This strategy of showing a very clean and well-conserved building with plenty of beautiful artwork makes visible the invisible. It empowers the Native community, providing them with a framework that challenges and rewrites the hegemonic narrative that situates Native people at subordinated positions because of their supposed lack of intellectual ability and capacity to perform. One of the founders described how important it is to empower employees and patients in general and the urban youth Native in particular, making visible a safe space that offers high-quality services from their cultural perspective:

> I think that's the thing that I want: staff, especially young staff, to get that it's kind of like a sanctuary place. And it's also a really good place to work that if you took any other dominant society business like ours and put us next to it, we would still score better. I mean, not only do they work in a brown place, they work in a really good brown place. (L22)

The organization contributes to the balancing of asymmetries of power in society between cultures and social groups by debunking myths that are part of the cultural violence against Native people that depict them as "primitive," lacking intelligence and education, or "objects" that belong to museums. Thus, observing Native people who act as role models struggling for social justice and challenging those myths contributes to raising personal awareness and interest in social activism. One of the young leaders described observing relatives getting involved and sacrificing to create the organization:

> [Members of my family] and a group of 13, 14 other people helped build this place, so as a child, I got to see it from the outside in. I saw a lot of the sacrifice and time that the board and staff made to this place. They put their own lines of credit on the

line. They put extra hours in. … But growing up seeing that, I was able to volunteer as a high school student. Me and a couple of my friends from a youth leadership program got to volunteer and be youth leaders in their Indian youth programs, so we volunteered a lot of our time in high school doing that. (L2)

Making visible Native people's struggles and successful experiences providing health services to the community regardless of whether they are Native or non-Native situates the organization at a better position in the social hierarchy. They can have a dialogue with other cultures with more horizontal conditions than if they would try to do it from the subordinated position that the system bestows them. One of the founders described American society as still colonized and named the need for a decolonized space as one of the main motivators for creating the organization:

I do see some people of color when they start working with systems they acquiesce, they change to be colonized, and then they become the colonizer. So, I always tell myself, "When I die I want to be the freest person in the room. I want to be decolonized." And it's really hard because I'm not. I'm not, you know? Especially at this age, we've been … like especially in our public school systems we've been really told a bunch of lies, and so you're deeply entrenched into really making good conscious decisions. We're not going to do that anymore. And when you don't do those anymore, it does make the dominant society uncomfortable. (L22)

In addition, within the organization, there is valuing of other epistemologies that go beyond the hegemonic epistemology that mainly focuses on positivism and science as being the only valid knowledge, which the system legitimates through the monopoly of bestowing academic degrees:

If I just worked in a regular hospital or clinic, I would have to worship the "God of intellect." Worship the "God of degrees." And to say, there's people here that can bring other things to the healing work we do, especially the therapy work we do. The most popular therapist we have does not have a degree, and the kids follow that person everywhere. He uses his power for good, and I'm like, "Should I have to eliminate him from our circle? No, no … we need that healing!" (L22)

Another strategy to raise awareness and critical consciousness for action is to offer a space where one can participate in "the struggle." It is within the struggle, and through living it daily, that employees become more empowered and critically conscious, and their commitment to social justice increases. It is individual empowerment to act through a collective action framework, combining the individuality of every person (and not neoliberal individualism) with the collective.

If you learn about the Native Americans, they have gone through a lot of stuff. But over the years, they have bounced back, even though we can still see the aftereffects in terms of comorbidities and things like that. Looking back at the Native American community in a greater panorama, I feel empowered. Also, tapped into the experiences and just that human spirit of keep moving, keep living regardless of adversity. I feel empowered by that because the things we deal with, you know, clinic, are very difficult. (S3)

Regarding "living" the struggle, the same employee noted:

Being able to identify vulnerable people, thinking about those social determinants of health, poverty, lack of housing, lack of transportation, cultural background, and things like that. I think when you're living it, in theory, is different than when you come to a particular community. And that has really changed the paradigm shift for me in terms of the lenses I see the world in. I have to kind of take their lenses and see from their aspect, not just how I'm seeing the world. (S3)

And another supporter affirmed:

I think broadening the perspective of other challenges of other people and growing up, coming as someone who's White from essentially a privileged background, not having to worry about basic challenges like food scarcity or domestic violence or drug abuse, I think being confronted with those issues here has just developed my consciousness for others in being more giving and being even more so willing to help out others with either volunteering or donating time or money. Whatever you can do to help because you just feel by broadening your perspective you're doing pretty well, and you should help other people get there too. (S4)

This awareness is raised among the different employees of the organization regardless of their ethnicity or nationality. As a non-Native employee said:

I have just gained a lot of insight just into Native American culture, seeing a lot of issues firsthand that are also present in every other society, but maybe more here in this population. I think it definitely shines a light on my life that you should be thankful and giving back, and I think this is a really good place to give back and help others. I think more than anything, it's kind of changing my own, broadening perspective and just kind of respect for other people's situation and empathy and contentment. (S4)

The health clinic is not just a Native organization but a women-led organization with a very matriarchal approach that has a strong influence on the organization's design and on providing holistic medicine. A non-Native leader explained how his awareness was raised not only about Native culture but also in terms of gender issues and biases:

I think I'm more culturally aware. There are things that I say and do that I'm more cognizant of now that I've been historically. I'd say that's probably the biggest thing, and some of that culture is just, again, working with women. Some of the Native Americans, some of it is in the context of this entity which is not the traditional medical clinic that I'm used to working in. (S25)

According to the leadership of the organization, when new employees are hired, they need to commit to at least one of the four big events the organization organizes every year for the community: the Healthy Pow Wow, leadership camp, the summer program graduation ceremony, or the Pow Wow Fun Run. As one employee argued:

> I've been at the Pow Wow before. And then we did like a school event, as well. And I think there's a lot of community involvement. It's almost expected that we all at some time get involved in the community. The community is our patients, yeah. (S3)

Through this involvement with the community outside the office, employees of the organization get more awareness about personal and collective struggles for social justice and raise their critical consciousness. As one employee stated:

> I think getting involved is key to raise critical consciousness. I've never been to a pow-wow before, so getting involved was really cool. Events like that. And just to see our patients outside of the healthcare setting is kind of interesting to see the dynamic there, you know? Kind of get to know them on a little more personal level. So that's nice. I think that's probably helped to raise it. (S6)

Besides having conversations about these social struggles with other employees and patients and experiencing "in your face" all these issues of social justice daily, the leadership encourages their staff to get involved with the community as employees of the organization but also as individuals in their free time. This is a very holistic concept of the person as not just a professional worker but also as a citizen and human being connected with a community as opposed to seeing the work at the organization as separated or compartmentalized from the community and the world. Thus, employees are expected to be involved with outside events organized by them and other events that, although they are not part of the organization, can bring back value for the community and contribute to the common good.

> Being an employee here brings awareness to some of the issues going on in the community, and where a lot of our staffs are involved in like the school boards, the parent committees, that type of thing. Just making them more aware of issues. And I think not necessarily me personally, but we have staff who serve on parent committees, and they're not even parents. But they know the issues that Native American children are facing in the community, and so they want to make sure that those are heard. I think that we do have a lot of staff more aware of issues, whether they have children or not, that it's affecting the community. (S24)

For the patients and the community, this strategy of bringing the providers and the staff outside the office to visit and socialize with them is very encouraging and empowering because they feel respected and valued. As noted before, most of the organization's patients belong to the most impoverished social groups—the invisible, the forgotten, the dehumanized—so being visited by their providers has a big impact on their self-esteem and individual empowerment process.

> I think the Pow Wows when we go to those and when we go to the diabetic screenings and the blood pressure. I think the community is surprised to see providers

out there, the doctors and the nurse practitioners, and the medical assistants out there working and needing them and learning about them and their lives and what's going on. I don't see that happening at other places. I just don't see it being that encouraged. (S1)

In terms of empowering patients, the key element of the organization is to make them realize that they need to take control of their health and their reality. They are not treated like passive agents and objects but as subjects and masters of their destinies despite the structural inequalities and injustices they face daily.

> I know a lot of our clients have some serious barriers that prevent them from moving forward. And I think because we have the diversity that we have, we can accept that these are real and true. We don't pretend like they don't exist. We don't try to say that's not fair, and people shouldn't do that to you and go and be strong. We don't do that. We go, "Hey, what can you do with this barrier? How can you deal with this? How can you live with this?" (S30)

Employees deconstruct a former framework of world-making that depicts the social groups their patients belong to as passive, useless, or objects by providing a new framework where they are active, powerful, and take charge of their own lives. Gradually, employees and patients become more empowered, increase their critical consciousness, and collectively decide to act for social change.

It may seem obvious that all employees working at the organization, particularly Native members, were already aware and critically conscious to a certain degree before joining the organization. However, there are different levels of critical consciousness and praxis, and although Native staff can be more aware than non-Native staff as a consequence of experiencing issues of social injustice and cultural resistance in their daily routines, joining the health clinic and living the decolonial struggle that the organization is developing further raises their awareness and critical consciousness to higher levels of social activism and change. For example, one Native employee stated that she not only raised her awareness working at the organization but also learned how to act and to contribute to social change, something she did not know before:

> I think [the organization] helps people in becoming more active. Like for example, the diabetes program that is going to end right now. They have cards where patients can fill them out and send to their legislators. I didn't know, when I started working here, I was [young age]. I had no idea how to contact my legislator and how to voice my concerns or whatever. So, I think not even so much being more conscious, but knowing how to make a change. (S24)

Going from a hegemonic framework and social order that create myths of inferiority that eventually may instill Native people with lack of confidence, a sense of helplessness, or a desire to become like the oppressor, the organization provides an emancipatory framework aimed to offer hope and empowerment through a path of collective action that can be shared and transmitted. It is a framework of critical intercultural leadership that works as a sort of charter of action, a guide to behavior for collective action that gives sense and meaning to many urban Native people in the city. One of the young leaders said:

> I got to come in here as a [young age] student, and I was treated with the same respect as an 80 years old elder. I was asked to sit at the same table, not a different one. That helped me find my own voice, and I learned a lot. And then, being an advocate from my community, using that same voice to speak up for others, and help give other opportunities to other people to be able to pass that down. I think [the organization] has really helped me with that. (L8)

This is a process of ethnogenesis where cultural identities and structures imposed through cultural violence are deconstructed while others are reconstructed that seek emancipation. As with every cultural process, this process of ethnogenesis that starts with individual empowerment is not individualistic as understood from a neoliberal perspective of empowering individuals to compete among themselves. Conversely, this cultural process of individual empowerment is designed through a collective action framework that raises critical consciousness as an action system for social justice and the cultural resistance of the community.

Particularities of the Leadership Process

In this process of individual empowerment through collective action, critical consciousness, praxis, and ethnogenesis, the leadership of the organization plays a central role in providing spaces for interaction, sharing information and knowledge, encouraging employees to be involved and to connect with patients within and outside the building, and creating frameworks of action that transmit values of cognitive and social justice. One cannot fail to notice that besides being a Native American health clinic, the main characteristic of the leadership of the organization is that it is a matriarchal organization led almost exclusively by women.

> This organization is pretty matriarchal. Strong woman who knows what she wants. And she is correct 99% of the time and always right. She believes in circles, and she does empower a lot of people. That was a hard one for me. Well, and they gave us a little more freedom, but she didn't at first. It's gotten a lot better over the years. It's been a growing experience for everybody, I think. (S1)

According to one of the young leaders:

> We have a very strong leadership model of women and from a lot of childhood friends and family. In the other places, it's predominantly men, and here we have all women. And being that [Northwest city], again, is conservative, they had to fight a lot to be able to be allowed to enter the room, to be allowed to have a voice. And they do that time and time again, even in 2017. And it just shows their passion for the work because they could've easily given up and say, "You know what? They're not going to invite me to the table, so I'm not going to go anymore." They still show up every single day. You have to admire them because they have something

to say, and they represent a patient population that needs help and needs to be recognized and served. … It's different, and I think it should be celebrated and recognized. (L8)

This strong leadership seems to be very focused on one person, the founder and CEO:

I think she's [the founder and CEO] very relationally based. If she gets along with you, life is good. If she doesn't get along with you, life is not good. Some of the people that have worked here haven't gotten along with her, and they disappear. So, I think that's important to figure out how to get along with her, what she likes, what she doesn't like. It's very interesting to me how she dominates this world … but she dominates this world. (S25)

Also, as a result of the rapid growth of the organization since its foundation, this leadership has been evolving in its structure, going from more horizontal and based on circles to more hierarchical and Western in style. As one of the founders put it:

When we first started, we tried to do a circle management where every voice was heard, but when you get to a certain size, you just have to become institutionalized, and you have to by law, and rule, and funding source. Every funding source has its own set of rules that they dictate upon you. You kind of have to start looking more and more like the dominant White culture. So, there's hierarchies now that didn't used to exist. (L33)

Although this approach of strong leadership personalized in one person appears to be well accepted by the staff, some employees expressed criticism:

I believe that a successful organization should be run with the horizontal type of leadership where employees are engaged in the decision-making. I think people in organizations have more success that way. The top-down or the vertical hierarchy organization model used to be commonplace used to be what used to run an organization. And still, we have an organization that is run that way, even though most organizations now are changing to be more horizontal. But in this organization, I would say there is a little bit of both. Some things I would feel are more engaged, some things are not. (S3)

In the future, this leadership model could bring about more difficulties in terms of succession processes that may spark potential struggles if not well managed. From the interviews conducted at the organization, different conversations emerged about the future of the leadership. One employee noted:

I look at this organization and say it's really built on one person's vision and one person having the strength to be able to make things happen and surrounding herself with other people that makes it happen and controlling that entirely and there's pros and cons to that. When you start something new, kind of like the grass roots level, that's the way you get things done, and at some point, you need to evolve into something different. And I think we're near that point of evolution potentially. (S25)

It seems complicated for the leadership who started this project to step out and let go. Notwithstanding, from observing and interviewing, I observed that this conversation occurs, at least in an informal manner, among leaders and supporters within the organization. According to one of the founders:

> Before, I worked 10, 12 hours a day and just all the time, all the time, all the time, probably at the expense of my family, at the expense of my health, and my sanity. But people always say that when they have a passion that they want to do. ... Now I've just learned that I don't have to do everything. I can trust other people that I've trained them well enough. I've indoctrinated them. I always think having indoctrinated a small army of Native kids. Lots who work here now. That's how I've changed. I've just like gone with the flow a little bit, but still feeling good about. (L22)

One of the young leaders involved in this future process of succession had an opinion regarding this particular issue but also regarding the growth of the organization:

> I think one of the challenges is that as we've grown, we might not be able to see and have more hands-on as we used to. We have to add more staff, and give some of that staff some of our original duties or possibilities, and charge them with handling things that we've always done. And having a little bit of anxiety about, "Well, I used to do that and now they're doing it." And being less control freaks, basically. And realizing that there's a new way of talent from here that we have to instill our mission of values and hope that they are making good decisions in faith for [the organization] and for the community. I think that's challenging here because we have staff who've been founders of this agency. Who has had to let some of those responsibilities go to other folks, and they have to step back a little bit and let other people who will be tasked with those job duties. (L8)

And the same leader was comparing the process of succession and letting go with that of parents who see their kids growing up and going to school:

> It's like you're going to have to send your kids off to school. Cannot be with them all the time now. You've got to let them be in the school. You're not going to watch them all day. You got to go and do your own thing, and then come back later and say, "Well, how was it? Did you do okay?" And having that responsibility. This was hard through the growth process, and it's going to happen even more if we have an organization full of patients. We cannot be at ever building so we have to charge somebody with that oversight and be comfortable enough to not be there and say, "Everything's okay so far" and that kind of thing. (L8)

As one of the employees summarized, "It's hard to let go and let somebody else take the steps and make mistakes, and let them make the mistakes. I mean it's not the end of the world if they do. I think that's a challenge" (S1).

Tacit and Explicit Understandings and Meanings

Among the main tacit and explicit understandings and meanings for employees within the organization is navigating between cultures. However, while for Native people the navigation seems more tacit and comes in a more natural way as part of their cultural assumptions, for non-Native employees, it appears to be more explicit and less embedded within their core values and beliefs. For example, one Native employee explained:

> I feel pretty comfortable with myself between the two cultures, and I try to be very conscious about other people's cultures. Even between people's cultures between medicines, like a naturopath versus Western medicine, versus Eastern medicine … I think I do it naturally. (S1)

Regarding the fluidity of identities and navigating between cultures in a smooth way, one of the founders said:

> The only time I'm a minority is when I drive home, when I drive to work on the street, and when I drive home. … Because in my community, I'm not a minority. In my home, I'm not a minority. In my tribe and family, I'm not a minority. So yeah, you just take that hat on, take it off, take it on, take it off. (L22)

And another founder described the process of not just navigating between Native and White/Western culture but between professional cultures too:

> I have a degree in [Western field], so I know what the rules are for the dominant White culture. But I'm still Indian, so I know what's expected of me in the [Western] culture. But I also know who I am. So, you do what you do. (L33)

As a result of navigating between the Native and the hegemonic White culture since they are born, Native people have developed a capacity to transition from different cultural perspectives in a fluid manner, and it appears they take it for granted. Besides, since the founders and most of the leadership of the organization are Indian women working in a White and male environment, in addition to ethnic and cultural discrimination, they often experience gender biases. As one woman leader noted: "In this environment, I could say something, and so a guy could say it a minute later. Then, somebody will hear what he says versus what I said, and I'm like, 'Wait a minute. I just said that.' Things like that" (L11).

On the other hand, non-Native staff—specifically, White employees—seem to require more effort to transition between cultures as a result of living within a system and society that have been designed for them. In addition, within the organization, non-Native employees represent a minority, particularly non-Native males.

> This is a women-dominated culture at this building, and I'm a guy. And then there's the Native American culture … I don't really think much about the other cultures, so I'm very well aware they're here. … The Native American culture is the dominant culture at this facility. (S25)

As noted before, although navigating between cultures requires more effort for non-Native people than for Native people, the daily experience of "living" between cultures contributes to improving their skills and raising their consciousness:

> I feel that navigating through different cultures has become easier over time. It used to be difficult, especially if you don't know people's way of living, what they believe in, cultural sensitivity about different subjects. … It was difficult. But I'm still learning, still trying to navigate through. (S3)

It seems that the process is not only about knowing and doing but also about being. It is a cultural consciousness and intelligence that contribute to easily navigating between different cultures and is developed through knowledge and immersion until it becomes a cultural value, belief, or even assumption. Thus, the ability to transition from one cultural perspective to another in a very fluid and natural manner is something that all employees eventually take for granted.

Curiosity, Openness, and a Lack of Fear

Another tacit understanding and meaning that all employees share is a curiosity for learning from other cultures and an openness and acceptance to be transformed by knowledge, experiences, theories, and practices, without fear of the "other" or the unknown. These characteristics of curiosity, openness, and a lack of fear appear to be essential to developing cultural sensitivity and learning to navigate between cultures in a fluid and natural way. Different way of knowing and doing are not enough. Different ways of being are required because the transformation of oneself is needed to establish authentic intercultural relations with even conditions. As one employee put it: "We're all humans, we all have our different ways of thinking, and you have to be accepting and curious about how other people, and why … how and why they do the things they do" (S1). For one of the founders of the organization, it is not just about cultures and an essentialism that attributes static characteristics to a social group but also about personal characteristics like openness and acceptance regardless of your cultural or ethnic background that make the employees so genuine:

> Even though there are different tribes and different countries, different ethnicities, [the organization's] employees are kind, they're generous, they're hopeful, they laugh. And so underneath, it's more like a characteristic rather than culture because we've had some honorary Indians here. We've had some honorary White people here. They didn't have those values and like they had to go work somewhere else. (L22)

Additionally, not being afraid is central to being able to encounter, interact with, and learn from other cultures instead of shutting down and avoiding communication:

> I think it is key one being open to other people and cultural experiences, not being necessarily afraid of others. Maybe that's just having a positive demeanor that people have overall good intentions and good values, letting that be open and not afraid to receiving other cultures. And even if they've not done right in front of you, giving them the benefit of the doubt. (S4)

These characteristics of curiosity, openness, and a lack of fear are embedded in employees' core values and beliefs and impact the treatment and serving of patients. It appears to be a cultural and professional humility that pushes the employees to learn and share. As one employee described:

> I think there's a willingness to learn. There's an open-mindedness. I mean there's respect. There's curiosity. There's acceptance. There's so many things that I would hope as medical providers or behavioral health counselors that we have these qualities, because how the hell are we going to serve our patients in an effective way if we don't carry these qualities ourselves? I think that is so important. There is such value to life and to culture. There's so much to experience and learn and to share. (S24)

It seems that within the organization there is a willingness to learn and share and an awareness of the differences, which are valued and understood as strengths. At the health clinic everyone is proud of their culture, and they just want to share it, learn from other cultures, and use all this knowledge to serve the patients better:

> I've learned things that if they say, "Well, I do this," and I'm like, "I have no idea what that means," and ask them. And then go ask around. "Does anyone know about this?" or "Has anyone ever participated in this?" So, it's more valued for our patients, too. It's not just a question we ask. We're able to incorporate that in how we treat them and how we connect with them. (S32)

Curiosity, openness, and a lack of fear of other cultures seem to be the core values and beliefs of the employees. It is a cultural humility that accepts the limitations of each culture and takes for granted the strengths that different ways of knowing, doing, and being can bring to the organization and the community in order to improve and grow. Besides, members of the organization understand different cultural encounters as opportunities to share and learn from each other and be more efficient in providing services, instead of seeing the cultural differences as barriers that complicate their work.

Intercultural Society and a Common Identity/Purpose

Since cultural differences are valued and shared within the organization and there is a continuous cultural dialogue with more or less even conditions where—although the Native culture is the majority—there is not a culture considered superior to others, the organization can be considered a critical intercultural organization or a critical micro-intercultural society. Interculturality and, more specifically, critical interculturality, is understood as a society or organization where cultural differences are valued and the relationship among cultures is developed without large asymmetries of power. Therefore, it is not about a multicultural society where cultural differences are tolerated but not appreciated and nonhegemonic cultures are situated at positions of subordination regarding a dominant culture or cultures. As one employee said, "It's not about tolerance. It needs to be like more about value. Tolerance isn't acceptable, that's all it is. It's not an understanding" (S1). Another employee added, "I think that more than anything [the organization] shows that just by one example these other cultures that you don't necessarily know have a lot to offer and you want to respect them and learn more about them" (S4).

One of the young leaders went deeper and explained that everyone has to be proud of their own culture and learn from other perspectives and worldviews without culturally appropriating them:

> I'm not trying to be a Vietnamese person. I'm not trying to be Kenyan. I do want to know about it and love it about you and try to understand it about you, so our patients are the community. We like to share that, and you're going to get more American Indian and Alaskan Native exposure to intercultural exchange in here. But yeah, there's still a lot that, you know, what do you call it ... supports it, supports that activity. And I like it when it happens because then I'm learning something new. But I'm not stealing your culture and trying to live it or coopt it either. (L2)

And this intercultural mentality is extended when it comes to treating the patients too:

> I think that no matter who walks in here, they're not looked at any differently than the next person that walks in here. It is more like as an individual person and like the needs that they need to better their health. I don't think that any person walks in here and says, "Well, they're Native American, so they're getting special treatment" versus, like, "I'm White and I'm not getting that same treatment." I think everybody that comes in here has a sense of community and a sense of belonging. That's a really important piece about, um ... community and multicultural, bringing people together in the community. (S21)

Regarding the establishment of relations with external institutions in the city, the health clinic contributes to making visible what was invisible, and because of the important role they play within the community, the organization can enter a dialogue with local actors with fewer asymmetries of power than the ones existing in society between Native people and the hegemonic culture in general. As one non-Native employee stated:

> There's a face, and [the organization] plays the role of having that face and saying, "Hello, we're here. There's Native Americans in your community and there are Native Americans in your medical community." And when you can put on a reasonable face to better health together with other institutions is very important. We're working with some of your clients and the hospitals that say, "Hey, we're trying to play together well." I think because this entity exists, it allows conversations that would not otherwise happen. It would be an individual who is Native American as opposed to an appreciation to a culture that exists within our city. (S25)

Having a dialogue with the institutions of the hegemonic culture with more horizontal conditions contributes to creating an intercultural society in the city because different perspectives are acknowledged and considered. For example, traditionally, when any Native person or group entered a conversation with the city's police department or the city council, it was exercised as a monologue where the hegemonic institutions talked and the subordinated cultures listened. Today, although still far away from an ideal and fair relationship in terms of asymmetries of power and with many barriers still to overcome, when the organization initiates a dialogue with the police department or the city council, what used to be a monologue has become a dialogue, with both sides talking and listening.

If the organization can be considered an intercultural society with internal and external relations, what would be the common identity of this society that differentiates them from others? What would be the values, beliefs, and assumptions of the critical intercultural society of the organization? Basically, besides the characteristics of curiosity, openness, and lack of fear noted earlier, it seems that two other characteristics are shared by the employees of the organization and are considered part of their common identity: (a) the will to create meaning transcending themselves, represented by the desire to help people and their capacity of experiencing empathy and (b) a high level of resilience to adjust to challenges, uncertainties, and changes, developed through flexibility and a sense of humor. Regarding helping people and empathy, one employee stated:

> We all share the identity of the client or the patient. They're always our main concern. Without them, we have no jobs. They are our number one priority, and I think we all share that. We all share the identity, the Sacred Hospitality that we talk about, of enabling the client. I think that would be something that we all share, and it centers around the client. (S1)

Following the same argument, another employee talked about the mission but emphasized how the desire to take care of and help people was the main goal:

> I think we all just really, as the common core, we all just care about other people. There's just no other way to put it. You can say it's the Mission. It could be the Mission, which deals with people, but I feel like we just want to help people. That's what we want to do. (L11)

In terms of empathy, one supporter agreed:

> Over here, it's very empathetic. That's almost a necessity just because of the huge amount of people with needs and diversity and different backgrounds. I think empathy is one of our common identities because sometimes it can be a very challenging patient population. (S6)

When it comes to developing resilience, understood as the capacity to adjust and overcome adversity, it appears that flexibility and humor are central mechanisms for releasing stress, coping with all suffering and injustices that the employees of the health clinic deal with daily, and adjusting to uncertainties and changes in an efficient manner. According to a young leader describing the organization:

> Here I think it is a sense of humor. I've noticed here that there's a lot of joking, and a lot of laughter, and a lot of having fun because you're dealing with teens and people who are dealing with some serious issues: broken families, domestic violence, health care diagnosis, just a variety of different things that really can hurt. And then, as a practitioner, you're working in different capacities with these patients and these

families, and you have to find an outlet to let that go and find some sort of release. And we all, collectively as a team, find ways just to laugh and have fun because if you did that every day and didn't laugh, your heart would be really heavy all time. You have to release that. We try to have fun here. We try to be as relaxed as possible, and then try to sit down and get to know each other, and share a good laugh, and make a happy workplace. (L8)

As a founder stated, the use of humor in the organization is one way of maintaining optimism and motivation:

One thing that I think [the organization] employees share as their identity is that they're funny, everybody laughs. They have a weird sense of humor, like a hopeful view. I mean, if you didn't have a hopeful view, nothing would be funny to you, right? I think everybody shows up like, "Yeah, this is going to go good today and we're just going to laugh about it!" I think those are the key things that I see collectively with people. (L22)

Transcending oneself while helping people and being empathetic toward causes of social justice, and developing resilience through flexibility and humor seem to be the common characteristics among employees of the organization and are part of the core values and beliefs of the organization. While valuing caring and helping people is essential to providing health services, feeling empathy and developing humor is central when it comes to the struggle for social justice and cultural resistance in order to be resilient and sustainable in a long-term struggle.

Safe Space and Sanctuary for Social Justice and Cultural Resistance

The organization, seen as an intercultural society where its members share a common identity, values, beliefs, and cultural assumptions, also represents a safe space and a project of struggle for social justice and cultural resistance. For any project to be trustworthy—especially this project, considering that the organization is a health clinic—the first step is to show congruency and professionalism with the organization's values to sensitize the community. Thus, the leadership tries to educate their employees to be role models for the patients and the community.

There's an element of service in our structure that you have to be seen in the community. So, if you're drinking, if you're doing drugs, if you're falling down, getting your name in the paper for domestic violence, then you probably shouldn't work here. I know people do it. I can't really mandate it. But we have a conversation about it, you know. ... But I'm talking to the staff, and so we're calling staff out to do your own work. (L22)

As noted before, besides the employee's image, the appearance of the building is also very important to transmitting these ideas of congruency and professionalism:

We want to have a very nice facility that people come in and not only do they feel welcome, but that it is clean and we don't have crappy furniture and where you know everyone is well dressed. Our staff over there have matching outfits, which you know is an investment. Because it's a lot of money. We just ordered shirts for all of us that have [the organization] thing on them. And the artwork, which I know a lot of people wouldn't know, but a lot of this artwork that is around this building it's expensive. Like if you tried to buy this stuff, you couldn't. And the agency invests in it. (S13)

Moreover, the employees are very aware of what they represent for the patients and the community and they see their job as a responsibility and commitment, not just toward the employer but above all toward the community. One employee who described sometimes feeling overwhelmed with work and was asking for more partnerships to help them said:

If I don't go out there and do that for that Native kid, nobody else would. And that's where if I had more community partners. … If we had more funding behind our community partners, who are kind of struggling compared to us, it would be better. (S10)

Another, describing the commitment of the employees, noted:

We are anxious about it. We are concerned about it. It's one of the last things I think about when I go to bed at night, first thing I think about when I get up in the morning. But I have the resources. I have enough money to buy food. I have health care. I can take care of my family. But these people who don't have that, it's just heartbreaking and embarrassing that we are going to allow these people who have been marginalized their entire lives to continue to fall through the cracks. I don't know. (S19)

Staff seem to go the extra mile to serve their patients because they are committed to the cause of social justice and cultural resistance and believe in what they do. One of the founders described the sacrifices they had to undergo to create and consolidate the organization:

If you are to lead a people, you must become their servant. And that is true. You can't be of the mindset of, "Oh, I'm above scrubbing the toilets, or mopping the floor, or working 17 hours days five days a week, six days a week." Oh, wait. I did it seven days a week for 12 years, but that kind of commitment is there. And it has to be there because if you truly are going to lead a people, you must be their servant. (L33)

The sacrifices were particularly immense during the first years of the organization, and the founders only persisted because of the strong values, beliefs, and commitment to a cause and a clear vision that gave them the energy to keep struggling:

For decades, we scrub toilets ourselves. We mop the floors after the group was done over there at night. Then we take out the garbage. We mopped the floors. We clean the bathrooms. We vacuum. That was part of our job before you went home. It didn't matter if you were the CEO, CFO … I was just the accountant at that point. There's just a department of one, and we just did that. We did the yard work on weekends.

We came in, and we just painted. We came in on weekends and did that kind of stuff because you have to make that big of a commitment. (L33)

And another founder noted when talking about energy and resilience:

People didn't realize how little money we had and how many hours a day we had to work to make this happen. But most of the time, I never felt tired, and I think the other people involved did not feel tired or exhausted or burned out. It was like a higher power. It's like energy from a spiritual source that you are supposed to do this. I think this is what I was supposed to do. I think I might do some other things, but I don't know. (L22)

It seems to have boiled down to the fact that if something needed to be done, it would get done even if the money was not there: "I mean, it's like Native Americans or other Indigenous people. ... It's like, 'We're going to survive, we're going to make the best of it and we're not going to whine about it,'" you know?" (L33). There appears to be within the organization a cultural ethic that fosters and promotes the struggle for social justice and cultural resistance, implementing a framework designed by the leadership that is transmitted and provides a project of a critical intercultural society while showing a path of social justice and cultural resistance to accomplish it.

Social Justice

It seems that members of the organization are committed to social justice for the community because they believe in a world where all individuals and groups can have the same opportunities to develop their capabilities and potential regardless of race, ethnicity, class, or gender.

We get to set our agenda based on the voice of the community of [Northwest city], and we get to answer to them. And our board of directors is really passionate about that. They've said, "Whatever the community needs are what our to do list needs to be," basically. Whereas it's not based on popularity. It's not based on money. It's not based on greed. It's really what do people need and how we, as 57 professionals who come to the same building every day, how are we going to tackle that. And I really like that about it. (L8)

As one leader noted:

We get people in here that have behavioral health problems. That have mental health problems. They're physically broken. All this stuff. And we're trying to come up with solutions, and work with them on ways to get better, and feel better, and help them as much as we can so that they don't have to navigate everything. I feel like it gives people optimism, and we try to be creative and use our resources to the best of our ability, in general. Things like that. It makes me happy. (L11)

The organization becomes a safety net for all disenfranchised people, regardless of culture, ethnicity, class, gender, age, and so on. Additionally, when it comes to non-Native employees, they are particularly committed to the organization because they are aware of both their privilege and the opportunity to serve the most impoverished and oppressed groups in the country. One of the employees said:

> I actually have a good affinity for Native populations, so I like working with this group of people. I think they're good people. I think they've been stepped on. I like working with people who have been stepped on, who are underserved or disenfranchised. (S25)

And another one stated, regarding the Native American community's health issues:

> I like the idea that I am here to serve the Native American community. And if you think about the Native American community when you look at the incidences and the prevalence of diseases … I'll just give you an example: Diabetes. Native Americans have about a four-fold risk of having diabetes as compared to the American White, ok? You look at something like hypertension. Similar incidents. If you look for something like obesity, alcohol use, tobacco dependence … All those things are at higher risk, and their culpabilities are higher, and I believe their life expectancy at best is also lower as compared to other communities. (S3)

It is about looking after those without insurance, those without health care access, and so on. They deserve to have access to quality health services. This is the commitment of the employees with social justice:

> Just serving the underprivileged, the uninsured. When that patient comes in and they're homeless, and they're sick, and they don't have a home, they don't have anything … and you are there, trying to figure out how they can just be able to afford and be able to have just the basic human right, which is basic health. I think it's a great privilege for me. (S3)

For the members of the organization, health care is not a business; it is a human right. And they are committed to fighting for it:

> Sometimes, the political administrations think that health is a privilege and not a right, and I think very differently. I think that is definitely something that I would hope that all men would fight for everyone to be able to have access to strong and good health care. (L8)

To bring the struggle for social justice to a higher level, some voices within the organization consider the necessity of developing more partnerships and networking with external organizations of the community:

> I believe that the CEO, and also the others, really tried to partner with other organizations and making the [organization], all the community around [Northwest city], all aware of what we do here and where we stand. We have been engaged in different levels in the community from the administrative point of view, at least from my understanding. On the other hand, I feel there is some aspect of multiculturality

where we're kind of like in an asylum, you know. And again, I'm not in the administrative. But in my opinion, I would say we can do better in terms of partnering with local organizations and creating that aspect of partnership and let's work together and let's remove, you know, like different barriers that are making us more isolated, you know, and things like that. (S10)

Another employee explained this in terms of how to improve the quality of the service:

I think it would be very nice to create better partnerships in the community to meet more community partners that are more inclusive so that they feel ownership and as much of a sense of responsibility as we do. Because it could only make more resource for our clients. (S34)

From the interviews, it is clear that this conversation about bringing the struggle to another level involving better partnerships with the community is going on in an informal way among different employees. However, right now it does not seem to be a priority for the leadership of the organization who appear to be more focused on consolidating the growth and the organizational culture of the organization before considering any sort of partnerships or common platforms that could influence the culture of the organization.

We Shall Overcome: Cultural Resistance

Resilience and sustainability are central to consistently keeping the momentum and adjusting to any different scenario or barrier that can emerge within any struggle. Thus, if one of the organization's shared characteristics is humor as a mechanism of relieving daily stress, optimism and resilience seem to be other central concepts that appear to be more effective for the long term. As one of the young leaders explained when talking about difficulties resulting from the current political climate:

I think there's hope, though. I think the future is going to be a lot better. I'll have to pick up on that. I think the future will be a lot better. I just think any time something like that happens, there's a cultural bonding between different communities where they kind of come together and bridge together. Because if they don't, then the oppressor wins, and we're just not going to let that happen. (L8)

And the same young leader continued describing the "dream," the framework that gives sense and meaning to their struggle:

Those conversations that happen in DC don't strip us away from being strong-minded and don't tear down the dream that we have as far as what [the organization] could be next. If we have a will, we'll find a way, and there's always a will, and there's always been a way. There's been administrations that have come through who wanted to do community help and needed help out of the budget. And in the midst of that, we built a brand new building. It wasn't about leading with fear, but it was about leading with love and compassion, and that's what made this building happen. It was we could sit there and just wait it out, or we can say,

You know what? Let's go full steam ahead because the patients need this." And that's what we did. And I feel [the organization] as being strong in the sense of not being afraid to make a change, and being able to fight for itself and advocate for itself, and to really be a strong agency to protect the community of [Northwest city] from using its services. (L8)

Regarding the optimism and resilience of the struggle, one of the founders stated:

I think in all of America, you still see hope. You still see someone saying, "Screw this. We're going to continue to do what we're going to do. We're going to continue, and we're not going to let ICE dictate. We will protect our neighbors." And you know, I don't think anyone's going to get deported from [Northwest city] without there being a huge outcry. I think we just need a little wake-up call. (L33)

In conclusion, the organization is not only a health center that offers high-quality services for Native and non-Native people from the city and the region but also a decolonial social movement and a project of struggle for social justice and cultural resistance that raises awareness and critical consciousness, gives hope, empowers individuals and communities through collective action, and shares strategies and frameworks for sense- and meaning-making to contribute to building a better society without large asymmetries of power.

Conclusion

Leadership is a relational process that implies sense- and meaning-making to create a culture and a social order. Additionally, leadership involves identity formation since the culture and social order create systems of classification and labels. Therefore, leadership can be a tool for creating organizational cultures and social orders where people are either controlled and oppressed or can thrive and be emancipated. Creating an inclusive and fair organizational culture and social order requires horizontal intercultural communication. Building an organizational culture from the bottom-up requires an intercultural dialogue where all voices are heard and difference is valued. This dialogue goes beyond language and includes empathy and emotions. In the following chapter we will see in detail how a critical intercultural leadership model works and can be implemented for organizational and social change.

Discussion Questions

1. What is the connection between critical consciousness and ethnogenesis for social change?
2. How can we combine vertical and horizontal structures of participation and decision-making in an organization?
3. Why is leadership central to processes of sense- and meaning-making and identity formation?
4. What are the key elements of an effective intercultural dialogue?

Chapter 7

Critical Intercultural Leadership Process

Objectives

In this chapter, we will see how a critical intercultural leadership process works and can be implemented for organizational and social change. The main ideas are:

- Within a context of a postcolonial world, it is key to denounce a situation of social injustice while debunking myths and imaginaries of the dominant culture and creating a safe space for critical reflection.
- It is critical to provide a platform for action because it is at this platform where critical consciousness can rise to the highest stages through the struggle. Additionally, the platform and the struggle function as a way of balancing asymmetries of power based on the monopoly of the hegemonic culture to control cultural assumptions that place negative value on difference.
- It is central to develop a framework of social order and a class consciousness within the organization that bonds through differences valuing diversity, reducing asymmetries of power, struggling for a common purpose, and enhancing a sense of belonging that ends up configuring an intercultural society among employees and patients.
- The critical intercultural leadership process will be eventually crystalized with a strong core of cultural assumptions, values, and beliefs regarding the emancipatory and decolonial project that act as lines in the sand and, although need to be reviewed constantly to avoid reproducing new oppressions, give stability to the culture of the organization.

In this chapter, I synthesize major themes and subthemes from Chapter 5 and 6 into four significant findings after reflecting thoroughly on their meaning and practical and theoretical implications. To interpret these findings, I put them into context to transcend the facts and engage in a productive discussion using the philosophical and theoretical frame designed throughout Chapters 1–4 to give them meaning, identify rival or competing explanations, and describe possible implications of my study for the fields of leadership studies, political sociology, and international relations.

The findings provide an understanding of how the critical intercultural leadership process that emerges at the health clinic creates an organizational culture that raises critical consciousness and unfolds ethnogenesis to move beyond a postcolonial society and a Eurocentric framework of leadership and toward an intercultural society.

The four findings of my research (see Figure 7.1) are:

- Making visible the invisible: the sanctuary
- We struggle; therefore, I am: the platform
- United by our differences: the intercultural society
- Emancipatory doxa/pluri-doxa and transformation: the lines in the sand

The first finding of this ethnographic case study is the necessity of making visible the invisible. Within a context of a postcolonial world, the health clinic makes visible the invisible by denouncing a situation of social injustice while debunking myths and imaginaries of the dominant culture that portrays Native people as primitive or inferior. Besides, the foundation of the health clinic creates a safe space and sanctuary for critical reflection for Native people in the area. The second finding suggests, "We struggle; therefore, I am." In other words, the organization provides a platform for action, and it is at this platform where critical consciousness can rise to the highest stages through the struggle. Additionally, the platform and the struggle function as a way of balancing asymmetries of power based on the monopoly of the hegemonic culture to control cultural assumptions that places negative value on difference. Individual empowerment and collective action contribute to decolonizing the minds of both the oppressed and the oppressors and "educating" hegemonic institutions to be transformed. The third finding presents the idea of "united by our differences." The health clinic develops a framework of social order and a class consciousness within the organization that bonds through valuing diversity, reducing asymmetries of power, struggling for a common purpose, and enhancing a sense of belonging that ends up configuring an intercultural society among employees and patients. A focus on an emancipatory doxa/pluri-doxa and transformation is the fourth finding. The critical intercultural leadership process within the sanctuary, the platform, and the intercultural organization is crystalized with a strong core of cultural assumptions, values, and beliefs regarding the emancipatory and decolonial project that act as lines in the sand and, although need to be reviewed constantly to avoid reproducing new oppressions, give stability to the culture of the organization. Its resilience characterizes this organizational culture's ability to be flexible and adjust to external and internal challenges and understand change and transformation, which results in the design of fluid and flexible organizational/ social structures.

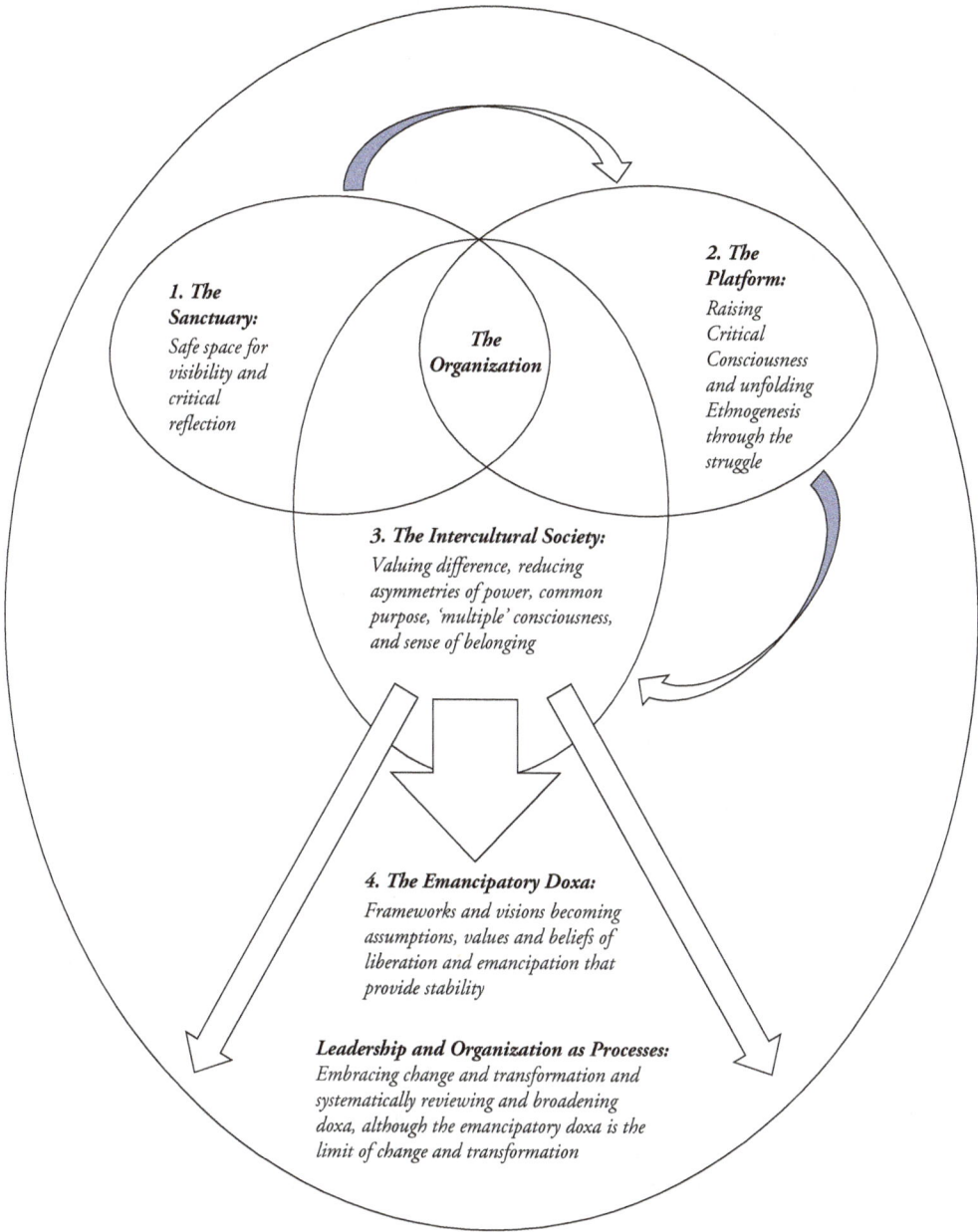

FIGURE 7.1 The Critical Intercultural Leadership Process.

Making Visible the Invisible: The Sanctuary

The first finding of my research is the need to make visible the invisible: those social groups that have been overlooked, forgotten, or demonized with the hegemonic discourse and narrative of a global system of domination and oppression that establishes a social hierarchy based on race, class, sex, and culture and where the dominant culture is at the top. As one of the leaders said,

"We're the forgotten. ... We were put aside on our little reservations, and hopefully never seen or heard of again" (L11). When it comes to the urban Native population, this invisibility is even more insidious because, according to the imagery of the dominant culture, Native people belong to museums and are part of the past, not the present. One of the employees denounced that history books used at schools and colleges in the United States are written solely from a White perspective: "When they do treat on topics of Native American history or more contemporary issues that we face, they are sort of glossed over and they sort of depict us as being ancient versus here today" (S14).

Through the process of modernity a lineal concept of the history of humanity was established that starts with a primitive stage and culminates in its most "sophisticated" phase, which is represented by Europe (Quijano, 2010). Thus, the European culture represents "modern civilization," and the other cultures are either made invisible or labeled as "primitive" and part of the past. This is why making visible what has been made invisible is central to any project of cultural resistance and cognitive justice. For example, another employee described her experience studying in a big city in the United States: "I was probably the only Native student at high school and some of the students thought I still lived in a teepee. Then, if I didn't live in a teepee, they didn't know I even existed" (S16). According to the Urban Indian Health Commission Report of 2007, although American Indians and Alaska Natives living in metropolitan regions in the United States represent nearly 67% of the nation's 4.1 million Natives, they are invisible for most of the country's population. This phenomenon results from Eurocentrism, or when western Europeans thought of themselves as the most developed culture in the history of humanity and protagonists of modernity while the rest were living in the past (Quijano, 2010). Thus, from a Western cultural assumption, if you are Native American, you should live in a teepee in the reservation because Native Americans cannot be "modern" and live in a city; only White people can. Using a Western mental framework to make sense of the world, a Native individual living in a city makes no sense, and this is why it is so important to make visible and raise awareness about the urban Native population and their social struggles.

Moreover, through Eurocentrism, Western culture is viewed as the only rational one; the rest are not rational and therefore are inferior by nature (Quijano, 2000). This ideology explains another stereotype of Native people as individuals who cannot adjust to modernity and progress and are passive victims of substance abuse and poverty because of their lack of intelligence, work ethic, and responsibility. Thus, the dominant culture conceptualizes the world only from its worldview and does not value other perspectives, making cognitive and social justice achievement almost impossible. For example, one of the founders talked about how Western culture worships the "God of degrees" and diminishes any other knowledge that the hegemonic institutions do not validate: "The most popular therapist we have does not have a degree and the kids follow that person everywhere" (L22). The lack of valuing a different knowledge that goes beyond the Western epistemology is what Santos (2014) calls *epistemicide*: the extermination of knowledge and different types of knowing.

In addition, since the organization provides holistic medicine with a Native American perspective based on the concept of sacred hospitality, it faces resistances from the hegemonic culture. After the Enlightenment, humans separated themselves from nature and became their masters, establishing a connection between the Enlightenment and the scientific method that situates science as the only legitimate model of explanation for reality, with the goal of overcoming tradition and "liberating" us from myth and superstition (Horkheimer & Adorno, 1996). Thus, the dominant culture only values scientific knowledge as the legitimate one, and concepts such as holistic medicine and sacred hospitality are considered either myth or superstition.

Regarding the Indian Health System (IHS), most of the employees shared a negative opinion: "It's a real crappy substandard subhuman way to treat Natives and it starts from birth if you have to go to IHS. Their standard of care is ridiculously low and it's caused a lot of deaths" (S18). In terms of the educational system, one of the founders, remembering the reasons behind founding the organization, stated:

> Only one out of every four kids were getting to high school. And of those one in four kids that got to high school, only one was going to graduate. And those are the super-achievers that were also going to go to college. But there's a lot of suicide, substance abuse. (L33)

These examples of institutional constraints that affect Native peoples' access to health care and education represent a system of oppression understood as an enclosing structure of forces and barriers that impact their immobilization and reduction as a particular cultural group. Oppression along with domination define injustice (Young, 2011). *Oppression* occurs when institutions constrain the self-development of individuals or groups of people, and *domination* occurs when these institutions limit the possibilities of self-determination. From Young's (2011) list of five dimensions that define oppression (exploitation, marginalization, powerlessness, cultural imperialism, and violence), Native people experience at least the last four. Thus, founding a health clinic made visible urban Native people and their particular struggles and, at the same time, attempted to address the different forms of oppression that urban Natives were experiencing.

As a result of this invisibility and the demonization of Native people and their ways of knowing—and also because of the structural violence experienced by urban Natives (e.g., lack of access to quality health services and education)—a group of 15 urban Native Americans from different tribes living in the city decided to found the health clinic. They made visible the invisible, denouncing a situation of domination and oppression in the American postcolonial society while debunking myths of cultural inferiority. Besides, the organization is led mainly by Native women who experience the domination and oppression of a patriarchal and sexist system that situates them in a position of double subordination for being both Native and women. As one of the young leaders said regarding the women's leadership of the organization:

> And being that [Northwest city], again, is conservative, they had to fight a lot to be able to be allowed to enter the room, to be allowed to have a voice. And they do that time and time again, even in 2017. And it just shows their passion for the work, because they could've easily given up. (L8)

To be successful in occupying a space in the field of political discourse limits the possibilities of certain groups while possibly reconfiguring the political opportunity structure for others (Jenson, 1995). In essence, the struggle of making visible the invisible and naming instead of being named involves understanding culture as a field for struggle and the exercise of cultural power relations.

One of the leaders argued regarding the need to make visible the invisible: "There's a face and [the organization] plays a role of having that face and saying, 'Hello, we're here. There's Native Americans in your community and there are Native Americans in your medical community.'" (S25). For Bourdieu (1977), "what goes without saying and what cannot be said for lack of an available discourse, represents the dividing-line between the most radical form of misrecognition and the awakening of political consciousness" (p. 170). Thus, the first step to an awakening of political consciousness is to make visible the invisible and say what cannot be said, contributing to broadening the space of doxa through new discourses, narratives, and frameworks. As Bourdieu argues, a group has power when it can make public and formulate experiences that have not been formulated before to make them official and legitimate them, which will give them strength.

Native people always have been "there" in the United States (Turtle Island)—even before the European arrived—but needed to make themselves visible for a hegemonic culture that either thinks that they do not exist, thinking that all Natives are in reservations or museums, or portrays Native people as inferior and not capable of adapting to progress.

This is why it was necessary to create this new reality with the foundation of the organization and be named by themselves instead of being named by the hegemonic culture: Symbolic power "is a power of consecration or revelation, the power to consecrate or to reveal things that are already there" (Bourdieu, 1989, p. 23).

Moreover, organization in general and political organization in particular are needed to gain recognition in the political sphere. In other words, by the end of the 1980s, it was not enough for urban Native people in the city to "be there," and that was the reason why a group of 15 urban Natives decided to initiate a process to organize themselves and create the health clinic. As Bourdieu (1989) states:

> In fact, as a constellation which, according to Nelson Goodman (1978), begins to exist only when it is selected and designated as such, a group, a class, a gender, a region or a nation begins to exist as such, for those who belong to it as well as for the others, only when it is distinguished, according to one principle or another, from other groups, that is, through knowledge and recognition (connaissance et reconnaissance). (p. 23)

One way of making visible the invisible urban Native people is creating a space that gives visibility to the struggle and, at the same time, is a safe space where Native people from the city can feel safe, celebrated, and valued. This sanctuary needs to be understood as a space for retreat where in particular young urban Natives can learn and appreciate their cultural traditions and critically reflect on the postcolonial system of oppression and domination and their particular reality. One of the leaders stated: "Just being Native in a non-diverse place, being gay in a very conservative city … it's nice because you can be what you want here, and celebrated. This is a place of diversity to the max, and in [Northwest city] it's hard to find places like that" (L8). Following the same line of the argument, one of the founders said, "I think that's the thing that I want: staff, especially young staff, to get that it's kind of like a sanctuary place" (L22). Subordinate groups operate in private, isolated from the control of the dominant groups of society, creating havens or free social spaces where the dominated can organize their challenge to the dominant narrative and ideologies, deconstruct old and create new meanings, construct emergent cultural forms, and transmit the culture (Fantasia & Hirsch, 1995).

Another strategy to provide visibility and debunk myths that portray Native people as primitive or not intelligent is through symbols and artifacts. For example, one supporter said: "We want to have a very nice facility that people come in and not only do they feel welcome, but that it is clean and we don't have crappy furniture and where you know everyone is well dressed" (S13). Symbols and artifacts like a beautiful building, nice furniture, or smart outfits create a consensus on the meaning of the social world, "a consensus which contributes fundamentally to the reproduction of the social order" (Bourdieu, 1991, p. 166). Thus, artifacts and symbols construct a social order by providing people with a social being that is recognized publicly. This is why the leadership is very focused on crafting a good image of the building, the furniture, the outfits, and the behavior and actions of all the employees. One leader stated: "If you're drinking, if you're doing drugs, if you're falling down, getting your name in the paper for domestic violence, then you probably shouldn't work here" (L22). Artifacts and symbols are political and embedded in power relations because they imply a space where general social relations can be represented and negotiated (Bourdieu, 1994). Additionally, since social movements are communities of discourse centered in creating new cultural codes that challenge hegemonic perspectives, the organization understands discourse as not only written in their mission and vision statements but also what the different members of the staff can say, the formal events and activities that they organize with the community, and the informal interactions when the employees are outside work in their private lives.

To make visible the invisible, it is also central to invest in outreach and encounter hegemonic institutions that either are not aware of your existence or view the world through cultural myths and stereotypes that need to be addressed and deconstructed. For example, one supporter said: "We have an outreach right now for postcards to our governors and senators to try to raise awareness for importance of a grant that helps subsidize some of our positions here. So, I think we're in pretty good communication" (S6). In essence, a group or a social class only exists and has force in the political field when representatives with the "plena potentia agenda" may be and feel authorized to speak in its name, like, for example, "the Party is the working class" or "the Pope is the Church" (Bourdieu, 1991, p. 250). Although the leadership insists that they do not represent Native people in the area, they get their strength in the political field by "representing" the Native community.

Initially, the health clinic was focused on the urban Native population from the city, but when the urban Native patients started to bring their relatives and friends from the reservation, including White, Latinx, Black, and Asian people, to the organization, the founders decided to broaden the focus and serve everyone. Thus, the organization became a safe space not just for the Native population but for all the invisible, the forgotten, and the demonized in a more transversal way that goes beyond Native people and broadens their class consciousness. One of the supporters said, "If the poor got together, the way that we were founded, no matter what color, there would be a lot more movement" (S10). Neoliberal ideology allowed a dehistoricized and desocialized political program "of methodical destruction of collectives" (Bourdieu, 1998, pp. 95–96). As a consequence of the process of destroying collectives and class solidarity, policies of redistribution in the United States were abandoned by the 1980s and substituted with policies seeking to integrate minorities and women in the political system (Navarro, 2016). These policies were prolific in the 1990s, but most of the people who benefited from them belonged to the upper-middle class as opposed to the majority of minority groups who belong to the working class (Navarro, 2016). With today's identity politics, an essentialist approach to the struggle for social justice does not consider the intersectionalities of race, class, gender that are dividing social movements and hindering the possibilities of emancipatory transversal and global projects of class consciousness.

As a result of the social justice motivations that created a safe space and a sanctuary to organize collective actions to struggle for decolonization and cultural resistance, the health clinic can be considered much more than a business or nonprofit in the field of health care. Since the foundation of the organization, the founders decided to organize leadership camps focused on the young urban Native Americans to give meaning to their lives and to encourage them to be proud of their cultural traditions and worldviews while training them as future Native leaders who will serve the urban Native community of the city and struggle for social justice and cultural resistance. In essence, any struggle for cognitive and social justice requires critical reflection, organization, and the decolonization of the minds of the oppressed so they can see the social order as arbitrary and not natural or inexorable. For Gramsci (1970), culture means organization, discipline, empowerment, and awareness of taking control of reality. Thus, the organization, understood as a Native organization that is part of a bigger social movement of decolonization, is seen as a reaction against a hegemonic culture and system to transform society. The main goals of social movements and SMOs are to influence and change the cultural order and perspectives of society in which they are embedded (Fine, 1995).

However, the organization does not try to threaten the state or its sovereignty; they struggle to create political spaces in the city that allow people to create their own forms of sociopolitical organization. Their goal is balancing asymmetries of power that result from placing a negative value on difference in terms of race, class, sex, and culture and unfolding a process of ethnogenesis that transforms the minds of both the oppressed and the oppressors to recognize and value other worldviews, narratives, and frameworks. One of the supporters said:

> There's genocide still happening in this country. And slavery in the prison system. We're being taught in our school system that that stuff was over with and done for and not happening because it was ancient history. ... There's a lot of ownership that's not been taken or taught about what's still happening in our country. (S10)

Any organizational project of emancipation needs a critical intercultural leadership process from their cultural perspective because "either they must organize authentically for their liberation, or they will be manipulated by the elites. Authentic organization is obviously not going to be stimulated by the dominators; it is the task of the revolutionary leaders" (Freire, 2012, p. 148). As one of the founders of the organization said: "Nobody rode in on their white horse and saved us" (L22). In other words, the urban Native community in the city needed to take control of their reality and destiny as active subjects instead of waiting to be saved.

Thus, the struggle needs to be carried out by themselves in their terms; otherwise, the hegemonic system can co-opt revolutionary projects and deactivate them as soon as they are implemented within the system. "The fate of democracy and the chances for social justice will depend on the movements' capacity to take ongoing responsibility for the social future" (Flacks, 1995, p. 263). The organization struggles for a social future of cognitive and social justice for all, and the first step of the process was to take control of their reality as a social group and to make visible the invisible. In essence, the power to control the naming and the history of a social group is perhaps the ultimate form of hegemony, and any organization or social movement that struggles for social justice and cultural resistance needs to start their emancipatory project by challenging this power.

We Struggle, Therefore I Am: The Platform

If the first step in the process of struggling for social justice and cultural resistance was to create a sanctuary for safety and critical reflection that made visible issues of social injustice in the area while debunking myths of Native people as inferior or not capable of organizing successful social, economic, and political projects, the following stage is to offer a platform for implementing action. As one of the members of the staff stated, "The [organization] allowed you more of a practice of interculturality and social justice. … I think it allows us to practice to that which is why I'm here" (S6).

According to Lederach (2005), platforms are useful to generate processes that may ultimately transform the relationships that lie at the root of social conflicts. This platform is essential for any process that aims to transition from a postcolonial world with large asymmetries of power to an intercultural society with fewer asymmetries because it is within the struggle (the action/praxis) where critical consciousness raises to the highest levels to decolonize the minds of the oppressed first, which will be able to start the process of decolonization of the oppressors without risk of being co-opted by them. As one employee argued: "I think getting involved is key to raise critical consciousness. I've never been to a Pow Wow before, so getting involved was really cool. Events like that. … I think that's probably helped to raise it" (S6). Another employee reiterated this sentiment: "When you're living it in theory is different than when you come to the particular community. And that has really changed the paradigm shift for me in terms of the lenses I see the world in" (S3). To overcome a situation of oppression requires transformative action that creates a new situation (Freire, 2012). However, before struggling, people must recognize and identify the causes of the oppression and design a new framework of the world and ethics. Thus, as the employee above said, the oppressed need to change the lenses through which they see the world, debunking myths created in the old order to develop new frameworks and social structures.

Moreover, the platform and its struggle function as a way of balancing asymmetries of power based on controlling and imposing cultural assumptions and myths that place negative value on what is different than dominant culture and are embedded in minds, resulting in feelings of powerlessness or hopelessness for the oppressed who end up internalizing and accepting the discourse of oppression. The domination of the mind is the most effective system of domination and violence because it is not visible and is reproduced unconsciously through individuals' daily dispositions and practices. In addition, the asymmetries of power are also embedded and reproduced through social structures and institutions created by individuals that at the same time shape their dispositions and practices. This process of imposing what can be thought and perceived upon the dominated who incorporate the social order of domination in their unconscious structures and take it as natural is called symbolic power (Bourdieu & Wacquant, 1996).

To balance these asymmetries of power embedded in minds, social structures, and institutions, a platform for action is central because it is the space where the struggle is carried out. Additionally, it is in this platform where collective frameworks of action that empower individuals to take control of reality and seek to transform the social order and educate hegemonic institutions to deconstruct social structures of domination and oppression are designed and developed. As one of the supporters said: "Providing the environment for me to meet with other people and to meet with Native American community. I think that by itself is empowerment" (S3). Thus, through new frameworks, the organization provides ways of perceiving and thinking that replace old ones while discarding old meanings, symbols, and erroneous beliefs.

If Descartes's famous quote "I think, therefore I am" was used to differentiate Europe from the rest of the world as being not worthy of existence or inferior (Maldonado-Torres, 2008), the platform at the organization offers a counterhegemonic option that gives meaning to the oppressed through the idea of "we struggle, therefore I am." According to one young leader at the organization: "Working here I have become prouder, and feel more celebrated, and hopeful. Before I came here, there wasn't really a place that had a bunch of professionals who were like, 'Hey, you're awesome as you are. Come join us.'" (L8). As Marcuse (1991) argued, all liberation depends first on deconstructing the consciousness of servitude and then reconstructing a consciousness of emancipation.

Empowerment Through Frameworks of Collective Action

Seeing other people struggling and having sense- and meaning-making frameworks to make sense of that struggle are essential elements in empowering individuals to take control of reality and transform it. One of the young leaders talked about witnessing all the sacrifices that her relatives made:

> Growing up seeing that, I was able to volunteer as a high school student. Me and a couple of my friends from a youth leadership program got to volunteer and be youth leaders in their Indian youth programs so we volunteered a lot of our time in high school doing that. (L2)

When one sees other people struggling, society is not perceived as natural or inexorable anymore but as a construction, something unfinished that can be transformed. It becomes a challenge rather than a frustrating limitation (Freire, 2012).

Another key element to getting empowered through collective action is class consciousness. As Freire (2012) argues, the oppressed are together by their solidarity, and they need to overcome their differences to develop class consciousness. For example, one of the employees explained:

> I think it's empowering as an employee or a patient to walk through those doors and to see a lot of different Natives specializing in a lot of different areas of medicine, social services, administration. I know when I started with them I was just like blown away. (S14)

To resist oppression and domination one needs to trust the other people who are struggling with them (Federici, 2016). That is why individualism is a barrier for any social struggle: There is no trust in the collective, which is the source of being empowered. It is the principle of "divide and conquer" complemented with the development of identity politics that hinders the possibility of unfolding transversal and emancipatory projects against a global system of domination and oppression. However, consciousness of being an oppressed class is preceded or at least accompanied by individual consciousness, which is different from individualistic consciousness (Freire, 2012). The same employee quoted above described his first visit to the health clinic: "I am like, 'Wow these tribal members from different tribes all coming here for the greater good of [the organization] of [Northwest city] community and our people!'" (S14). Since the subaltern needs to transition from being conscious of themselves as oppressed individuals to an oppressed class consciousness, the leadership of the organization empowers individually through a framework of collective action. As one employee argued regarding the leadership's emphasis on empowering their employees and patients: "[The founder and CEO] is a great mentor and she believes in empowering her staff. She believes in mentoring the young ones to follow up" (S1).

Collective action is understood as a social construction with purpose and meaning that is derived from structural constraints and cannot be reduced either to leaders' discourses or militants' options or public behavior (Melucci, 1995). There are three components of collective action frames: injustice, agency, and identity (Gamson, 1995). *Injustice* refers to moral indignation; *agency* refers to the consciousness that through collective action it is possible to transform society; and *identity* refers to the process of defining the "we" versus the "they" with different interests or values (Gamson, 1995). These three components are described in a similar vein by Snow and Benford (1992) but identified as (a) punctuation, or bringing attention to the injustice suffered; (b) attribution, or describing the causes and solutions for the injustice; and (c) articulation, or connecting different experiences. The organization emphasizes injustice/punctuation in all their meetings and events, but it is central for the emancipatory project that they also focus on agency/attribution by empowering people and providing them with ways of acting collectively. This creates a collective identity for the employees through a common purpose. As one employee stated:

> [The organization] helps people in becoming more active. … I didn't know, when I started working here, I was [young age]. I had no idea how to contact my legislator and how to voice my concerns or whatever. So, I think not even so much being more conscious, but knowing how to make a change. (S24)

Instead of remaining in the component of injustice and identity (i.e., we versus them), the organization tries to empower employees and patients through collective action, describing the causes and solutions for the injustice.

Deconstructing and Reconstructing Social Structures

The most effective way to deconstruct and reconstruct social structures is to approach this process in a holistic way, focusing on macro structures (systems of stratification, institutions, and patterned relations between groups), meso structures (social networks ties between individuals and also between organizations), and micro structures (norms that shape the behavior of individuals and groups within a society).

Thus, it is a process of ethnogenesis that decolonizes minds, dispositions, and practices on one side and reconstructs hegemonic institutions that have the capacity of reproduction of structures that shape the dispositions and practices of individuals and groups on the other.

The relationship between Western culture and other cultures that began during the 16th century continues to be one of colonial domination whose results are a relationship that consists, in the first place, of a colonization of the imagination of the dominated (Quijano, 2010). Thus, it is central to decolonize the minds of the people. One employee recounted her own experience: "Coming as someone who's White from essentially a privileged background, not having to worry about basic challenges like food scarcity or domestic violence or drug abuse, I think being confronted with those issues here has just developed my consciousness for others" (S4).

Through Eurocentrism and its leadership process, intersubjectivity is dominated, and the world is only conceptualized from a Western worldview, which makes the achievement of social and cognitive justice nearly impossible because other cultures are either completely ignored or deemed inferior. As one leader of the organization argued, talking about the relationship of the dominant culture with subordinated ones, "I think we might not be aware of our own prejudices, and our own biases, and things like that. And when we look at viewing other cultures [it is done as if they were] inferior or less than your own" (L8). For example, one of the founders was very clear about a hegemonic system that reproduces both the invisibility of nondominant cultures and a feeling of superiority over them: "It's been a challenge sometimes because I think some professions like social work, medicine, or counseling have an unhealthy part that teaches people to be codependents and take care of other people ... that is not our culture" (L22). In essence, the system implements paternalist and assistentialist approaches to control and deactivate any possibility of social revolution that could transform a system configurated with structures that privilege certain social sectors of society over others. Besides, paternalism reinforces the Eurocentric doxa of the oppressor because it makes them feel satisfied with their actions and creates the imaginary illusion of solidarity and social justice while the real causes of the injustice are hidden.

One of the ideologies that results from Eurocentrism during modernity and its darker side, colonialism, is racism. Racism reproduces racial inequality in contemporary America in a very covert way because it is embedded in normal operations of institutions and is invisible to most White people (Bonilla-Silva, 1996). For example, one of the leaders said: "Some of my White colleagues don't necessarily understand why the Native population has a different set of needs than the White population does" (S25). The hegemonic culture is successful in holding power over social institutions and, through them, influences the thoughts and behaviors of the rest of society, establishing normative ideas, values, and beliefs that eventually will become the hegemonic worldview of the society (Strinati, 1995). Thus, since the dominant culture views the world through cultural assumptions of racism, classism, sexism, and cultural superiority/ inferiority, these ideas need to be challenged and reconstructed through an emancipatory struggle.

Subaltern groups are dominated and manipulated by the force of the myths imposed by the hegemonic sectors of society who, after internalizing the opinion the oppressors hold of them, eventually become convinced of their inferiority and see it as natural (Freire, 2012). A similar phenomenon of cultural domination is *learned helplessness*, which arises when prior learning in a situation that cannot be solved undermines motivation for future responses in a similar situation and distorts the ability to change the environment (Rabow et al., 1983).

Another element of control implemented during the last several decades has consisted of embedding the minds of the oppressed with individualism and a bourgeois concept of personal success to dismantle ideas of solidarity and social class. Cultural conquest leads to the cultural inauthenticity of those who are invaded, who begin to respond to the values and goals of the invaders (Freire, 2012). As one of the employees stated regarding the division between subordinated social groups: "If the poor got together, the way that we were founded, no matter what color, there would be a lot more movement" (S10). At a certain level, the organization began to represent a transversal and intercultural movement seeking cognitive and social justice since the very first moment that non-Native people started to be treated at the clinic. Although the organization's leadership could have denied providing health services to non-Native people, this decision implied the transformation of a Native American emancipatory project into a subordinated emancipatory endeavor.

For Freire (2012), since the oppressed are divided through an ideology of oppression, they can be emancipated with a form of cultural action that requires de-ideologizing and re-ideologizing. It is the start of a process of ethnogenesis at an individual, organizational, and societal level that deconstructs social structures of domination and oppression and reconstructs new structures for liberation and emancipation. In terms of de-ideologizing/decolonizing minds, the leadership of the organization is very concerned about decolonizing the minds of all their employees and patients as the first step for struggling for social justice. As one of the founders stated:

> They need to know like oral history. They need to know the historical context of why they work here. They need to know about trauma. They need to know the truth about what happened to Native people. We're sitting in this building today as a direct result of historical trauma. The genocide and how it shows up now. They killed almost most of us, so we better be on-board all hands-on deck to save what is rest of us. (L22)

Thus, the leadership, understanding culture as a field for struggle, empowers staff and patients by debunking myths of inferiority and offering collective action frameworks to transform an oppressive reality. As one employee stated, describing how they empower the patients to be active, "We don't try to say that's not fair and people shouldn't do that to you and go and be strong. We don't do that. We go, 'Hey, what can you do with this barrier? How can you deal with this?' (S30). And one of the founders stated, "To be free is to be independent. We teach people to be autonomous, healthy, independent, to live on their own, and to take care of their own health and their mental health" (L22).

Gradually, the health clinic creates an organizational culture that raises critical consciousness and unfolds ethnogenesis, changing the frameworks through which employees and patients view the world. One of the employees said: "I'm an enrolled [Indian tribe], but I never lived on the reservation, so I was very White. I did have to learn to navigate between cultures then and get educated" (S1). The creation of meaning, naming and constructing discourses and narratives, and rituals are central processes of cultural production. To create meaning in a social movement, Klandermans (1992) suggests three processes that use public discourses, persuasive communication, and consciousness-raising during episodes of collective action. At the organization, there is a discourse outside and inside the organization centered on social justice and cultural resistance transmitted with sense- and meaning-making frameworks. Regarding naming, discourses and narratives involve a struggle for discursive space to imagine the past, the present, and the future of the communities. The organization emphasizes that their employees need to know the history of Native people, their struggles, and their emancipatory projects. Rituals are understood as the cultural mechanisms that collective actors implement to express their emotions and are central to mobilize and sustain the struggle (Taylor & Whittier, 1995). Emotions are the glue of solidarity (Collins, 1990) and are expressed at the health clinic through formal rituals (e.g., Pow Wows or graduation ceremonies) and informal ones (e.g., time for sharing different types of food and jokes and laughter) as mechanisms to create solidarity and make the struggle more sustainable.

When it comes to the formation of cultural assumptions that represent the core of a culture, there are two basic mechanisms that are connected with positive problem solving to cope with external adaptation issues, on the one hand, and anxiety avoidance to cope with internal integration issues, on the other (Schein, 2010). Thus, the critical intercultural leadership process at the organization

- creates a culture for resistance;
- establishes norms and behaviors for navigating external adaptation issues and avoiding anxiety while coping with internal integration challenges;
- deconstructs hegemonic assumptions; and
- consolidates emancipatory ones.

As one employee stated regarding the social injustices and the system of oppression and domination that is internalized and seen as natural by the oppressed: "It's affecting our lives. Affecting our cultures. And we're not taking ownership. There's a lot of ownership that's not been taken or taught about what's still happening in our country" (S10). Thus, if assumptions are not challenged because they are taken for granted, the organization aims to make them visible and to show that they are not natural or inexorable but a social construction, an arbitrary and unfair social order that must be challenged and transformed.

Regarding the de-ideologizing/decolonizing of social structures and institutions, the leadership focuses part of their activities on establishing fluid communication with hegemonic institutions to raise visibility and awareness about their struggles and educate them about Native culture and social struggles. State institutions are central to deciding criteria of inclusion, exclusion, and funding; this is why, besides balancing asymmetries of power, the organization seeks recognition by public institutions. As one employee described: "I have watched the improvement in the relationships with the city and I think [the founder and CEO] does a wonderful job of educating people about Native culture and people of color" (S1).

The categories that make the world order possible are key for any political struggle, "a struggle which is inseparably theoretical and practical, over the power of preserving or transforming the social world by preserving or transforming the categories of perception of that world" (Bourdieu, 1991, p. 236). That is why it is central to make visible the invisible and, with a parallel process of critical reflection debunk myths about nonhegemonic cultures while empowering through collective action subordinated individuals and social groups who will have a less asymmetric dialogue with hegemonic institutions. One employee said:

> [The founder and CEO] has sent people to the hospital to meet our clientele and invite them over to see the clinic and see what we do, the fire department, the ambulance, the police. ... We've had people from senators and their staff come over to be introduced. (S1)

World-making consists of "carrying out a decomposition, an analysis, and a composition, a synthesis, often by the use of labels" (p. 22). Symbolic power, the power that through naming reproduces or transforms objective principles that unite and separate, along with social classifications, is needed to carry out this process of world-making.

Balancing Asymmetries of Power

The processes of decolonizing the minds of both the oppressed and the oppressors and educating and reconstructing hegemonic institutions to not reproduce colonial dispositions and practices contribute to the balancing of asymmetries of power because they are central to the transformation of objective principles of union and separation and social classifications that define power relations in postcolonial societies. According to one of the founders, on the possibility of working in a hegemonic organization or institution: "If I were to work in those systems I would never have power. I would have to always acquiesce to the power and control of the colonizer because they own every system in this country" (L22).

Since the hegemonic culture possesses the most cultural capital, any group's struggle for improving the position within the system and increasing power will reinforce the structure that serves the interests of the dominant class (Chopra, 2003). As one founder said:

> I do see some people of color when they start working with systems they acquiesce, they change to be colonized and then they become the colonizer. So, I always tell myself, "When I die I want to be the freest person in the room. I want to be decolonized." (L22)

Thus, the founders understood that the struggle was not just about increasing the capital of urban Native people within the dominant system but also redefining the conversation's terms to challenge the postcolonial system and its doxa. It was not about getting a bigger piece of the cake; it was—and still is—about changing the cake. As one of the founders stated regarding when they decided to found the organization: "We can do this ourselves, we can make systems that maybe from the outside look like their system so if it's palatable enough they'll give us money ... but underneath really like nurture the spirit or the core of it" (L22). Therefore, to dismantle the dominant hegemony, a new and alternative hegemony in the area had to arise: what Gramsci (1995) called a "war of position."

According to Arendt (1970), power belongs to a group and remains with the group as long as the group keeps together. Similarly, Bourdieu (1977, 1990) argues that today there is a struggle for social recognition as a type of power he called symbolic power. This is a struggle

> to win everything which, in the social world, is of the order of belief, credit and discredit, perception and appreciation, knowledge and recognition—name, renown, prestige, honor, glory, authority, everything which constitutes symbolic power as recognized power. (Bourdieu, 1984, p. 251)

The struggle for this symbolic power was central to the creation the organization because, as one of the founders stated, "In our public school systems we've been really told a bunch of lies and so you're deeply entrenched into really make good conscious decisions. We're not going to do that anymore. And when you don't do those anymore it does make the dominant society uncomfortable" (L22). Thus, the organization tries to acquire symbolic power and increase the value of existing assets, seeking to impose its worldview and frameworks to make sense and meaning of reality as most valuable (or at least valuable) to secure symbolic power.

The organization understands the privilege of authenticity, and they do not try to be like the oppressor. They are proud of the culture of their ancestors, and they channel the frustration from historical injustices to energy to keep struggling for social justice and emancipation. When some social groups begin to see themselves and their society from their perspective and not from the perspective and the narratives of the oppressors, they become aware of their potentialities (Freire, 2013). As one young leader said regarding the struggle for social justice at the organization: "[The organization] has taught me how to have that conversation, and taught me how to really be who I am and stand my ground. And to share with others my gift" (L8). In addition, as soon as the oppressed start decolonizing their minds about their inferiority and powerlessness, they contribute to decolonizing the minds of the oppressors because the assumptions and frameworks to make sense of the world of the oppressors start to be shaken as a consequence of the quasi-perfect correspondence between the objective order and the subjective principles of organization not being evident anymore, and it stops being taken for granted.

These processes taking place at the health clinic of construction of different knowledges, political practices, and social power that go beyond the Eurocentric leadership frameworks and social orders from modernity and colonialism started shaping the emancipatory project of an intercultural society. The intercultural society involves a thought, a praxis, a power, and a paradigm of and from the difference that goes beyond the dominant forms while at the same time challenging them (Walsh, 2007).

United by Our Differences: The Intercultural Society

The critical intercultural leadership process that emerges at the health clinic contributes to creating a particular organizational culture characterized by a prominent diversity that is valued. There is a "multiple" consciousness developed by the employees as a result of navigating between cultures daily that facilitates them to interact with different cultures in a more fluid and empathetic way and provides a common purpose at the organization that enhances a sense of belonging among the staff. Overall, their differences unite the organization's leaders, employees, and patients because they are aware that what all of them have in common are the differences and the capacity to be diverse, and it is from that cultural assumption at the core of the organizational culture that they develop values and beliefs that allow them to see differences in a positive light while reducing asymmetries of power between cultures. Therefore, it is not about homogenizing from a dominant culture but creating a permeable and fluid "culture of many cultures" where the common characteristic is the difference and the heterogeneity. An organizational culture does not necessarily require homogeneity to hold together the members of the organization (Feldman, 1991). Heterogenous and diverse members of an organization can develop a sense of belonging through the articulation of common frames of reference or the fact that everybody recognizes the same relevant issues. As noted before, the health clinic is a very diverse organization where there are people from 17 different tribes and seven nationalities corresponding to five different continents. Employees are aware of the diversity of the organization and also of the fact that what all of them have in common are their differences, which are valued and celebrated.

To make sense of an experience, a person creates a frame that explains the world and helps them act and behave in the world (Bruner, 1986). In terms of meaning-making, the most general tool in society to make meaning is culture, which, at the same time, is also the primary leadership process (Drath & Palus, 1994). Thus, through a framework of an intercultural society where diversity is valued and there are fewer asymmetries of power, employees start developing similar patterns of interpretation that give them a sense of belonging and contribute to developing a multiple consciousness to navigate comfortably between different cultures.

People need a goal, a purpose, meaning in what they do, and this is what unites employees, a common project and purpose represented through a framework of intercultural organization that ends up creating an intercultural organization/society. Frames and framing have material consequences because it is through them that people create the realities to which they must then respond (Fairhurst, 2011) and social structures and institutions are produced and reproduced to create a specific social order.

Valuing Different Cultures

Since negatively valuing difference is common to all ideologies of domination and oppression, such as racism, classism, or sexism, and is also key to reproducing asymmetries of power between cultures, to place positive value on what is different will contribute to processes of liberation and emancipation and reduce power differences. The intersectionality of social hierarchies that configured the colonial matrix of power inherited from modernity and colonialism could not be possible without assigning to the difference and diversity negative cultural value. Therefore, for the political struggle carried out at the organization to be effective, the organization needs to transform the categories of perception of the world in the struggle for recognition and appreciation, or, in essence, the struggle for symbolic power.

Concerning race, the first form of racism consisted of stressing the difference between accuser and victim (Memmi, 1996). However, revealing a characteristic differentiating two individuals or two groups does not, in and of itself, constitute a racist attitude. Rather, it depends in part on how difference is perceived. As a result of the asymmetries of power between cultures and valuing the difference negatively, the dominant culture is ignorant about other cultures because, as part of the privilege of belonging to the dominant culture, they do not need to know about different traditions and worldviews to survive. For example, one of the non-Native employees recognized the lack of knowledge about Native people: "One of the things about making myself more accustomed to the Native American culture is to acknowledge that I know nothing about them" (S4).

As a part of valuing and recognizing different cultures, the organization fosters and promotes cultural diversity by inviting employees to share, ask, and enhance curiosity for other ways of viewing the world, doing, and being. As one of the employees stated: "I think there's a willingness to learn. There's an open-mindedness. I mean there's respect. There's curiosity. There's acceptance. ... There is such value to life and to culture. There's so much to experience and learn, and to share" (S24). The organization is aware of being one of the most diverse places in the area, and they are proud of it and celebrate it. They go beyond multiculturalism, which tolerates the difference but does not value or celebrate it and is a process where asymmetries of power are maintained, relegating the rest of the cultures just to folklore. As one employee said: "It's not about tolerance, it needs to be like more about value. Tolerance isn't acceptable, that's all it is. It's not an understanding" (S1). Besides, following this idea, another employee stated: "I think that more than anything [the organization] shows that just by one example these other cultures that you don't necessarily know have a lot to offer and you want to respect them and learn more about them" (S4).

To be successful, the dominated need to have "the material and symbolic means of rejecting the definition of the real that is imposed on them through logical structures reproducing the social structures (i.e. the state of the power relations) and to lift the (institutionalized or internalized) censorships which it implies" (Bourdieu, 1977, p. 168). Thus, valuing difference and celebrating diversity are central in the struggle against a hegemonic culture based on the power to invisibilize, homogenize, and demonize.

Navigating Between Cultures to Develop a Multiple Consciousness

The organization is one of the most diverse places in the city, and employees and patients who enter the organization are obliged to navigate between different cultures daily. As one employee stated, "You have to be open to the different cultures because we have Vietnamese, we have

Russian, we have Caucasians, we have Blacks, we have Natives, and I think you have to be open to that" (S1).

When it comes to cultures at the organization, it is not only about different races and ethnicities but also about class and gender. As one of the employees said, "We try to relate to their ethnic or cultural backgrounds. Different socioeconomic backgrounds. We have homelessness, we have people with mental health issues and minorities. People who are impoverished" (S6). In terms of gender differences, one of the young leaders argued regarding a social and medical field dominated by men: "In the other places it's predominantly men, and here we have all women. And being that [Northwest city], again, is conservative, they had to fight a lot to be able to be allowed to enter the room, to be allowed to have a voice" (L8).

Individuals learn and carry out activities and competencies in a particular social space, which at the same time enable them to have interactions with other people in that social space. Additionally, it is from these particular social spaces where individuals and groups develop specific dispositions or inclinations toward certain responses. Thus, the particular social space that represents the health clinic as a diverse organization where individuals encounter and navigate between cultures daily contributes to developing among the employees a habitus that enacts the worldview of their employees through their practices. Staff at the organization are characterized by the relative ease with which they navigate between cultures and—although to a different degree depending on different groups—the development of a multiple consciousness to navigate between cultures in a fluid and almost unconscious way. As one of the founders stated: "I think the old days in a lot of Native language mix blooded people will call the interpreter. People that could explain both sides, and a lot of times I see that as my role" (L22).

Culture is seen as "a system of schemes of perception, expression and historically constituted and socially conditioned thinking" (Bourdieu, 1993, p. 233) that consecrates a social order and is achieved only when this system becomes natural (a habitus) after the objective structures of society are embodied in the categories of perception of individuals and groups of people. Thus, a culture of cultures, like the organization, requires a habitus where employees feel like a fish in water, where navigating between cultures and shifting from one cultural consciousness to another is seen as natural. One of the employees said, "I feel pretty comfortable with myself between the two cultures, and I try to be very conscious about other people's cultures. Even between people's cultures between medicines, like a naturopath versus Western medicine, versus Eastern medicine. … I think I do it naturally" (S1).

In terms of cultural assumptions, Argyris and Schön (1996) define them as "theories-in-use" that guide behavior and inform group members how to perceive, think, and feel. At the organization—since navigating and learning with and from other cultures is the best solution for providing a good service and fitting in the organization—this idea is eventually taken for granted and considered natural, becoming a basic assumption for the employees and becoming part of the core of the organizational culture.

Enhancing a Sense of Belonging Through a Common Purpose

Regardless of race, ethnicity, class, or gender, employees have a common goal, a common purpose that unites them to work together in a synergistic way: to help the patients. This purpose is what gives sense and is meaningful for employees at the organization, and it is also central to keeping them together as a group. As one of the employees stated regarding the patients, "We want to make sure that we can help them to do whatever they want, but we'll do a White, Yellow, Black, Red ... It doesn't matter; they all need help" (S18). Meaning-making enables the members of an organization to work together toward a common interpretation of reality, to provide the organizational activity with coherence and common direction (Ladkin, 2010).

Collective action in social movements and SMOs as a social construction with purpose and meaning that emerges from framing to legitimate the action (Melucci, 1995). Framing and action are interconnected, and both influence each other in the creation of a shared reality, a new social order. As one leader stated: "We all share the identity of the client or the patient. They're always our main concern. Without them we have no jobs. They are our number one priority and I think we all share that" (S1). A shared reality contributes to what Hofstede et al. (2010) describe as a "collective programming of the mind" (p. 5), an organizational culture that distinguishes the members of the organization from others. Besides, during the process of creating a particular organizational culture, the "moral circles" of culture that define criteria of inclusion and, therefore, of exclusion are broadened and become more inclusive, contributing to the creation of solidarity of class among nonhegemonic cultures that focus on shared identities of domination and oppression and their common position of subordination within the colonial matrix of power that characterizes today's postcolonial societies.

From that solidarity of class and shared reality that results from a common purpose and meaning, a sense of belonging is raised among the employees. For example, as one of the employees said regarding what the organization meant to her: "It's more of like a sense of family. I like that feeling. There's a familiar feeling" (S27). Feelings of group membership arise with the awareness of subconscious practices that people have in common (Bentley, 1991), or as Bourdieu (1990) argues, these shared practices arise from the habitus with which people identify because of the similarity to their practices. At the organization, the habitus of the employees generates practices that reinforce those same dispositions, and although they are not physically similar, they turn to each other as a result of similar conduct while avoiding those who seem to act differently.

However, as Barth (1976) states, even if ethnic groups establish boundaries among themselves in terms of ethnicity, nationality, class, and so on, these boundaries are still permeable because ethnicity is dynamic. At the organization, ethnicity is understood in terms similar to Poutignat (2008): as a system of organization, a principle to divide the social world that can change according to situations and historical periods. In other words, ethnic groups are not static or bearers of a culture, as an essentialist approach can suggest; they are social constructions that try to organize their social life and are subjected to constant change (Luna Penna, 2014). This is why the organization is not an essentialist project where one homogeneous culture is imposed upon the organization, but since ethnicity is dynamic and its boundaries are flexible, it represents a process of ethnogenesis that creates a system of organization, a culture of cultures where the common characteristics are their differences, and all employees are united by the common purpose of helping the patients.

Taylor and Whittier (1992) describe collective identity as three interrelated processes of (a) construction of group boundaries, (b) development of consciousness or interpretive frameworks that came up from the struggle, and (c) politicization of everyday life using symbols and under-taking actions. At the health clinic, the leadership work for developing a collective identity that unites them through a common purpose and their differences, focuses on organizing in terms of boundaries differentiating them from the dominant culture; interpretive frameworks identifying the interests of the organization; and the politicization of everyday life resisting and transforming the dominant system.

Emancipatory Doxa/Pluri-Doxa and Transformation: The Lines in the Sand

Since leadership is a process of transformation (Burns, 1978), mobilization of people (Heifetz & Sinder, 1988), and through which a particular social order is created and changed (Hosking & Morley, 1988), a critical intercultural leadership process is needed to be able to transform the current postcolonial society of domination and oppression and mobilize people to create an emancipatory social order. This particular approach of critical intercultural leadership is the leadership process that emerges at the organization and raises critical consciousness and unfolds ethnogenesis among employees, patients, and also hegemonic institutions of the city, providing them with new frameworks to make sense of the world and give meaning to their lives. According to Fairclough (1992), sense-making is political because meaning is political; and the organizational culture created at the health clinic through the implementation of different frameworks (e.g., framework of a postcolonial society that identifies the causes for the domination and oppression, framework of empowering through collective action, the framework for an intercultural society united by the differences, etc.) is complemented in a transversal way by a framework of an emancipatory doxa/pluri-doxa: a space where many doxas can fit.

Each habitus is differentiated from the others because there is a different range of possibilities of dispositions and practices influencing the individual or the group in each habitus (Bourdieu, 1998). In essence, for each habitus, some different limitations and constraints influence the possibilities of thinking and doing of a person or group. These limitations and constraints of what can be thought or said is what Bourdieu calls "doxa." However, these limitations when it comes to thinking and acting are not inexorable, and when there is either cultural contact or political and economic crises, doxa is questioned, emerging with a critique that brings what is indisputable into dispute, what is not formulated into formulation (Bourdieu, 1977).

Since the founders of the health clinic occupy a position of subordinated culture that goes beyond the Western canon, they have been able to keep an emancipatory critique that disputes the indisputable and formulates what has not been formulated. Thus, the critical intercultural leadership process that emerges at the organization broadens a narrow and exclusive doxa that reproduces the current system of domination and oppression in an effort to create a more inclusive space for thinking, doing, and being.

Doxa is more than common belief and domination because it also has the potential to give rise to common action and liberation (Bourdieu & Eagleton, 1992). Therefore, the leadership understands doxa as a field for struggle and seeks to broaden it by going beyond the hegemonic narratives and discourses to create an emancipatory doxa/pluri-doxa that will contribute to the creation of a new social order where diversity is valued and appreciated with fewer asymmetries of power. Doxa gives strength to the dominant discourse and is re-created through partisan groups of academics, media outlets, businessmen, and others who spread ideas and narratives that reinforce and contribute to the acceptance of the propositions of a system that is seen as an inexorable truth about the social world (Bourdieu, 1998).

Therefore, to initiate the struggle for cognitive and social justice, the organization decided to develop a critical consciousness, a project that transcends itself, an emancipatory doxa/pluri-doxa that will change the rules of the game, thinking what cannot be thought and formulating what cannot be formulated. It is a struggle for imposing ideas, narratives, and frameworks that reinforce and contribute to the challenge and dispute of the propositions of a system that is seen as natural and inexorable. "Radical new social movements seek to change the rules of the game, 'not just the distribution of relative advantages in a given organization.' Indeed, only by changing those rules can their ends be achieved" (Hunter, 1995, p. 331).

A broadened doxa contributes to building an intercultural society where different cultural and epistemic perspectives are valued and asymmetries of power between cultures are reduced. An emancipatory doxa/pluri-doxa:

- expands the limits and constraints of the hegemonic doxa with the inclusion of other ways of thinking and being
- designs a pluriversal world resulting from a true and efficient dialogue without big asymmetries of power between cultures and epistemologies
- constantly reviews the internalization of cultural assumptions that limit and constrain the possibilities of thinking and being

In other words, an emancipatory doxa/pluri-doxa offers stability to a culture, but since this "doxa of many doxas" is constantly reviewed to avoid the creation of cultural assumptions of superiority/inferiority, it is a fluid process without an end, making it better suited for embracing change and social transformation.

Resilience: Flexibility and Capacity to Adjust

One of the characteristics of the critical intercultural leadership process that emerges at the organization is resilience to adjust to external and internal challenges. *Organizational culture* is a pattern of shared basic assumptions that a group learns as it efficiently solves external adaptation and internal integration problems (Schein, 2010). Thus, adjusting is central to solving problems of external adaptation and internal integration, which will contribute to configuring shared assumptions that will create an organizational culture.

Although contemporary researchers, educators, and social service providers became familiar with the concept of cultural resilience by the end of the 1990s, the concept has been present in Native American communities for centuries (Heavy Runner & Morris, 1997). According to Heavy Runner and Morris (1997), "Resilience is not new in our people; it is a concept that has been taught for centuries. The word is new but the meaning is old" (p. 28). As one of the founders of the organization stated regarding the relationship between resilience and Native people: "It's like Native Americans or other Indigenous people. It's like, 'We're going to survive, we're going to make the best of it and we're not going to whine about it'" (L33).

For Greene and Conrad (2002), resilience is a static personal quality and a continuous process developed through interaction between people and their environment. It is a positive emotion central to upholding adjustment (Cheung & Yue, 2013). One of the founders explained how she had to adjust throughout the time to different challenges while working at the health clinic:

> I personally worked for 11 years with no benefits, with no healthcare, no savings or 401(k)s. So now here I am [mature age]. I look at my 401(k) on my retirement and there's this over a decade gap of no retirement. But, you know, I was willing to do that. (L22)

At the core idea of resilience theory is the ability to adjust and thrive regardless of the presence of a stressful environment, and since its foundation, the organization has been obliged to adjust to external challenges and internal problems to be successful in providing health services, celebrating and resisting with their culture, and struggling for cognitive and social justice. Resilience factors can be considered as either external or internal (Brownlee et al., 2013). The external factors include peers, family, school, and community, whereas the internal ones encompass such personal qualities as empowerment, self-control, self-efficacy, and personal strengths. At the organization, a strong focus on community and family on one side and a process of empowerment to take control of reality through collective action on the other has been central to developing resilience among employees and patients and improving their capacity to adjust. As one of the founders remembered regarding all the challenges and sacrifices they had to make since the organization's foundation: "Most of the time I never felt tired and I think the other people involved did not feel tired or exhausted or burned out. It was like higher powered. It's like energy from a spiritual source that you are supposed to do this" (L22).

One characteristic of the employees that contributes to developing their capacity of resilience and adjustment is humor. At the organization, jokes and laughter are used as a mechanism to release stress and cope with the challenges and frustrations that they face daily. As one of the young leaders said:

> As a practitioner, you're working in different capacities with these patients and these families, and you have to find an outlet to let that go and find some sort of release. And we all, collectively as a team, find ways to just laugh and have fun, because if you did that every day and didn't laugh, your heart would be really heavy all time. You have to release that. (L8)

Resilience prevents depression and involves beliefs, practices, and, eventually, conditions for problem solving and overcoming difficulties (Lee et al., 2007). In addition, it is a precursor to adjustment that tends to contribute to self-esteem, life satisfaction, existential well-being, mental health, and resisting distress. In other words, any long-term struggle for social justice and cultural resistance needs mechanisms that contribute to their sustainability. At the organization, developing resilience and the capacity to adjust to different challenges and use humor as a coping mechanism for mental health are essential for carrying out their emancipatory project that aims to be successful in the long term.

Embracing Change and Transformation

The health clinic, as an emancipatory endeavor, is about change and transformation of the current postcolonial social order, but the organization also understands reality as change, a reality that is constantly moving and being transformed instead of being static and inexorable. The coexistence of the present system with its negation represents two dimensions, which in terms of culture would be expressed in the role of culture as a critique of the social order (Marcuse, 1991). Thus, this critique is needed to unfold any social change because the two dimensions create a space between what can be thought and what exists, and it is within this space where critical thinking can emerge.

As Marcuse (1991) argues, "Contemporary society seems to be capable of containing social change—qualitative change which would establish essentially different institutions, a new direction of the productive process, new modes of human existence" (p. xliv). However, the health clinic, through an organizational culture that raises critical consciousness and unfolds ethnogenesis, aims to enhance social change by providing frameworks for sense- and meaning-making that transform and change the current social order while navigating the uncertainty and ambiguity that any process of change implies. As one of the employees explained: "We never just shoot for the status quo, which I see a lot in Native culture. … And our leadership will not let us be status quo. It's like we're always going to be a step above. That's where we're aiming. We're not aiming for the bottom tier" (S10).

According to Weick et al. (2005), a cue is an observation, what people particularly notice in an organization, and when people notice certain cues is when the process of sense-making begins. In addition, there are two main types of cues that normally contribute to initiating sense-making in organizations: ambiguity and uncertainty. While the former means that experiences and situations are equivocal, the latter refers to the inability to predict the consequences of the actions (Weick, 1995). Thus, when a person is faced with either ambiguity or uncertainty, the act of noticing emerges, and it initiates the process of sense-making. This sense-making process contains three main elements: a cue, a frame, and a connection. It is when an individual can make a connection between a cue and a frame that meaning is created (Weick, 1995).

In terms of frames, they are useful to situate, perceive, identify, and label what is happening around a person and enable people to make interpretations, understand, and respond to events. In other words, frames provide a structure of assumptions, rules, and boundaries that guide the process of sense-making (Luscher & Lewis, 2008). When it comes to frame transformation, this process unfolds when new concepts and values replace old ones; old meanings, symbols, and artifacts are discarded; and erroneous beliefs and misframings are addressed (Taylor, 2000). In essence, frame transformation is part of the process of ethnogenesis and implies a general reframing of the main issues regarding a social movement. This process is key to the success and sustainability of social movements because "numerous social movements have risen and fallen partly as a result of atrophy and lack of reflexivity" (Pellow & Brehm, 2015, p. 187). At the organization, change and transformation are experienced constantly and are part of a way of viewing the world and the necessity to adjust to different challenges before and since their foundation. This process of rethinking and change is not easy, because it involves uncertainty and ambiguity, and according to one of the young leaders, arguments and discussions often occur within the organization: "This building wasn't built in quiet rooms. There was shouting. There was yelling … and when you want to really impact change, affect change, and really help people, it's not a quiet process" (L8).

For the modern human being, ambiguity means chaos and anarchy, and the framework imposed with modernity seeks for stability and order through binary classifications. The project of modernity that aims to control and dominate ambiguity and heterogeneity is unachievable because ambiguity constantly emerges, producing more ambiguity that cannot be classified (Bauman, 1991). Conversely, the critical intercultural leadership process at the organization, as an emancipatory endeavor, embraces change, transformation, and ambiguity because this critical approach understands leadership effectiveness with versatile and agile practices that accept uncertainty, unpredictability, and even paradox as part of the real world. The essence of leadership remains in organizational systems that thrive on paradox wherein leaders need to embrace tensions and contradictions (Storey & Salaman, 2009). Besides, the organization is one of the most diverse and heterogeneous places in the city, with many different cultures working together with a common purpose going beyond the binary social order of modernity, and conceptualizes the boundaries of their organizational culture as permeable and fluid instead of static, allowing intercultural exchange and cultural transformation to unfold.

Leadership and Organization as Processes

A leadership approach that seeks change and transformation while embracing uncertainty and ambiguity is a perspective that views leadership as a process and, when it comes to creating an organization and a culture, designs flexible and fluid structures. Culture is a dynamic phenomenon that is not static. It flows because culture is constantly created, re-created, and even deconstructed by our interactions with others. According to Schein (2010), "When we are influential in shaping the behavior and values of others, we think of that as 'leadership' and creates the conditions for new culture formation" (p. 3). However, leadership is a broader phenomenon that goes beyond a conceptualization of positional leadership because "the formal scheme of an organization will always be different from the way in which the organization itself operates, that is, through a number of interpersonal relations, which are absent from a formal scheme" (De Giosa, 2009, p. 180).

Thus, leadership is a complex web of people and institutions working toward achieving goals that influence other people, structures, institutions, cultures, and the environment and are also shaped by all those elements that configure the deep and holistic phenomenon of leadership. As one of the young leaders stated when describing the depth and complexity of the leadership:

> There's a lot of depth. It looks superficial on the outside, but there's a lot of depth. It looks like a clear, clean water on top of the lake but then there's so much movement going on under. You're not seeing it, but it's happening and it's awesome. (L2)

Therefore, what leaders and supporters do is to impulse a trend, to point out a direction, articulating and implementing frameworks that aim to transform a social order of domination and that at the same time provides the organization with stability within the uncertainty and ambiguity of reality. As Elias (2000) argues, the relations between individuals regarding their actions, plans, and purposes cannot be foreseen just because multiple combinations cannot be calculated. For example, one of the young leaders said regarding the consistent political changes that affect the organization: "You're always keeping your eye on that to make sure the policy changes. What's plan A, B and C for the viability and sustainability of building as a whole" (L8). Another argued, in terms of fluid and flexible organizational structures: "Here there's a structure, but it's not as strict as corporations would like it. We take on the title like a corporation, but I feel like it's fluid, like horizontal" (L2).

Within that context of change, uncertainty, and ambiguity, the frameworks that the leadership designs to make sense and give meaning to their work are fluid and flexible, same as the organizational structures developed to cope and adjust with external uncertainties and turbulences. As one of the employees argued: "There's always things in flux, like plans. And I think in order to be successful here you definitely need to be able to adapt. That's probably one of the key elements of success here, I think is adaptability" (S6).

Moreover, understanding leadership and organization as processes involves adjusting to new challenges and changes in society and reviewing an organizational culture that aims to liberate and emancipate. The oppressed "must not, in seeking to regain their humanity (which is a way to create it), become in turn oppressors of the oppressors, but rather restorers of the humanity of both" (Freire, 2012, p. 44). This is the task of the oppressed: to seek their liberation and the liberation of the oppressors in a constant critical process of reflecting and questioning. Because "only power that springs from the weakness of the oppressed will be sufficiently strong to free both" (Freire, 2012, p. 44).

Drawing Lines in the Sand

Although the critical intercultural leadership process that emerges at the organization is characterized by seeking change and transformation along with fluid and flexible organizational structures that cope and adjust better to external challenges of adaptation and internal issues of integration, when it comes to disputes or reformulating the emancipatory doxa/pluri-doxa, the leadership of the organization draws a line in the sand, and there is no possibility of change or flexibility. Like democracy, which can be defined as deliberation of everything but deliberation in itself, because deliberation is the only path that guarantees democracy, an emancipatory doxa/pluri-doxa implies constantly broadening the space for thinking, doing, and being. We must seek to be more inclusive and value other cultures and epistemologies but cannot accept any perspective resulting from modernity and its darker side, colonialism, that could jeopardize the emancipatory project.

Although leaders cannot control events or the whole leadership process, they can control the context through which events are seen through the process of framing. For example, one of the founders said regarding employees who arrive to the health clinic bringing Western perspectives of organization and medicine: "I don't care what you do at [Northwest city's] Mental Health. I don't care what you did at Sacred Heart Hospital. You're at [the organization] now. But that's part of the colonization, too" (L22). To successfully challenge doxa, subordinated cultures need to have material and symbolic means of rejecting the hegemonic definition of what is real. When it comes to reproducing an emancipatory doxa/pluri-doxa at the organization, what is needed is to reject that definition of the real that is imposed through the hegemonic doxa. At the same time, they must consolidate stable objective structures and reproduce them in the employees' dispositions until they internalize them and see the new social order as self-evident and natural. For example, one of the young leaders shared their response when employees at the organization try to implement external structures and practices different than the ones that characterize the organization: "That's a Western model, can we have this conversation again?' Honestly, I feel like I have the Western concept model or White privilege model or the White male privileged discussion one to five times a week" (L2). Thus, when it comes to certain concepts, ideas, or philosophies at the core of the organizational culture, there is no discussion. They cannot be disputed or reformulated, and the leadership of the organization draws a line in the sand to preserve the emancipatory project from being co-opted or (re)colonized. According to one of the leaders regarding these lines in the sand that cannot be trespassed: "I think she's [founder and CEO] very relationally based. If she gets along with you, life is good. If she doesn't get along with you, life is not good. Some of the people that have worked here haven't gotten along with her and they disappear" (S25).

Delegates or leaders base universal value on themselves and "monopolize the notions of God, Truth, Wisdom, People, Message, Freedom, etc. They make them synonyms. What of? Of themselves. 'I am the Truth.'" (Bourdieu, 1991, p. 210). Thus, they become sacred and establish a division between them and ordinary people that can create tensions when other leaders struggle for power or disagree with certain aspects of the project. Additionally, with organizations where the leadership is very personalized, if the environment changes and those assumptions that used to work start to fail, the organization will need to change part of its culture, which will be extremely difficult due to how founders and leaders have been embedding and transmitting their assumptions to the different members of the organization (Schein, 2010). As one of the leaders explained:

> I look at this organization and say it's really built on one person's vision and one person having the strength to be able to make things happen and surrounding herself with other people that makes it happen and controlling that entirely and there's pros and cons to that. (S25)

Notwithstanding the lines in the sand, the emancipatory doxa/pluri-doxa is what gives strength to the project, and for almost 30 years, the frameworks, narratives, and values of the habitus suggested by the leaders have been successful and—despite some resistances—have made sense for most of the employees of the organization who have supported their leaders for the last 3 decades.

Today, while for certain leaders and supporters at the organization the emancipatory doxa/ pluri-doxa is embedded and internalized in their mental structures and affect their dispositions and practices, other members of the organization are still navigating between the hegemonic and emancipatory doxas and cultural frameworks. However, ambiguity, paradox, and in particular heterogeneity of thinking, doing, and being is what characterizes culture in general and the organizational culture of the health clinic in particular. Above all, what unites all employees of the organization are their differences and a common purpose: to help the patients, the invisibilized, the impoverished, the demonized.

The organization is a health clinic that provides high-quality services for the most vulnerable sectors of society in the area, but beyond the agency and the business, the organization can be considered an emancipatory endeavor that aims to struggle for social justice and cultural resistance while uniting different subordinated cultures to establish a dialogue with fewer asymmetries of power with the hegemonic culture and institutions that will end up in the construction of a better world for all. As one young leader summarized:

> I think the future will be a lot better. I just think any time something like that happens there's a cultural bonding between different communities where they kind of come together and bridge together. Because if they don't, then the oppressor wins, and we're just not going to let that happen. (L8)

The challenge is immense, but building an intercultural world of cognitive and social justice where different worldviews can coexist and the different ways of thinking and being are valued cannot wait anymore.

Conclusion

Social change leadership requires a combination of theory and action. Thus, it is key to offer spaces for reflection where cognitive deconstruction and reconstruction can be considered and platforms for action where critical consciousness and empowerment raise to the highest levels can be created. Therefore, the leadership work unfolded in these spaces is based on designing frameworks for sense- and meaning-making, organizing collective actions for empowerment and identity development, and creating new structures for a more inclusive organizational culture and social order. It is a leadership process of world-making. Throughout this process, power in general and symbolic power in particular will be critical since building power starts with changing the relationships established by the dominant social order regarding systems of classification and labels that people (both oppressors and oppressed) end up with internalizing and reproducing. Eventually, this power can be leveraged for social change.

Discussion Questions

1. How can an inclusive organizational culture or social order where everyone feels that they belong be created?
2. Why is designing sense- and meaning-making frameworks critical for social change leadership?
3. How can you apply this critical intercultural leadership process to another organization that you know?

References

Arendt, H. (1970). *On violence*. Penguin.

Barth, F. (1976). *Los grupos étnicos y sus fronteras: La organización social de las diferencias culturales*. Fondo de cultura económica.

Bauman, Z. (1991). *Modernity and ambivalence*. Polity Press.

Bentley, G. C. (1991). Response to Yelvington. *Comparative Studies in Society and History, 33*(1), 169–175.

Bonilla-Silva, E. (1996). Rethinking racism: Toward a structural interpretation. *American Sociological Review, 62*(3), 465–480.

Bourdieu, P. (1977). *Outline of a theory of practice*. Cambridge University Press.

Bourdieu, P. (1984). *Distinction: A social critique of the judgment of taste*. Harvard University Press.

Bourdieu, P. (1989). Social space and symbolic power. *Sociological Theory, 7*(1), 14–25.

Bourdieu, P. (1990). *The logic of practice*. Stanford University Press.

Bourdieu, P. (Ed.). (1991). *Language and symbolic power*. Harvard University Press.

Bourdieu, P. (1993). *The field of cultural production*. Columbia University Press.

Bourdieu, P. (1994). Rethinking the state: Genesis and structure of the bureaucratic field. *Sociological Theory, 12*(1), 1–18.

Bourdieu, P. (1998). Neo-liberalism, the utopia (becoming a reality) of unlimited exploitation. In P. Bourdieu (Ed.), *Acts of resistance: Against the tyranny of the market* (pp. 94–105). The New Press.

Bourdieu, P., & Eagleton, T. (1992). Doxa and the common life. *New Left Review, 191*, 111–121.

Bourdieu, P., & Wacquant, L. (1996). *An invitation to reflexive sociology*. Polity.

Brownlee, K., Rawana, J., Franks, J., Harper, J., Bajwa, J., O'Brien, E., & Clarkson, A. (2013). A systematic review of strengths and resilience outcome literature relevant to children and adolescents. *Children and Adolescents Social Work Journal, 30*(5), 435–459.

Bruner, J. (1986). *Actual minds, possible worlds*. Harvard University Press.

Burns, J. M. (1978). *Leadership*. Harper and Row.

Chopra, R. (2003). Neoliberalism as doxa: Bourdieu's theory of the state and the contemporary Indian discourse on globalization and liberalization. *Journal of Cultural Studies, 17*(3–4), 419–444.

Collins, R. (1990). Stratification, emotional energy and the transient emotions. In T. D. Kemper (Ed.), Research agendas in the sociology of emotions (pp. 27–57). State Universtiy of New York Press.

De Giosa, V. (2009). The cultural management of leadership. *Anales de Estudios Económicos y Empresariales, 19*(1), 167–191.

Drath, W. H., & Palus, C. J. (1994). *Making common sense: Leadership as meaningmaking in a community of practice*. Center for Creative Leadership.

Elias, N. (2000). *The civilizing process*. Blackwell.

Fairclough, N. (1992). *Discourse and social change*. Blackwell.

Fairhurst, G. T. (2011). *The power of framing: Creating the language of leadership*. Jossey-Bass.

Fantasia, R., & Hirsch, E. L. (1995). Culture in rebellion: The appropriation and transformation of the veil in the Algerian revolution. In H. Johnston & B. Klandermans (Eds.), *Social movements and culture* (pp. 114–159). University of Minnesota Press.

Federici, S. (2016). No puedes resistir a la opresión si no tienes confianza en que otros lo harán contigo. *Desinformémonos*. Retrieved September 1, 2021 from https://desinformemonos.org/

no-puedes-resistir-a-la-opresion-si-no-tienes-confianza-en-que-otros-lo-haran-contigo-silvia-federici/

Feldman, M. (1991). The meanings of ambiguity: Learning from stories and metaphors. In P. Frost, L. Moore, M. Louis, C. Lundberg, & J. Martin (Eds.), *Reframing organizational culture* (pp. 145–156). Sage.

Fine, G. A. (1995). Public narration and group culture: Discerning discourse in social movements. In H. Johnston & B. Klandermans (Eds.), *Social movements and culture* (pp. 127–143). University of Minnesota Press.

Flacks, R. (1995). Think globally, act politically: Some notes toward new movement strategy. In M. Darnovsky, B. Epstein, & R. Flacks (Eds.), *Cultural politics and social movements* (pp. 251–263). Temple University Press.

Freire, P. (2012). *Pedagogy of the oppressed*. Bloomsbury.

Freire, P. (2013). *Education for critical consciousness*. Bloomsbury.

Gamson, W. A. (1992). The social psychology of collective action. In A. Morris & C. McClurg Mueller (Eds.), *Frontiers in social movement theory* (pp. 53–76). Yale University Press.

Gramsci, A. (1970). *Antología*. Siglo XXI.

Greene, R., & Conrad, N. (2002). Basic assumptions and terms. In R. Greene (Ed.), *Resiliency: An integrated approach to practice, policy, and research* (pp. 1–27). National Association of Social Workers Press.

Heavy Runner, I., & Morris, J. S. (1997). Traditional Native culture and resilience. *Research and Practice, 5*(1), 28–33.

Heifetz, R. A., & Sinder, R. M. (1988). Political leadership: Managing the public's problem solving. In R. B. Reich (Ed.), *The power of public ideas* (pp. 179–203). Ballinger.

Hofstede, G., Hofstede, G. J., & Minkov, M. (2010). *Cultures and organizations: Software of the mind*. McGraw Hill.

Horkheimer, M., & Adorno, T. (1996). *Dialectic of enlightenment*. Continuum.

Hosking, D. M., & Morley, I. E. (1988). The skills of leadership. In J. G. Hunt, B. R. Baliga, H. P. Dachler, & C. A. Schriesheim (Eds.), *Emerging leadership vistas* (pp. 89–106). Lexington Books.

Hunter, A. (1995). Rethinking revolution in light of the new social movements. In M. Darnovsky, B. Epstein, & R. Flacks (Eds.), *Cultural politics and social movements* (pp. 320–343). Temple University Press.

Jenson, J. (1995). What's in a name? Nationalist movements and public discourse. In H. Johnston & B. Klandermans (Eds.), *Social movements and culture* (pp. 107–126). University of Minnesota Press.

Klandermans, B. (1992). The social construction of protest and multiorganizational fields. In A. Morris & C. McClurg Mueller (Eds.), *Frontiers in social movement theory* (pp. 77–103). Yale University Press.

Ladkin, D. (2010). *Rethinking leadership: A new look at old leadership questions*. Edward Elgar.

Lederach, J. P. (2005). *The moral imagination: The art and soul of building peace*. Oxford University Press.

Lee, T., Shek, D., & Kwong, W. (2007). Chinese approaches to understanding and building resilience in at-risk children and adolescents. *Child and Adolescent Psychiatric Clinics of North America, 16*(2), 377–392.

Luna Penna, G. (2014). Trayectoria crítica del concepto de entnogénesis. *Logos: Revista de Lingüística, Filosofía y Literatura, 24*(2), 167–179.

Luscher, L. S., & Lewis, M. W. (2008). Organizational change and managerial sensemaking: Working through paradox. *Academy of Management Journal, 51*(2), 221–240.

Maldonado-Torres, N. (2008). *Against war.* Duke University Press.

Marcuse, H. (1991). *One-dimensional man.* Beacon Press.

Melucci, A. (1995). The process of collective identity. In H. Johnston & B. Klandermans (Eds.), *Social movements and culture* (pp. 41–63). University of Minnesota Press.

Memmi, A. (1996). Assigning value to difference. In S. P. Rothenberg (Ed.), *Beyond borders: Thinking critically about global issues* (pp. 173–179). Worth Publishers.

Navarro, V. (2016, October 18). De lo que no se informa y/o se conoce sobre las elecciones en EEUU. Diario Público. Retrieved September 1, 2021, from http://blogs.publico.es/vicenc-navarro/2016/10/18/de-lo-que-no-se-informa-yo-se-conocesobre-las-elecciones-en-eeuu/

Pellow, N. P., & Brehm, H. N. (2015). From the new ecological paradigm to total liberation: The emergence of a social movement frame. *The Sociological Quarterly, 56*(1), 185–212.

Poutignat, P., & Streiff-Fénart, J. (2008). *Théories de l'ethnicité.* Presses universitaires de France.

Quijano, A. (2010). Coloniality and modernity/rationality. In W. Mignolo, & A. Escobar (Eds.), *Globalization and the decolonial option* (pp. 22–32). Routledge.

Rabow, J., Berkman, S. L., & Kessler, R. (1983). The culture of poverty and learned helplessness: A social psychological perspective. *Sociological Inquiry, 53*(4), 419–434.

Santos, B. de S. (2014). *Epistemologies of the South: Justice against Epistemicide.* Paradigm Publishers.

Schein, E. (2010). *Organizational culture and leadership* (4th ed.). Jossey-Bass.

Storey, J., & Salaman, G. (2009). *Managerial dilemmas.* John Wiley.

Strinati, D. (1995). *An introduction to theories of popular culture.* Routledge.

Taylor, D. (2000). The rise of the environmental justice paradigm: Injustice framing and the social construction of environmental discourses. *American Behavioral Scientist, 43*(4), 508–580.

Taylor, V., & Whittier, N. (1995). Analytical approaches to social movement culture: The culture of the women's movement. In H. Johnston, & B. Klandermans (Eds.), *Social movements and culture* (pp. 163–187). University of Minnesota Press.

Urban Indian Health Commission. (2007). *Invisible tribes: Urban Indians and their health in a changing world.* https://www2.census.gov/cac/nac/meetings/2015-10-13/invisible-tribes.pdf

Walsh, C. (2007). Interculturalidad y colonialidad del poder: Un pensamiento y posicionamiento otro desde la diferencia colonial. In S. Castro-Gómez, & R. Grosfoguel (Eds.), *El giro decolonial: Reflexiones para una diversidad epistémica más allá del capitalismo* (pp. 47–62). Siglo del Hombre.

Weick, K. (1995). *Sensemaking in organizations.* Sage.

Weick, K. E., Sutcliffe, K. M., & Obstfeld, D. (2005). Organizing and the process of sensemaking. *Organization Science, 16*(4), 409–421.

Wuthnow, R. (1989). *Communities of discourses: Ideology and social structure in the reformation, the Enlightenment, and European socialism.* Harvard University Press.

Young (2011). *Justice and the politics of difference.* Princeton University Press.

Conclusions and Recommendations

Objectives

In this chapter, I discuss the major findings and conclusions drawn from my research and suggest some recommendations to apply these conclusions for policy and practice from a perspective of a model of critical intercultural leadership process. Finally, I culminate with a reflection on my study and a note of intentionality.

The conclusions of my study follow the findings from Chapter 5 and therefore address four areas:

- Making visible the invisible: the sanctuary
- We struggle, therefore I am: the platform
- United by our differences: the intercultural society
- Emancipatory doxa/pluri-doxa and transformation: the lines in the sand

Making Visible the Invisible: The Sanctuary

The first finding of this mini-ethnographic case study is the necessity of making visible the invisible. Within the context of a postcolonial world, the health clinic makes visible the invisible by denouncing a situation of domination and oppression while debunking myths and stereotypes of the hegemonic culture that portray Native people as primitive or inferior. Besides, when the health clinic was founded, it also created a safe space and a sanctuary for critical reflection for Native people and other subordinated cultures in the area.

A conclusion to be drawn from this finding is the need to deconstruct dominant cultural assumptions and frameworks that make other perspectives invisible or demonize what is different. Therefore, creating a society with cognitive and social justice can only be accomplished in broadening what can be thought by reflecting about and challenging hegemonic cultural assumptions resulting from modernity and its darker side, colonialism, and bringing attention to make visible other projects, perspectives, and epistemologies. In this regard, it also may be concluded that any struggle for social justice that is not brought about from the decolonization of the minds and the deconstruction of hegemonic cultural assumptions and frameworks will not be effective or complete, because, eventually, the struggle will end up reproducing the same mechanisms of domination and oppression embedded in our minds by the colonial narrative of modernity.

A further and related conclusion that can be drawn is that the challenging of the dominant system cannot be carried out within the system and with the tools that this system provides to be "challenged." This challenge would represent a position of heterodoxy that the system can accept because it does not contribute to its transformation and all these heterodox processes will be eventually co-opted by the system and either neutralized or deactivated, contributing to reinforcing the status quo. Thus, it is essential to create alternative spaces that, although still within the system, can preserve enough autonomy to challenge the hegemonic cultural assumptions and imaginaries and to create new emancipatory mental frameworks and social structures.

We Struggle, Therefore I Am: The Platform

The second finding suggests that "we struggle, therefore I am." The organization represents a platform for action, and it is at this platform where critical consciousness raises to its highest stages through the struggle. Additionally, the platform and the struggle are central to balance asymmetries of power based on the monopoly of the hegemonic culture to control and impose cultural assumptions that place negative value on difference. It is within the struggle when the oppressed decolonize their minds about the superior-inferior divide and contribute to decolonizing the minds of the oppressors because their assumptions and frameworks to make sense of the world start to be shaken as a consequence that the quasi-perfect correspondence between the objective order and the subjective principles of organization is not evident anymore and stops being taken for granted. From there, the oppressed will start to educate hegemonic institutions with the aim of transforming the social structures that reproduce the system and beginning to create emancipatory ones.

A conclusion that can be drawn from this finding is that the phenomenon of critical consciousness has different stages, and it is only through the struggle and praxis that the highest stages can be reached. In other words, the theory is needed to contribute to raising critical consciousness because it allows one to understand the interconnection of the different elements of a system of domination and oppression that hinders the potential and capabilities of millions of human beings daily. However, without praxis, the critical consciousness will not raise to its highest levels, and when it comes to critical consciousness, it needs to be toward something and requires a practical application; otherwise, it is useless.

A related conclusion is that there is a correspondence between the lack of critical consciousness and perceptions and feelings of powerlessness and learned helplessness that facilitates manipulation and exploitation, perpetuating a paternalist system that avoids real change and transformation. Conversely, there is a connection between raising critical consciousness and empowerment through collective action because the oppressed do not feel inferior anymore and contribute to liberating the oppressor by challenging cultural assumptions and mental frameworks. In today's postcolonial societies with large asymmetries of power between cultures, a balance of the relations of power is needed to build communities of cognitive and social justice. However, the accumulation of power in itself as the hegemonic culture perpetuates it is not the solution, because it contributes to develop a fetishism for power that reproduces the same system of domination and oppression, with the only difference being that the subjects at the top of the social hierarchy have changed. A critical intercultural struggle for emancipation sees power as a means for an end that is balancing asymmetries of power to have an intercultural dialogue with horizontal conditions, not an end in itself that seeks to be in control, impose another monologue, and become a new dominant hegemony.

United by Our Differences: The Intercultural Society

The third finding presents the topic of being united by our differences. The organization provides a framework of social order that contributes to the unfolding of a class consciousness within the organization that unites employees and patients through differences, valuing diversity, reducing asymmetries of power, struggling for a common purpose, and enhancing a sense of belonging that eventually configures an intercultural society.

A conclusion to be drawn from this finding is that what is inherent to all human beings is the capacity of every individual and social group to be diverse. This diversity and these differences can be understood as what we all have in common as opposed to viewing culture as being the same for all people. The integrative view of culture that looks for similarities contributes to homogenization and minimization of differences and does not understand that culture is a fluid and fragmented phenomenon that tends toward heterogeneity and diversity, just as nature does. Thus, an organization, society, or country can be united by their differences, and culture and ethnicity can be seen as a system of organization where every person has the right to be different while sharing the same rights and common purposes.

Emancipatory Doxa/Pluri-Doxa and Transformation: The Lines in the Sand

The fourth finding focuses on an emancipatory doxa/pluri-doxa. The critical intercultural leadership process within the sanctuary, the platform, and the intercultural organization establishes a strong core of cultural assumptions, values, and beliefs regarding the emancipatory and decolonial project that are like lines in the sand that shape and give stability to the culture of the organization. Among the main characteristics of the organizational culture of the health clinic, there is a willingness to be flexible and adjust to external and internal challenges and the ability to understand change and transformation, which results in the design of fluid and flexible organizational/social structures.

The primary conclusion drawn from this finding is that doxa is more than homogenization, passivity, and domination because it can also be understood as heterogeneity, action, and liberation. Although doxa represents a limit and constraint to what can be disputed or formulated, at the same time, it is necessary to provide stability and sustainability to any culture, framework, or project. More specifically, in a context of domination and oppression, any emancipatory project needs a doxa that establishes limits that protect the project from the being co-opted and neutralized by the hegemonic system.

A related conclusion is that in a context of globalization where the world is getting smaller, changes and uncertainty are more visible than ever, new technologic advances appear and disappear faster than a human's capacity to assimilate and manage them, and where trying to control every element of a process seems almost impossible, the ability to embrace change and complexity is necessary in order to understand the phenomenon of leadership as a process that points out a direction and controls the context but not the outcome. A further and related conclusion connected with the idea of leadership as a process is the concept of organizations as a process. Organizations that develop fluid and flexible organizational structures (physical and relational) that configure more horizontal designs and distribute power for decision-making while at the same time can maintaining certain hierarchy are better able to adjust to a world that is rapidly changing.

Recommendations

Based on the findings, analysis, and conclusions of my study, I offer the following recommendations from a theoretical perspective of critical intercultural leadership process for social movement organizations (SMOs), educational institutions, political administrations, organizations and corporations, and for further research. These recommendations are intended to be applied as both policy and practice for these SMOs, institutions, administrations, and corporations.

Social Movement Organizations

Among possibilities for implementing a critical intercultural leadership process, SMOs could:

- Develop strategies and campaigns to make visible the invisible, bringing attention to their cause, and gaining recognition in the field of political struggle to be able to participate in the design of political agendas.
- Implement a process of challenging the hegemonic culture and its assumptions and imaginaries as a system of domination and control regardless of the cause of every particular SMO struggling for social justice. In essence, without cognitive justice, there is no social justice.
- Consider their processes of struggle from a perspective of decolonizing mental and social structures of both the oppressed and the oppressors as essential for any struggle for cognitive and social justice. Only focusing on decolonizing the external will not be effective, because the process also needs to be implemented at an internal level.
- Rethink the struggle within the system and use the tools provided by the system. Only an alternative and autonomous project carried out outside of the system (at least at a mental level by implementing other logics) and thought from the difference can be truly emancipatory.

- Review paternalistic approaches that are not addressing the real causes of the system of domination and oppression that needs to be transformed. Although paternalism and assistentialism can be useful in a temporal way and as a complementary parallel process of deep transformation, on their own they will never be able to transform any single structure of society and will reinforce the status quo of domination and oppression.
- Design frameworks of collective action that make sense and are meaningful to mobilize people while empowering them, seeking to transform society. In a postcolonial world where human beings are used as means and not ends in themselves, people need frameworks that make sense and give meaning to their lives.
- Consider balancing asymmetries of power between cultures as central for any struggle; otherwise, there is no possibility of intercultural dialogue, just a monologue of the hegemonic culture. However, it is essential to understand power as a means for social justice and not an end in and of itself, because the accumulation of power can result in changing the subjects at the top of the social hierarchy but not the hierarchy itself, which is the root of the system of domination and oppression.
- Reflect on developing transversal social movements that go beyond identity politics based on differences that divide the subordinated social groups, diluting their power and real capacity to challenge the system as a whole oppressed class.
- Be aware that in a context of domination and oppression, it is essential to design a framework that, although inclusive and horizontal, establishes limits that protect the struggle from being co-opted and neutralized by the system.

Educational Institutions

Educational institutions could:

- Review academic programs, courses, and syllabi to broaden the perspectives offered, including other worldviews and epistemologies that go beyond the Western canon.
- Acknowledge the need to decolonize minds and structures in the field of education designed from a perspective resulting from Modernity and colonialism that is embedded in dispositions and reproduced through practices daily.
- Consider culture as fragmentation and diversity when it comes to design and shape the organizational culture of an institution to be more inclusive and appreciative of the difference. Besides, it is essential to value diversity at every decision-making level and not limit diversity to folklore. In other words, culture is more than food, dances, and costumes; culture is also politics and economics. It is a social order and a field for struggle.
- Develop projects for action and praxis that complement philosophy and theory to both raise the critical consciousness of the students to their highest levels and empower them through frameworks of collective action to take control of reality and believe in the transformation of an unfair system. According to the Nasa tribe in Colombia, all action without the word is blind, and all word without action is empty.
- Rethink the policy of creating multicultural centers as safe spaces for diversity that eventually can result in ghettos of marginalization and isolation. In essence, safe spaces

and sanctuaries for diverse students are needed but should be complemented with the promotion of diversity in a more holistic way that permeates all the spaces of the educational institution and leadership positions of decision-making.

Political Administrations

Political administrations could:

- Implement more inclusive processes of decision-making wherein different views and cultures are represented at all leadership levels.
- Design more inclusive social and public policies, including different perspectives that go beyond Western approaches.
- Review vertical analysis and decision-making processes and implement bottom-up structures that distribute power in a more horizontal way.
- Consider more decentralized political systems, instruments, and mechanisms that provide autonomous spaces where alternative perspectives can emerge and contribute to the political agendas.
- Empower the citizenship to be active and well informed as part of their rights and duties as citizens in a democratic society. Democracy can be understood as a culture, a system of values, where citizens are involved and engaged instead of a procedural and mechanic system emptied of content that configures most of today's pseudo-democracies.
- Establish the limits of what would represent a "healthy" democracy and be vigilant of not violating any of those basic principles. Democracy means deliberation and the possibility of deliberating about everything, but the limit is deliberation in itself and the respect for the minority who is not in power.
- Rethink the concepts of nation-state, nationality, and citizenship to create a broader and more inclusive concept where people can be united by their differences while sharing the same rights and a common purpose reflected, for example, in legal instruments, like a constitution, or crystallized in the concept of a plurinational state.
- Consider understanding political administrations as social movements to struggle for social justice, which are more flexible to better adjust to a context of globalization where, although politics remained at a national level, power fled to a global sphere.

Organizations and Corporations

Organizations and corporations could:

- Design frameworks that make sense and give meaning to their employees and at the same time are inclusive and value difference.
- Implement intercultural decision-making mechanisms where different perspectives can be acknowledged and recognized.
- Provide spaces for intercultural communication and hermeneutic translation of meanings.

- Acknowledge the culture of the organization as fluid and fragmented and as a system of organization where every person has the right to be different while sharing the same rights and one or more specific purposes.
- Empower employees through meaningful frameworks of collective action for them that give them a purpose, unites them, and eventually creates a particular organizational culture and ethics where everybody can thrive.
- Embrace the concept of organization as a process, understood as organizations that develop fluid and flexible organizational structures (physical and relational) to better adjust to an uncertain and complex world that is rapidly changing.
- Provide a framework that gives stability and sustainability to the organization for the long term while understanding and embracing change and complexity.
- Rethink leadership as a process to point out a direction and control the context but not the outcome due to the infinite elements involved in the process.

Final Note of Intentionality

Today we are living in a historical period of turbulences and complexity that seems to navigate between a late modernity/postmodernity that is still very embedded in our minds and practices. There is a new paradigm that has started to emerge, but it is not clear enough to be understood and analyzed without a holistic approach. Within this scenario of uncertainty and ambiguity, many political and social projects emerging from a Western perspective try to look for answers by going back to idealized societies from the past or simply building walls (literally and figuratively) and isolating themselves from a reality that they fear and are incapable of understanding. Thus, different perspectives that go beyond the Western canon can shed light on the complexity and the main challenges that we are experiencing in our current postcolonial societies. In particular, a critical approach thought from an interdisciplinary and intercultural perspective can become a possibility for the reconstruction and legitimation of a freer and fairer society.

Leadership studies, as an interdisciplinary and holistic field, can be central to promoting a dialogue between disciplines and cultures to interpret all different processes of resistance to colonialism, capitalism, and patriarchy in a more comprehensive way. However, an epistemological project would be needed that goes beyond the Euro-American interpretation of the world and that will complement a critical theory centered on the Global North that contributes to social justice. Only with cognitive justice and less asymmetric relations of power between cultures will there be social justice. To better understand the leadership of different emancipatory projects in the Global South (including subaltern cultures within the Global North) means to go beyond academic conventions that contribute to the isolation between disciplines and make visible the wide space of economic, social, cultural, and political innovation and diversity existing all around the world.

For example, the Native American organization from this study implies a different political and epistemic perspective that comes from the oppressed, those who suffer the injustice of a system of domination and oppression resulting from modernity and colonialism. Their knowledge and projects have been made invisible and demonized for hundreds of years, but the time has come when what was invisible has become visible and what used to be a doxa for domination has turned into a doxa of emancipation/pluri-doxa. Leadership can be understood as a social myth that functions to legitimize a social order that results from colonialism and is based on individualism and hierarchies of race, culture, and identity. Therefore, any leadership process led by subaltern social groups represents a challenge to the dominant social order and the individualistic assumptions of leadership that support it. This study suggests that illuminating the relationship between cultural identity as a resource and symbolic power can help to advance our understanding of how social change can happen. By implementing the concept of symbolic power, this research combines identity and power in organizations with emancipatory purposes. Symbolic power is built through the deconstruction of old and construction of emergent frameworks and cultural forms. Thus, a critical intercultural leadership process develops different strategies to build symbolic power using frames that, beyond language, can be created through role-modeling, architecture, artwork, clothing, and so on. This process brings nuances regarding the power embedded in identities and implies a holistic perspective. In addition, the concept of symbolic power is directly linked to a process of liberation and emancipation.

Moreover, by drawing from the social movements' concept of collective action, this study provides a lens to understand the collective work of leadership and how groups of people make collective sense and meaning of this phenomenon. Since mainstream perspectives of leadership focus on the leader—typically positional leaders—this research shows a more distributive and participatory way of exercising leadership that, instead of annihilating people, can empower them in a more emancipatory way. Through the concept of collective action, this study describes the collective sense- and meaning-making frames that use culture and identity for social change. These collective frames result in the creation of a collective identity that gives a particular orientation and meaning to the group's actions based on who they were and who they want to become. These frames are the result of the work within the organization between leaders and supporters and external actors of the dominant culture. Thus, some of these collective frameworks are a combination of the amplification of the frames of subaltern groups, the bridging of frames with those of the dominant society, or the transformation of the dominant ones. Collective processes of leadership imply that one no longer perceives leadership as a phenomenon that belongs to a few chosen ones but as a process wherein everybody needs to lead.

The struggles of resistance of subaltern social groups that go beyond mainstream canons of leadership can be crucial to learning more about how social change can be implemented and making collective and participatory processes of leadership more visible. These power-sharing perspectives of leadership from nonmainstream leadership actors who belong to nondominant cultures can contribute to a more epistemological and theoretical eclecticism in the field. Also, learning from their perspectives and struggles can be essential to improving the quality of our democracies and political systems and learning about new tools to build a better world.

The time for intercultural dialogue between cultures with horizontal relations and valuing different views and epistemologies cannot wait anymore. This intercultural dialogue of knowledges and struggles will make visible subordinated groups and peoples from all around the world who will develop other narratives and discourses, think using different logics, and bring new perspectives and solutions to address the main challenges of our turbulent times. Critical interculturality is about reconceptualizing and refounding social and epistemic structures where different worlds can fit within a broader canon of thought than simply the Western canon. Besides, critical interculturality is characterized for valuing the difference and designing permeable and fluid frameworks for sense- and meaning-making resulting from the critical dialogue between diverse cultures, epistemologies, ethics, and emancipatory political projects. The endeavor of building a critical intercultural society will be neither easy nor fast, but as José Carlos Mariátegui said in 1925: "*Vivir peligrosamente significa correr riesgos a veces grandes, pero la alternativa es demasiado mediocre: vivir en espera, pero sin esperanza*" ("Living dangerously means to experience risks that sometimes can be big. However, the alternative is too mediocre: Living waiting and without hope").

Afterword

Arthur W. Blume, PhD
Washington State University

I t is a great honor to write an afterword to this fascinating book that examines the workings and leadership of a community organization dedicated to Indigenous American conceptualizations of well-being and health. In his book, Dr. Jiménez-Luque reports several key interpretations of his findings I wish to highlight here that have significant implications for the future of colonial societies. To begin with, Dr. Jiménez-Luque's scholarship conveys the importance of decolonization processes to extend the presence of cultural sanctuaries while eliminating the invisibility of certain disempowered peoples, including Indigenous Americans.

Decolonization from an Indigenous American perspective will require broad-based transformation of the whole rather than simply transforming organizational entities within the whole. Challenging the injustices of colonial social systems will foster the expansion of cultural sanctuaries in society, places where people feel safe to be authentically themselves, Indigenous or otherwise, without threats of dehumanization. The benefits of a fully decolonized society include only reducing risks to traditionally disempowered and minoritized people, such as Indigenous Americans but also reducing the stress of social disharmony created by the imbalances of colonialism imposed on us all.

Challenging Colonial Hierarchies

Challenging colonial assumptions of superiority will be an important first step, as suggested in the final chapters of the book. By challenging superiority, the circumstances of victimization and perpetration will also be challenged. Beliefs of superiority and inferiority are the consequences of artificial hierarchical assumptions about the natural world. Interestingly, the preponderance of evidence from the life sciences challenges the existence of hierarchies in an interdependent natural world, a world where both predator and prey are symbiotically vulnerable to imbalances and a world in which a virus has the capacity to humble the human creature. The artificial hierarchies have been used to maintain inequitable status quos in societies: to control certain groups to the advantage of others and to justify privilege in the face of intergenerational oppression and poverty.

Chapter 1 suggests that the hegemonic worldview of the colonial ruling class has ensnared all who live within the society. The framing of the American Dream is an excellent example of how a colonial myth has been used to capture the hearts and minds of generations, promising social class mobility through education and hard work but ignoring the inherent social inequities that represent hierarchical barriers to that mobility. The American Dream has been used as subterfuge to justify intergenerational privilege while assigning blame to the victims of intergenerational poverty. Part of the decolonization process involves exposing the irrationality of the American Dream in the context of expansive intergenerational education, health, income, and wealth inequities for many citizens.

The process of decolonizing societies in an interdependent world must begin with egalitarian assumptions. Justice and freedom cannot thrive under the inherent inequality of colonial superiority–inferiority hierarchies. However, an egalitarian perspective insists upon equity for all entities. Assuming a state of privilege comes across as dysfunctional, delusional, and pathological though egalitarian lenses. Intergenerational planetary harm to benefit the privileged few is ethically indefensible if one assumes an interdependent existence. Egalitarianism in action resides in acts of social and environmental justice toward others. Seeking the health and well-being of the whole of the global community is the only reasonable course from an Indigenous American perspective.

Egalitarian organizations and leadership are at the heart of Indigenous American social structures. The destruction of Indigenous cultural wisdom through assimilation, as discussed in this book, has hampered the colonial social order with a very limited perspective of reality. The result is a wounded society, a society that is left without the essential tools to peacefully coexist with egalitarian others in an interdependent world. The individualism of colonialism has inflicted a wound upon itself by jeopardizing global sustainability and well-being. Assimilation efforts may have initially targeted Indigenous people, but the harm from assimilation tactics expanded exponentially in the context of an interdependent world. An important part of decolonizing social structures is reconstructing an egalitarian vision, a vision still protected within Indigenous American sanctuaries. Thankfully, assimilation was not entirely successful, with collective wisdom for healing from colonialism safeguarded in Indigenous sanctuaries. Wisdom within those sanctuaries may be used to restore right relationships to empower just and equitable organizations and social systems, moving us toward a sustainable existence and potentially saving our children, the forests, other species, and the air, land, and water as a result.

Decolonization requires the coming together of people in order to restore harmony and balance. As discussed in Chapter 5, for reconciliation to be posible, disempowered peoples must be joined by postcolonial allies. Our allies must step forward and elevate awareness of the damaging aspects of exercising privilege that subordinates the needs of others. Allies who comprehend the collective pain and suffering of colonial hierarchies—those who also may have experienced colonial consequences themselves—will be important ambassadors for decolonization processes. Our interdependent world demands a coalition of the likeminded to stop the dysfunction of self-orientation and of relational psychopathology that inevitably harms others. Allies who understand and reject the harmful nature of colonialism are needed to support an egalitarian transformation of social structures.

Together, the disempowered and allies can reclaim society as a sanctuary for the whole. Cultural sanctuaries can help to transform the rest of society with increased visibility in times of collective trauma and injustice. They represent the authenticity of an Indigenous vision of how to restore and heal a broken society. The cultural sanctuaries (from the two concluding chapters) have the capacity to lead the movement to transform hierarchy and exceptionalism into a realistic vision aligned with the realities of an interdependent planetary order.

The Resilience of an Indigenous Worldview

Dr. Jiménez-Luque also discusses important lessons concerning Indigenous American resilience, valuable lessons for understanding and addressing global colonial consequences with inter-generational impact. Ensnared by the worldview of the ruling class, minoritized people may find it easy to stray from an "emancipatory framework" (Chapter 6) toward the temptations of colonial individualism, especially when under constant societal pressures to assimilate. Taking on the identity of the oppressor—a colonial identity—is an ever-present threat to authenticity. Pressures toward conformity within colonial social orders encourage and coerce participation in the artificial hierarchies of colonial societies, tempting people to seek the material well-being as a poor substitute for egalitarian relationships centered in harmony and balance.

As discussed in Chapter 6, cultural humility liberates people from colonialism through an accurate understanding of the social structures that coerce hierarchy. Cultural humility flows naturally from an Indigenous American worldview that views holism rather than individualism as foundational and views egalitarian relationships as a prosocial alternative to self-orientations and self-interests. Cultural humility allows for accurate self-examination in the context of the well-being of whole: a form of honesty that tends not to take one's self too seriously. Cultural humility provides a balanced perspective on the limits and shortcomings of the self when con-trasted to the healing strength of the whole. When one grasps personal limits, one is liberated with flexibility to seek harmony and balance with others. Cultural humility enables the naturally self-deprecating humor of Indigenous Americans who laugh at their own troubles and failings routinely. This level of resilience, as discussed in Chapter 7, allows people to find meaning and purpose in the adversity that drives their resolve to resist suffering from colonization and its hierarchical myths. The ability to rise above self-pride and self-pity—to be able to laugh amidst the darkness—has been a great source of collective resilience for Indigenous Americans during the darkest of times.

Chapter 6 also examines how resilience is linked to both optimism and sustainability. Indige-nous American resilience during colonialism has persisted against all odds, sustaining optimism despite the darkness of the colonial era. The persistence and patience apparent in Indigenous American resilience is well-aligned with the persistence and patience needed to pursue and support a sustainable world order. The depth of the spiritual power inherent in Indigenous American resilience energizes the decolonization process, empowering those who have been enslaved by hierarchical inequity and injustice. Collective resilience of this magnitude unleashes transformative power for cultural emancipation from false hierarchies: Life will thrive amidst the emancipation.

Indigenous American resilience mediates the colonial mindset by rejecting the colonial centrality of immediate material gratification that threatens present and future generations

(Chapter 5). Indigenous resilience is centered in holistic well-being, contributing to a sustainable and egalitarian approach to human and planetary survival. When considering the realities of an interdependent natural order, a resilient world must be reconstructed selflessly in order to fully emancipate the planet.

Transformative Leadership

A third important point made within this book concerns the important lessons from Indigenous models of leadership and how those lessons might help to create societies of sanctuary. Leaders selected or elected as a result of economic or political power typically preserve the inherent flaws of hierarchical social orders, maintaining the status quo as apologists and defenders of inherent colonial assumptions within the organizations or societies they lead. Hierarchical leaders implicitly and unwittingly perpetuate privilege and other inherent social inequities that granted them the power to leverage their positions in the first place. Transformative change comes from a different kind of leader, not one who is committed to hierarchical assumptions and their consequential inequities.

To deconstruct inequitable structures and organizations, a nonhierarchical conceptualization is required where leadership is no longer considered an upwardly mobile career path but, instead, is considered a transitory calling from the people to serve. Decolonized leadership will be collectively oriented and highly participatory, as suggested in Chapter 7. Decolonized leaders understand the nature of an interdependent planetary order that drives an egalitarian perspective. As discussed in the concluding chapter of the book, decolonizing social structures and organizations requires an appropriate theory to support and underpin decolonization activities to transform societies. An Indigenous paradigm offers such a theoretical perspective. Therefore, Indigenous leadership models may be very helpful to facilitate the decolonization process.

Indigenous leaders have long resisted colonization; thereby, they naturally assume a decolonizing perspective. Decolonized leadership is a relational process (Chapter 2) and therefore is better understood by those operating within a relational worldview. Indigenous leaders emphasize holistic social and environmental responsibility to respect relationships with all others. A collective vision and egalitarian approach make it easy to operate with transparency, an important aspect of decolonization. Indigenous leadership thrives on consensus. Decolonized leaders serve the people (the whole) rather than themselves and the privileged, respecting egalitarian relationships in an interdependent existence.

Indigenous leaders operate from the strengths of cultural resilience. Decolonizing culture means transforming assumptions and potentially managing fear and anxiety as a result of those transformative changes (Chapter 4). Addressing fear and anger through transparency and egalitarian processes instills trust that a leader has the communal best interests of the organization/community/planet at heart. These skills would come naturally to a competent leader who has led a resilient community successfully through dark days and years. Competent Indigenous leaders are optimistic and highly adaptable and flexible, operating with cultural humility. They advocate for sustainable initiatives and activities to serve the generations rather than serving only the impulses of the present. Indigenous leaders have the responsibility to protect the community—past, present, and future—honoring the traditions and values of the ancestors, advocating for the needs of the present, and anticipating the sustainable needs of the future. They view every collective concern through timeless lenses that respect past, present, and future.

Reconstructing Truly Democratic Organizations and Systems

Dr. Jiménez-Luque discussed the importance of instilling a culture of democracy in order to decolonize social structures and organizations (Chapter 7 and following chapters). Democracy is an appropriate choice for an egalitarian restructuring of hierarchical societies. However, as demonstrated through the historical mistreatment of minoritized groups, democracy has never been ensured by colonial social orders. For example, Indigenous Americans did not fully gain voting rights in the United States until the middle of the 20th century or gain religious freedom protections until 1978. Only a privileged few have been consistently empowered by and benefitted from colonial political processes. Recent U.S. political events have illustrated again that voting rights may be fleeting and overturned by those who claim superiority.

Democracy is in many ways incompatible with the artificial hierarchies that underpin the colonial worldview. Colonists from Europe, people who lived under the strong and unquestioned authority of the ruling classes, found Indigenous American democracy appealing and co-opted many of the practices to formulate American democracy. However, Indigenous American democracy was constructed within an egalitarian worldview that does not assume superiority or inferiority. Whereas democracy in Indigenous American communities was extended to all members, colonial powers have not extended democracy to all their people. In order to nurture and maintain truly democratic social structures and organizations, hierarchies must be dismantled.

This book also calls attention to the importance of advancing democratic principles within businesses and other organizations. Those entities hold significant power in colonial social orders due to the centrality of materialism in the colonial worldview. An Indigenous American conceptualization of democracy, assuming an interdependent and egalitarian world, would expect businesses and organizations to serve others rather than others serving businesses and organizations. Orienting organizational missions toward serving the well-being of the whole rather than simply operating for the benefit of a few would be a transformative leap toward an emancipatory organizational framework.

As Dr. Jiménez-Luque suggests, the hope is to find unity amidst our differences to advance the well-being of all. That will only be possible if our differences are interpreted under egalitarian assumptions that empower all the differences. Decolonizing how differences are interpreted is an important step (i.e., negotiating our differences as equal partners in the reconstruction of social structures). An Indigenous leadership style that encourages consensus and seeks to advance and protect the well-being of the whole offers hope for modeling a different way of being and becoming during the deconstruction and reconstruction process discussed in Chapter 4.

A Renewed Vision of Equity

Dr. Jiménez-Luque has astutely interpreted his scholarship to anticipate what social structures can become under the influence of a collective vision of justice. An Indigenous American organizational model provides one interpretation for how such a vision may unfold. In the final chapters, Dr. Jiménez-Luque reflects upon the asymmetries of power in colonial structures as barriers to the collective vision of justice. The importance of maintaining harmony and balance in social systems and organizations through right relationships will challenge the asymmetries of colonial social structures. As Dr. Jiménez-Luque discussed, "Emancipatory doxa/pluri-doxa offer stability to a culture" because hierarchical injustices inherently create instability in social structures due to the consequences of self-oriented behavior. The social unrest apparent in many colonial nations, compounded by the stressors of a pandemic, is an example of the instability of colonial social structures.

Dr. Jiménez-Luque also wrote that "without cognitive justice there is no social justice," and I would simply add that without social justice there is no sustainable peace. Indigenous leaders have known for centuries that the pathway to peace is through collective justice. Egalitarian models that align with the realities of an interdependent existence are essentially reasonable approaches for leading the people toward sustainable peace and progress—to adequately respond to needs and protect the well-being of the whole in just and equitable ways. An egalitarian vision of leadership wisely protects the rights of the whole of the planetary system, now and into the future. An egalitarian organizational vision is a logical pathway toward emancipation of all impacted by the activities of the organization.

One result of the very interesting study discussed in this book is a vision for how these transformations may be possible with the assistance of people like you. Decolonization of organizations, social systems, societies, and their leadership is possible if colonial hierarchies are challenged as baseless. Resilient people, cultures, and their worldviews serve as models for how transformation can occur. Truly democratic organizations and systems rooted in cultural humility, egalitarianism, interdependent respect and concern, resilience, and transparency will emerge from the transformation, rebuilding sustainable societies of sanctuary designed to benefit all entities equally and end the dehumanization and invisibility of the disempowered. I personally believe that the world may be at a crossroads of sorts: psychologically ready to decolonize businesses, economies, leadership, organizations, and other social structures and systems. Like Dr. Jiménez-Luque, I also believe that Indigenous models may be helpful to facilitate the transformative change that many have desired. The crises of present circumstances have opened doors to new pathways for societies, if we will choose to walk through those doors. Personally, I believe it is time to take that walk—for our collective well-being and for our psychological health.

Index

A

Adorno, T., 5–6, 42
Affordable Care Act, 94
agency, 18–19, 143
American Revolution of 1776, xv
Amselle, J. L., 40
Arendt, H., xix, 148
artifacts, 56, 139
assumptions, 15, 57, 62, 64
asymmetries of power, 90–91, 147–149
Ausseralltäglichkeit, 11
authority, defined, 22
awareness, 85–86

B

Barbour, J. D., 59, 64
Barker, R., 25
Bauman, Z., 21
Benford, R. D., 47, 143
Bennis, W. G., 68
Bentley, A. F., 18
Beyer, J. M., 1–2
Blake, R., 19
Bonté, P., 40
Bourdieu, P., xix–xx, 7–11, 16, 18, 34, 42, 55, 57, 62–68, 138, 148, 152–153
Bureau of Indian Affairs (BIA), 78

C

capital, 62. *See also* metacapital
   concept of, 18
   cultural, 10, 147
   symbolic, 69
capitalism, xix
case study
   macro context of organiza-tion, 77–99
   micro context of organization, 99–131
Chia, R., 25
classism, xx, 17, 78, 85, 145, 149–150
coercive organizations, 54
collective action, 28, 45, 47, 69, 115, 118–119, 142–144
collective frames, 47
collective identity, 44
colonial matrix of power (CMP), xvii–xviii, 17
colonialism, xv, xvi–xvii, 16, 41, 70–71, 144, 148, 166, 171
Columbus, C., xvi
common identity/purpose, 124–127
communication, 63–64
complexity, 20–22
conceptual framework, xxiv–xxv
Condorcet, xv
Conrad, N., 155
consensus and commitment, 17
consensus mobilization, 47
Cooper, R., 24
corporations, 170–173
creativity and fluidity of organizational structures, 110–113
critical consciousness, 33–38
critical intercultural leadership, xxiv–xxvi, 12, 133–160
critical intercultural leadership, xxiv–xxvi
   emancipatory doxa/ pluri-doxa, 153–158
   intercultural society, 149–153, 167
   platform, 141–149, 166–167
   sanctuary, 135–141
critical interculturality, 47–48
critical leadership studies (CLS), 20–22
cultural and symbolic approaches, 22–23
cultural arbitrary, 66
cultural capital, 10, 147
cultural differences, 2–3
cultural frames, 28
cultural resistance, 114–119, 127–132
cultural studies, 43–45
cultural violence, 78
culture(s), xxiii–xxiv, 20, 33–49, 58, 60–61. *See also* organizational culture
   as a critique of social order, 6
   as a field for struggle, 42
   changes, 67–70
   characteristics of, 2–3
   concept of, 1–2, 43
   defined, 54
   hegemony and, 3–8
   ideology, 4–5
   industry, 5
   levels of, 55–57
   management of, 22
   mass, 6
   navigation between, 105–107, 150–151
   organization and, 22, 54
   popular, 5–6
   social movements and, 43–48
   valuing difference, 149–150
curiosity, 123–124

D

de Sousa Santos, B., xxii, 42, 136
De Giosa, V., 22
decolonization, xix, 16, 40, 71, 91, 140–141, 166, 175–178, 180
Descartes, R., xxii, 142
Devanna, M. A., 67
Dewey, J., 18
differentiation, 58–60

direct violence, 78
disciplinary technologies of
     power, 7
discourses, 45–46
dispositions, 8
domination, xxii–xxiii, 41–42,
     137
doxa, 8–12, 33
     as an act of heresy, 9–10
     emancipatory/pluri, 153–158,
       167–168
     Eurocentric, 144
     nomos, 10–11
Drath, W. H., 17, 27
dualisms, 20–22

E

economic exploitation, xv
educating hegemonic institu-
     tions, 91–94
educational institutions, xi, 65,
     169
Elias, N., 18, 25, 158
emancipatory doxa/pluri-doxa,
     153–158, 167–168
embedding mechanisms, 66–67
Emirbayer, M., 18
empathy, 85–86
Engels, F., 4
Enlightenment, 5
epistemicide, xxi–xxii, 136
espoused beliefs and values,
     56–57
ethnic identity, 39, 47–48
ethnogenesis, 38–42
Etzioni, A., 54
Eurocentric doxa, 144
Eurocentric leadership, 17–18
Eurocentrism, xv–xvi, xxi–xxii,
     70, 136, 144
explicit understandings, 122–123
external formal and informal
     relationships, 87–89

F

fachpromotor, 67
Fairclough, N., 3, 153
Fairhurst, G. T., 16
family, 107–110
Fine, G. A., 45
formal and informal
     relationships

external, 87–89
     internal, 100–121
formal statement, 67
Foucault, M., 7
fragmentation, 58–60
framing, 28, 43, 47
Freire, P., 11–12, 33, 34–38, 70,
     142–143, 145
French Revolution of 1789, xv

G

Galtung, J., 78
Gamson, W. A., 47
Gardner, J. W., 20
Giordano, J., xxi
Goodman, N., 69, 138
Gordon, S., 46
Gramsci, A., 4–5, 7, 42, 140, 148
Greene, R., 155
Grosfoguel, R., xviii, xix

H

Harter, N., 20
Heavy Runner, I., 154
hegemony
     concept, 5
     culture and, 3–7
     institutions, 91–94
     rule vs., 4–5
Hernes, T., 26
heroes, 2
Hill, D. J., 40
Hiroto, D., 38
Hofstede, G., 1, 3, 54–55, 152
Horkheimer, M., 5–6
Hosking, D. M., 16, 25

I

identity, 38–42, 143
ideology, 4–5
idioculture, 45
Indian Health Service (IHS),
     80–81, 137
inequities, 17, 176, 178
injustice, 143
instrumental rationality, 26
integration, 58–60
intentionality, 171–173
intercultural society, 70–72,
     124–127, 149–153, 167
interculturality, 48

internalization, 56, 62
Italian Renaissance, xv
Izard, M., 40

K

King, M. L. Jr., 41
Klandermans, B., 45, 47, 146
knowledge, 63–64

L

lack of fear, 123–124
Ladkin, D., 17, 26
language, 63–64
leaders, 23–25, 26
leadership, 15–28
     as a process, 17, 25–27
     complexity, 20–22
     conceptualizations of, 15
     consensus and commitment,
       17
     cultural and symbolic
       approaches, 22–23
     defined, 20, 25
     dualisms, 20–22
     Eurocentric, 17–18
     mainstream, 15–16, 21, 24
     misplaced, 24–25
     ontological challenge of, 23
     organization and, 157–158
     particularities of, 119–121
     phenomenon of, 24
     revolutionary, 36
     role in mobilizing, 16
     substantialist approaches,
       18–19
     theories, 19–29
Leadership Conference, 78
learned helplessness, 38–39
Lederach, J. P., 141
legitimizing inequities, 17
Luhmann, N., 17

M

M'Bokolo, E., 40
Maalouf, A., 26
machtpromotor, 67
macro context of organization
     asymmetries of power, 90–91
     awareness, 91–94
     case study, 77–99
     challenges, 94–97

characteristics, 82–84
decolonization, 90–91
employees, 85–86
external formal and informal
    relationships, 87–89
foundation and evolution,
    79–82
hegemonic institutions, 91–94
history, 78–79
openness, empathy, and
    awareness, 85–86
macrocultures, 60–61
make sense/meaning of world,
    27–28
Maldonado-Torres, N., xxii
Mann, R. D., 19
Manz, C. C., 20
Marcuse, H., 6–7, 142, 156
Mariátegui, J. C., 173
Martin, J., 2, 55–56, 60, 68
Marx, K., xvi, 4, 18
mass culture, 6
McGoldrick, M., xxi
meaning creation/making, 17,
    28, 45–46
Meindl, J. R., 62
Melucci, A., 28, 44, 47
Memmi, A., xviii
metacapital, 10
micro context of organization
    case study, 99–132
    common identity/purpose,
        124–127
    cultural resistance, 127–132
    curiosity, 123–124
    explicit understandings,
        122–123
    formal and informal internal
        relationships, 100–121
    intercultural society, 124–127
    lack of fear, 123–124
    meanings, 122–123
    openness, 123–124
    social justice, 127–131
    tacit, 122–123
misplaced leadership, 24–25
modern civilization, 136
modernity, xv–xvi
    as a European phenomenon,
        xv
    concept, xv
    origin, xv
modernity, xv–xvi. See also
    Eurocentrism

colonialism and, 41, 70–71,
    144, 148, 166, 171
culture, 3
Enlightenment and, 5
humanity, 136
rationality and, 70–71
Morgan, G., 24
Morris, J. S., 154
Mouton, J., 19
movement community, 45
myth, 5

N

naming, 45–46
Nanus, B., 68
narratives, 45–46
Native American organization,
    77
Native employees/staffs, 87–88,
    91, 101–106, 118, 122
navigation between cultures,
    105–107
nomos, 10–11
non-Native employees/staffs,
    86–88, 91, 96, 100–106,
    110, 116, 118, 122–123,
    125, 129, 132, 145, 150
normative organizations, 54

O

Obadia, L., 40
openness, 85–86, 123–124
oppression, xxii–xxiii, 41–42, 137
organizational culture, 22,
    53–73, 154
    described, 54–55
    formation, 62–63
    from academic approach,
        57–60
    levels of, 55–57
    social movements organiza-
        tions, 60
    towards an intercultural
        society, 70–72
organizational structures,
    creativity and fluidity of,
    110–113
organizational theory, 21
organization(s), 54, 170–171.
    See also macro context of
    organization; micro context
    of organization

coercive, 54
cultures and, 54
leadership and, 157–158
normative, 54
power within, 22
social movements organiza-
    tions (SMO), 42–43, 48, 53,
    55, 60, 69, 168–169
utilitarian, 54
Outline of a Theory of Practice
    (Bourdieu), 8

P

Palus, C. J., 17, 27
patient-centered care, 91
patriarchy, xxi
Peters, T., 54
Pfeffer, J., 23
platform, 141–149, 166–167
political administrations,
    170
popular culture, 5–6
postmodernity, xx
Poutignat, P., 39, 152
power
    bases of, 19
    concept, xix–xx
    symbolic, xix–xx
    within organizations, 22
primary embedding
    mechanisms, 66
primitive accumulation, xvi
process change, 68
process studies, 23–24

Q

Quijano, A., xvi–xviii, 71

R

racism, xxi, 17, 78, 83, 85, 89,
    144–145, 149–150
raising awareness, 91–94
relational sociology, 18–19
resilience, 96, 110, 126–127, 129,
    131–132, 134, 154–156
resistance
    against domination and
        oppression, 41–42
    cultural, 114–119
revolutionary leadership, 36
rituals, 2, 46–47

Rost, J. C., 25
Rothenberg, S. P., xxi

S

Salaman, G., 21
sanctuary, 90–91, 135–141,
    165–168
Sartre, 11
Schein, E., 2–3, 20, 54–56, 60,
    157
secondary embedding
    mechanisms, 66–67
self-leadership, 20. *See also*
    leadership
Seligman, M., 38
sense-making, 17
sense of belonging, 151–153
sexism, xxi, 17, 78, 83, 85, 145,
    149–150
Shamir, B., 62
shared experiences of group,
    63
Simondon, G., 24
Sims, H. P., Jr., 20
Smircich, L., 24
Snow, D. A., 47, 143
social contagion, 62
social identification, 56, 62
social justice, 114–119, 127–131
social movements, 43–48
    culture production, 45–47
    defined, 48
    discourses, 45–46
    evolution of, 43–45
    meaning, 45
    naming, 45–46
    narratives, 45–46

organizations, 168–169
    rituals, 46–47
social movements organizations
    (SMO), 42–43, 48, 53, 55,
    60, 69, 168–169
social orders, 8, 16–17, 25, 28–29
social space, 8, 10
social structures, xviii–xx,
    144–147
social theory, 21
socioeconomic stratification, xix
Stacey, R., 26
Stogdill, R. M., 19
Storey, J., 21
structural violence, 78
subcultures, 60–61
Swindler, A., 43
symbolic capital, 69
symbolic power, xix–xx, 42, 138,
    142, 147–148
symbolic violence, 7–8
symbol(s), 2, 139

T

tacit understanding, 122–123
Tarrow, S., 45, 48
Taylor, V., 44
Tichy, N. M., 67
Tilly, C., 48
Trice, H. M., 1–2
Tsoukas, H., 25

U

United States, 34, 78, 136, 140
    Native people in, 138
    race, culture, and identity in, 16

Urban Indian Health Commission, 78
Urban Indian Health Commission Report (2007), 136
urban reservation, 108
utilitarian organizations, 54

V

values, 2–3, 105, 119, 137, 143,
    156–157
    assumptions and, 58
    beliefs and, 22, 28, 46, 56–57
    ethics and, 56
    oppositional, 47
    organization, 127
violence, 7–8, 78
Voss, B., 41

W

Wacquant, L., 18
Walsh, C., 48
Waterman, R. H., 54
Weber, M., 11, 39
Weick, K., 22, 156
Western culture, xvii
Western imperialism, xvii
Western worldview, xxii
Whitehead, A. N., 24
Whittier, N., 44
Williams, R., 5
Winant, H., 34
world-making process, 25–27,
    69
Wuthnow, R., 46

www.ingramcontent.com/pod-product-compliance
Lightning Source LLC
Chambersburg PA
CBHW081434270326
41932CB00019B/3198